Acknowledgements

The Code for Sustainable Homes Technical Guidance has been drafted by the BREEAM Centre at the Building Research Establishment (BRE) under contract to the Department for Communities and Local Government.

Contents

Preface

The Code for Sustainable Homes (the Code) is an environmental assessment method for rating and certifying the performance of new homes. It is a national standard for use in the design and construction of new homes with a view to encouraging continuous improvement in sustainable home building. It was launched in December 2006 with the publication of *Code for Sustainable Homes: A step-change in sustainable home building practice* (Communities and Local Government, 2006) and became operational in April 2007. Where Building Regulations apply, compliance is necessary at all times.

The implementation of the Code is managed by BRE Global (formerly BRE Certification Ltd) under contract to Communities and Local Government under arrangements based on the EcoHomes© operating systems. BRE Global is the main licence holder. Under the terms of its agreement with Communities and Local Government, BRE Global issues licences to both assessors and other Code service providers. BRE Global provides training, licensing and registration of Code assessors to standards ISO 17024 and EN 45011, within a UKAS accredited 'competent person's certification scheme'.

Code service providers are licensed organisations offering all or part of the range of Code services, including assessor training; registration and monitoring; quality assurance of assessments; certification; investigation and resolution of complaints; and maintenance of records (BRE Global, 2007). At the time of publishing, Stroma Certification Ltd and Robust Details Limited are the other organisations licensed to provide Code services. Further information about Code service providers can be found at www.communities.gov.uk/thecode.

The Code for Sustainable Homes covers nine categories of sustainable design:

- Energy and CO_2 Emissions
- Water
- Materials
- Surface Water Run-off
- Waste
- Pollution
- Heath and Well-being
- Management
- Ecology.

Each category includes a number of environmental issues, see table 1.1.

Each issue is a source of environmental impact which can be assessed against a performance target and awarded one or more credits. Performance targets are more demanding than the minimum standard needed to satisfy Building Regulations or other legislation. They represent good or best practice, are technically feasible, and can be delivered by the building industry.

In addition to meeting mandatory standards, achievement of the requirements in each design category scores a number of percentage points. This establishes the Code level or rating for the dwelling. The Code certificate illustrates the rating achieved with a row of stars. A blue star is awarded for each level achieved. Where an assessment has taken place and no rating is achieved, the certificate states that zero stars have been awarded.

Figure 1.1: Final Code Certificate

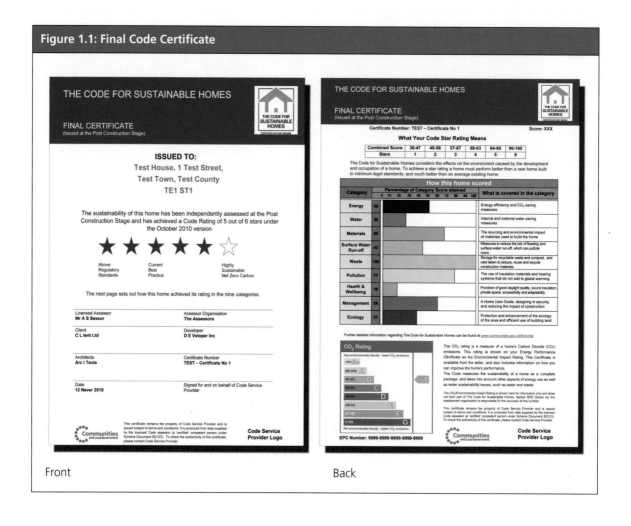

Front   Back

1 Purpose of the Technical Guide

The purpose of this technical guide is to enable Code service providers and licensed assessors to deliver environmental assessments of new dwellings on the basis of the Code scheme requirements. The guide includes a list of issues associated with the building process which are known to impact on the environment, and for which performance measures to reduce their impacts can be objectively assessed, evaluated and delivered in a practical and cost-effective way by the construction industry. Results of the Code assessment are recorded on a certificate assigned to the dwelling. The process of gaining a Code assessment rating and certificate is described in Section 2. The guide includes a comprehensive list of definitions and reference material for everyone involved in the process. The system of evaluating environmental performance in the Code is both transparent and open to scrutiny. A Technical Group consisting of industry representatives, sustainability specialists and Government representatives advise on the content of the guidance and any necessary updates. Significant future changes will be subject to consultation.

This technical guide includes:

Part One

- The Code for Sustainable Homes assessment procedure
- The scoring system.

Part Two

- The environmental issues to be assessed
- Performance requirements and their evaluation
- Evidence required to confirm performance evaluation
- Calculation algorithms, checklists and other tools used in the assessment method.

1.1 Summary of the assessment system

The Code for Sustainable Homes is an environmental assessment rating method for new homes which assesses environmental performance in a two-stage process (design stage and post construction stage) using objective criteria and verification. The results of the Code assessment are recorded on a certificate assigned to the dwelling.

The report Code for Sustainable Homes: A step-change in sustainable home building practice (Communities and Local Government, 2006) defined a set of nine categories of environmental impact, see Table 1.1.

Table 1.1: Summary of Environmental Categories and Issues	
Categories	**Issue**
Energy and CO_2 Emissions	Dwelling emission rate (M)
	Fabric energy efficiency (M)
	Energy display devices
	Drying space
	Energy labelled white goods
	External lighting
	Low and zero carbon technologies
	Cycle storage
	Home office
Water	Indoor water use (M)
	External water use
Materials	Environmental impact of materials (M)
	Responsible sourcing of materials – basic building elements
	Responsible sourcing of materials – finishing elements
Surface Water Run-off	Management of surface water run-off from developments (M)
	Flood risk
Waste	Storage of non-recyclable waste and recyclable household waste (M)
	Construction site waste management
	Composting
Pollution	Global warming potential (GWP) of insulants
	NO_X emissions
Health and Well-being	Daylighting
	Sound insulation
	Private space
	Lifetime Homes (M)
Management	Home user guide
	Considerate Constructors Scheme
	Construction site impacts
	Security
Ecology	Ecological value of site
	Ecological enhancement
	Protection of ecological features
	Change in ecological value of site
	Building footprint

(M) denotes issues with mandatory elements.

The Code assigns one or more performance requirements (assessment criteria) to all of the environmental issues. When each performance requirement is achieved, a credit is awarded (except the three mandatory requirements with no associated credits). The total number of credits available to a category is the sum of credits available for all the issues within it.

Mandatory minimum performance standards are set for some issues. For three of these, a single mandatory requirement is set which must be met, whatever Code level rating is sought. Credits are not awarded for these issues. Confirmation that the performance requirements are met for all three is a minimum entry requirement for achieving a Level 1 rating. The three un-credited issues are:

- Environmental impact of materials

- Management of surface water run-off from developments

- Storage of non-recyclable waste and recyclable household waste

If the mandatory minimum performance standard is met for the three un-credited issues, four further mandatory issues need to be considered. These are agreed to be such important issues that separate Government policies are being pursued to mitigate their effects. For two of these, credits are awarded for increasing levels of achievement recognised within the Code.

The two issues with increasing mandatory minimum standards are:

- Dwelling emission rate

- Indoor water use.

The final two issues with mandatory requirements are Fabric Energy Efficiency and Lifetime Homes. To achieve an overall Code rating of level 5 it is necessary to achieve at lease 7 credits in Ene 2. To achieve an overall Code rating of level 6 it is necessary to achieve at least 7 credits in Ene 2 and 3 credits in Hea 4 – Lifetime Homes.

Tables 1.2 and 1.3 below illustrate how, for the creditable mandatory issues, the minimum mandatory standards increase with increasing rating levels. For CO_2 emissions there are increased mandatory minimum standards for each increase in Code level.

Table 1.2: Code Levels for Mandatory Minimum Standards in CO_2 Emissions (Ene 1)	
Code Level	Minimum Percentage Improvement in Dwelling Emission Rate over Target Emission Rate
Level 1 (★)	0% (Compliance with Part L 2010 only is required)
Level 2 (★★)	0% (Compliance with Part L 2010 only is required)
Level 3 (★★★)	0% (Compliance with Part L 2010 only is required)
Level 4 (★★★★)	25%
Level 5 (★★★★★)	100%
Level 6 (★★★★★★)	Net Zero CO_2 Emissions

For indoor water use there are increased mandatory standards at Code Levels 1, 3 and 5.

Table 1.3: Code Levels for Mandatory Maximum Standards in Indoor Water Consumption	
Code Level	Maximum Indoor Water Consumption in Litres per Person per Day
Level 1 (★)	120
Level 2 (★★)	120
Level 3 (★★★)	105
Level 4 (★★★★)	105
Level 5 (★★★★★)	80
Level 6 (★★★★★★)	80

Further credits are available on a free-choice or tradable basis from other issues so that the developer may choose how to add performance credits (converted through weighting to percentage points) to achieve the rating for which they are aiming.

The environmental impact categories within the Code are not of equal importance. Their relative value is conveyed by applying a consensus-based environmental weighting factor (see details below) to the sum of all the raw credit scores in a category, resulting in a score expressed as percentage points. The points for each category add up to 100, see table 1.4.

1.2   Weightings, credits and percentage points

Table 1.4 shows how weightings are applied across all Code categories of environmental impact to adjust the relative values of credits within different categories. Within each category, credits are awarded for achieving specified degrees of performance. The weighting factors show the contribution made by each category to the total performance recognised and rewarded by the Code. The total available contribution is expressed as 100 per cent. The weighting of each category is expressed as a fraction of this, such that the sum of all the category contributions equals 100 per cent.

As an example, the 31 credits available for energy and CO_2 emissions contribute 36.4 per cent of the total available performance. Similarly, the four credits available for pollution contribute 2.8 per cent of the total available performance. By dividing the weighting factor by the number of credits for each category, we arrive at an approximate weighted value for each credit. For instance, within the energy and CO_2 emissions category, 36.4 per cent contribution to the total, divided by the 31 credits available, means that each credit in this category is worth roughly 1.17 percentage points. Similarly, for the Pollution category, 2.8 per cent contribution to the total, divided by the four credits available, means that each credit in this category is worth roughly 0.70 percentage points.

It is important to note that weightings apply at the category level and not to individual credits to avoid rounding errors. For instance, for the Energy and CO_2 Emissions category, 36.4 per cent weighted contribution divided by 31 credits equals 1.1741935 expressed to seven decimal places, but 1.17 when expressed to two decimal places.

It is also important to note that achieving high performance in one category of environmental impact can sometimes result in a lower level of performance for another. For instance, if biomass is used to meet heating demand, credits will be available for performance in respect of energy supplied from a renewable source, but credits cannot be awarded for low NO_x emissions. It is therefore impossible to achieve a total percentage points score of 100.

Table 1.4: Total Credits Available, Weighting Factors and Points

Categories of Environmental Impact	Total Credits in each Category	Weighting Factor (% points contribution)	Approximate Weighted Value of each Credit
Category 1 Energy and CO_2 Emissions	31	36.4%	1.17
Category 2 Water	6	9.0%	1.50
Category 3 Materials	24	7.2%	0.30
Category 4 Surface Water Run-off	4	2.2%	0.55
Category 5 Waste	8	6.4%	0.80
Category 6 Pollution	4	2.8%	0.70
Category 7 Health and Well-being	12	14.0%	1.17
Category 8 Management	9	10.0%	1.11
Category 9 Ecology	9	12.0%	1.33
Total	–	100.0%	–

Table 1.5 summarises the environmental impact categories, issues, credits and weighting factors.

Table 1.5: Summary of Environmental Impact Categories, Issues, Credits and Weighting		
Code Categories	Available Credits	Category Weighting Factor
Energy and CO$_2$ Emissions		
Dwelling emission rate	10	
Fabric energy efficiency	9	
Energy display devices	2	
Drying space	1	
Energy labelled white goods	2	
External lighting	2	
Low and zero carbon technologies	2	
Cycle storage	2	
Home office	1	
Category Total	**31**	**36.40**
Water		
Indoor water use	5	
External water use	1	
Category Total	**6**	**9.00**
Materials		
Environmental impact of materials	15	
Responsible sourcing of materials – basic building elements	6	
Responsible sourcing of materials – finishing elements	3	
Category Total	**24**	**7.20**
Surface Water Run-off		
Management of surface water run-off from developments	2	
Flood risk	2	
Category Total	**4**	**2.20**
Waste		
Storage of non-recyclable waste and recyclable household waste	4	
Construction site waste management	3	
Composting	1	
Category Total	**8**	**6.40**
Pollution		
Global warming potential (GWP) of insulants	1	
NOx emissions	3	
Category Total	**4**	**2.80**
Health & Well-being		
Daylighting	3	
Sound insulation	4	
Private space	1	*continued*

Code Categories	Available Credits	Category Weighting Factor
Table 1.5: Summary of Environmental Impact Categories, Issues, Credits and Weighting		
Lifetime Homes	4	
Category Total	**12**	**14.00**
Management		
Home user guide	3	
Considerate Constructors Scheme	2	
Construction site impacts	2	
Security	2	
Category Total	**9**	**10.00**
Ecology		
Ecological value of site	1	
Ecological enhancement	1	
Protection of ecological features	1	
Change in ecological value of site	4	
Building footprint	2	
Category Total	**9**	**12.00**
Total	**107**	**100.00**

1.3 Calculating an assessment score

The assessment process should proceed in a logical order through the environmental impact categories and issues, summarised in figure 1.3 below:

- It should begin with a check that the three mandatory issues for which no credits are awarded have been achieved.

- The mandatory requirements for CO_2 emissions, fabric energy efficiency, internal water use and Lifetime homes should be checked and confirmed at the minimum values required to meet the Code level sought.

- The remaining tradable credits should be checked and confirmed so that they also, contribute to the required Code level.

If any of the standards for the three non-creditable issues are not met, then a zero rating will result, regardless of the other credits achieved, including the creditable mandatory issues.

If all the non-creditable mandatory standards are met, but one or other of the creditable mandatory issues fails to reach the minimum required to achieve a higher level, the rating will be determined by the lowest mandatory level met.

1.4 Total percentage points score and resulting Code level

Figure 1.3 illustrates the calculation method to obtain the total percentage points score. For each category, the number of credits achieved is divided by the total available and multiplied by the category weighting factor to derive the percentage points score. **This number should be rounded down to two decimal places before the next step.**

The rounded percentage points scores for each category are then summed to arrive at the total percentage points score for the dwelling. **The total percentage points score must be rounded down to the nearest whole number.**

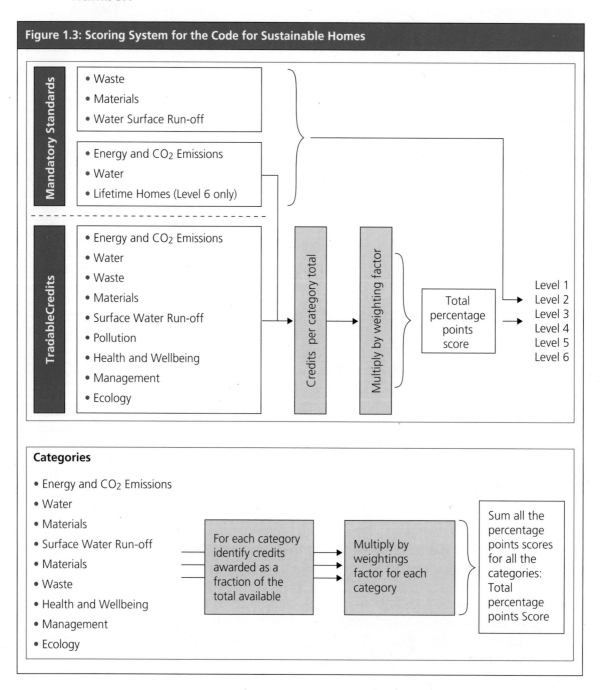

Figure 1.3: Scoring System for the Code for Sustainable Homes

The Code level is then derived from the total percentage points according to table 1.6. Each Code level is represented on the certificate by an equivalent number of stars from 1 to 6.

Table 1.6: Relationship Between Total Percentage Points Score and Code Level	
Total Percentage Points Score (equal to or greater than)	Code Levels
36 Points	Level 1 (★)
48 Points	Level 2 (★★)
57 Points	Level 3 (★★★)
68 Points	Level 4 (★★★★)
84 Points	Level 5 (★★★★★)
90 Points	Level 6 (★★★★★★)

The report submission tool (available for assessors from the Code service provider) must be used to determine an accurate score for an assessment.

2 Obtaining a Code rating – The Process

2.1 Registering a site (before detailed designs are finished)

1. The client for the assessment chooses a service provider for the Code from the register at www.communities.gov.uk/thecode. The service provider will offer a register of licensed and trained Code assessors from which the client can choose and appoint an assessor.

2. The appointed Code assessor registers the development formally with the service provider as early as possible. This registration is valid for a maximum of five years between expiry of the Technical Guide version at registration and submission of the design stage report. So far, there is no time limit on the delivery of the associated post construction stage or final certificates for the development. This enables the version of the Code to be set such that even if the Code is updated the version used can remain the same across the site.

3. It is only possible to register developments/dwellings against the current version of the Code for Sustainable Homes. The only exception is where there is a documented contractual or legal requirement to meet a specific level of the Code against a previous version. Documentary evidence would need to be provided to the Code service provider in order to have this exception approved prior to assessment taking place. Sites already registered under a previous version can be re-registered under the current version of the Code.

4. Once a site is registered by the assessor on the service provider database, it is given a unique registration number.

2.2 Performing Code assessments

Code assessments are normally carried out in two stages:

- Design stage (DS), leading to an interim certificate
- Post construction stage (PCS), leading to a final certificate.

The assessment process for these two stages is very similar. Evidence is collated and used as the basis for the assessor to determine how many credits are to be awarded for each issue. A summary report is submitted to the Code service provider for quality assurance and certification.

Figure 2.1: The Code Assessment Process

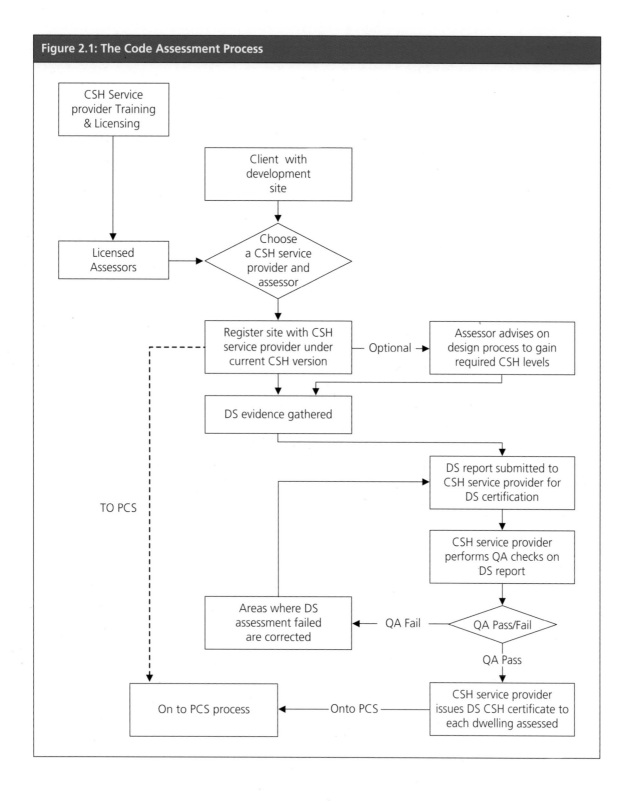

Figure 2.1 (*Cont.*) The Code Assessment Process

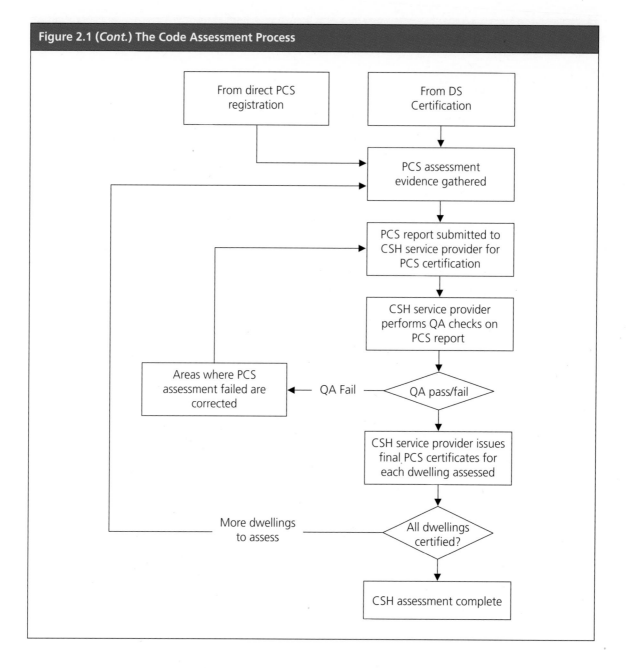

The licensed organisation has responsibility for the assessment and the Code assessor has responsibility for producing the report. It is possible for different licensed organisations to undertake the DS and PCS assessments for a particular site. Code assessors are required to make DS assessment evidence available to the post construction assessor where this is the case.

Licensed organisations are required to keep full supporting documentation of all assessments carried out. Assessors are required to retain this information for a period of 10 years from submission of the report. Each licensed organisation is required to establish and maintain internal quality management procedures relating to record-keeping.

2.2.1 *Design stage assessment*

The aim of the design stage assessment is:

- To assess the design specifications (i.e. before construction begins) for each individual dwelling to determine the design stage or interim rating

- To award (subject to quality assurance) a design stage or interim certificate.

The DS assessment is carried out on the detailed design of each dwelling in the period up to the issue of tender documents, sometimes referred to as RIBA Stages A–G. A Code assessment requires a more detailed specification than Building Regulations compliance because the Code covers many more aspects of the performance of the dwelling. For instance, specification details of all the sanitary fittings are required to calculate the score for the Code indoor water issue.

The assessor will also be able to calculate, at this initial design stage assessment, any site-related credits. Therefore, details of final landscaping and ecological enhancement measures will also need to be known.

The assessor should work closely with the design team to:

- Demonstrate that the performance requirements set for each of the three non-creditable mandatory issues of environmental impact are met for each dwelling.

- Demonstrate that the performance requirements set for each of the credited mandatory issues of environmental impact (dwelling emission rate, fabric energy efficiency, indoor water use and Lifetime Homes) are met for the desired rating for each dwelling.

- Choose the remaining tradable issues which are required to achieve the desired overall rating.

- Evaluate the performance of each dwelling against the requirements set for each of the chosen issues to confirm that the required standards are met for the desired overall rating.

- Assemble and check the evidence required for the developer, design team and other consultants to show the intended performance will be met.

When the assessor is satisfied with the performance under the Code, they shall submit the assessment report to the service provider for quality assurance and to receive design stage or interim Code certification. The report must contain references to documentary evidence describing how performance requirements are met, creating a clear audit trail linking the rating awarded to the evidence used to justify it. The service provider may issue a standard report format for the assessor to complete.

2.2.2 *Post construction stage assessment*

The aim of the PCS assessment is to assess each individual dwelling as built to determine the final score and Code level for the dwelling.

If a DS assessment has been undertaken, this can be used as the starting point for the PCS assessment. The PCS assessment is carried out to confirm that dwellings are either built to the DS specifications or, if there are variations from the DS, that they are documented, reassessed, and a new score and Code level calculated for each dwelling that is affected. The assessor organisation should carry out an appropriate level of checking to be satisfied that commitments made have been achieved.

If there has been no prior DS assessment, then the full assessment shall be completed against the as-built dwelling(s).

Licensed organisations are required to set up robust and auditable post construction stage assessment procedures. These are to include:

- An appropriate number of site visits for each development site (at least once per site). The appropriate number of site visits is dependent on the particular situation. It is the assessor's responsibility to determine the necessary number of site visits required to satisfy themselves that the assessment properly reflects the dwelling

- Every different specification for each issue shall be reviewed and evidence recorded to confirm that it complies with the requirements for PCS assessment

- Where dwellings of identical construction type are planned to be released in phases, the assessment evidence must show that the same specifications have been incorporated into dwellings completed following the initial release. If there are variances to the specification in subsequent releases, the assessor shall reassess the dwellings based on the new specifications.

The number of PCS assessment reports is likely to be based on the phased completion of dwellings within a development. The number of PCS assessment reports submitted to cover a particular development is entirely at the discretion of the assessor (and developer).

For a large or phased development, there are some issues that will not be complete when a post construction stage assessment for the first dwelling(s) is submitted to the service provider. For example, these could include some ecology credits or community-based facilities. It is possible to certify the first dwellings without certain issues being complete. The details of these exceptions are contained within the relevant issues, but are also highlighted in table 2.1 below. This is not intended to be a comprehensive list; its purpose is to provide guidance to assessors on the type of exceptions that are acceptable.

Table 2.1: Post Construction Stage Assessment Exceptions		
Categories	Issues	Exception
Energy and CO$_2$ Emissions	Ene 1: Dwelling emission rate	Centralised energy supply infrastructure on multi-phase developments may not be commissioned in the first phase but should be operational before more than 60 per cent of the dwellings are completed/certified. This requirement is variable where there is an alternative statutory requirement in place for the system to be operational at a different stage.
		For community heating systems; the infrastructure to allow a future connection must be provided to each dwelling for credits to be awarded, regardless of the percentage of total dwellings completed.
		Note: Where exemption from SDLT Regulations is sought in addition to a Code rating, these exceptions do not apply.
	Ene 4: Drying space	Provision of external drying fittings or footings for later parts of the development, as this would form part of the 'externals' and be one of the last finishes.
	Ene 5: Energy labelled white goods	White goods may not be fitted owing to security risk until just prior to handover to new residents. Orders must be in place.
	Ene 6: External lighting	External light fittings may be in place but may not have bulbs until handover. This is acceptable.
	Ene 7: Low and zero carbon technologies	Centralised energy supply infrastructure on multi-phase developments may not be commissioned in the first phase but should be operational before more than 60 per cent of the dwellings are completed/certified. This requirement is variable where there is an alternative statutory requirement in place for the system to be operational at a different stage.
		For community heating systems; the infrastructure to allow a future connection must be provided to each dwelling for credits to be awarded, regardless of the percentage of total dwellings completed.
		Note: Where exemption from SDLT Regulations is sought in addition to a Code rating, these exceptions do not apply.
	Ene 8: Cycle storage	Some cycle storage may not be in place in later stages of the development as this would form part of the 'externals' and be the last of the finishes installed.
Water	Wat 1: Indoor water use	Communal grey water or rainwater systems may not be installed yet but should be operational before more than 60 per cent of the dwellings are completed/certified.
	Wat 2: External water use	Communal rainwater collection systems may not be installed yet but should be operational before more than 60 per cent of the dwellings are completed/certified. (Water butts should be installed although they are often left until just before completion.)

continued

Table 2.1: Post Construction Stage Assessment Exceptions		
Categories	**Issues**	**Exception**
Surface Water Run-off	Sur 1: Management of surface water run-off from developments	Specific infiltration measures, such as soakaways and permeable paving, may not be fully installed when initial phases are released, but evidence of the devices to be used and any relevant calculations need to be available. They need to be operational before more than 60 per cent of the dwellings are completed/certified.
	Sur 2: Flood risk	All of the flood protection measures should be planned and a programme for their construction finalised which indicates that they will be operational before more than 60 per cent of the dwellings are completed/certified.
Waste	Was 1: Storage of non-recyclable waste and recyclable household waste	Local authority collection schemes, kitchen waste collection schemes and private recycling schemes will need to be operational within one year of the completion date of this dwelling.
	Was 3: Composting	A communal/community composting service will need to be operational within 18 months of completion.
Pollution	Pol 2: NO_x emissions	Centralised energy supply infrastructure on multi-phase developments may not be commissioned in the first phase but should be operational before more than 60 per cent of the dwellings are completed/certified. This requirement is variable where there is an alternative statutory requirement in place for the system to be operational at a different stage. For community heating systems; the infrastructure to allow a future connection must be provided to each dwelling for credits to be awarded, regardless of the percentage of total dwellings completed.
Ecology	Eco 1: Ecological value of site	It will not be possible to check that all features outside of the construction zone have been undisturbed until construction is completed.
	Eco 2: Ecological enhancement	Features are often not in place until the whole site is complete or until the appropriate planting season. A design and programme are required; demonstrating that all such enhancement works will be completed normally within a single annual cycle from the completion of construction works on the site's final dwellings.
	Eco 3: Protection of ecological features	It will not be possible to confirm that the credit has been achieved for an individual plot being assessed until the entire development site has been assessed to confirm all features have been protected. The assessor should check that features relating to areas of the site where construction has been completed have been protected. For areas where construction is not yet complete, it should be checked that protection measures are in place to protect features during construction works as detailed at design stage.
	Eco 4: Change in ecological value of site	Planting is often delayed until the whole site is complete. A design and programme are required; demonstrating that all such enhancement works will be completed normally within a single annual cycle from the completion of construction works on the site's final dwellings.

2.3 Evidence Requirements

The information within this section will clarify how the evidence requirements tables should be used, the roles and responsibilities of individuals involved and the definitions of the terminology used within the tables. Clarification of the routes to certification has also been provided to emphasise the importance of the design stage assessment.

2.4 Using the Schedule of Evidence Required

The Schedule of Evidence Required lists the basic information that is needed to demonstrate compliance for certification. They are not exhaustive lists of every document necessary to conduct the assessment or calculate performance.

Assessors will need to consider what information to request during the assessment to enable them to fulfil the requirement for an audit trail.

2.5 Roles and Responsibilities

2.5.1 Role of the Code Assessor

The role of the Code assessor is to undertake credit score calculations and verify the validity and authenticity of evidence provided. The assessor will also carry out calculations which are pertinent only to the Code assessment, where these are not undertaken by a professional under an appropriate regulatory requirement, competent persons scheme or specialist requirement. At the post construction stage, the assessor is required to carry out sufficient site inspections to audit the as-built evidence. At least one visit will be required for all sites. Each specification employed to meet the criteria at the design stage and/or post construction stage must be reviewed or assessed as appropriate, and detailed documentary evidence recorded, to confirm that it complies with the requirements for post construction assessment given in the Technical Guidance manual. The Code assessor is at all times responsible for the content and scoring within the assessment report.

It may be that assessors have competencies in other disciplines and as such are employed to undertake additional tasks that feed into the Code assessment, but these fall outside their role as an assessor.

2.5.2 Role of the Code Service Provider

The Code service provider operates the UKAS Accredited Product Scheme for the Code to ensure that assessors are technically competent, accurate and professional when carrying out assessment services on behalf of their clients. The service provider will audit assessment services for quality assurance (QA) purposes. The QA process is in place to help protect the credibility of both the Code scheme and the assessor, as well as to safeguard the interests of developers and their customers. Through a process of random checking, the QA audit will provide a reasonable degree of confidence that assessment reports correctly reflect the requirements of the scheme, so allowing a certificate to be issued. The QA process will not seek to check every aspect of a Code assessment.

2.5.3 Role of the Developer

The developer is responsible for providing accurate evidence as required by the assessor to carry out their assessment. At post construction stage, the developer must confirm which dwellings are built to the same specification as those types inspected by the assessor on site.

At post construction stage, written confirmation from the developer must be in the form of a letter on company headed paper and must be signed by a senior individual who is deemed responsible for the development by the board of directors or equivalent senior management group of that developer. The letter must refer to specific criteria within the issues and explain how the criteria or design stage commitment have been satisfied. The letter must be explicit in terms of the assessment and the site under development, and must confirm which dwellings are built to the same specification as those types inspected by the assessor on site.

2.6 Definitions of Terminology Used in the Evidence Requirements Tables

2.6.1 Definition of 'Developer'

This is an organisation or individual(s) with the responsibility for delivering the dwelling being assessed.

2.6.2 Definition of 'Detailed Documentary Evidence'

'Detailed documentary evidence' may be any written documentation confirming compliance. Across the assessment, evidence will include a mix of letters, the site inspection report, and specification text or drawings as appropriate. The assessor must satisfy themselves that the evidence is robust and traceable. A letter of intent from the developer is not acceptable where the requirement is for 'detailed documentary evidence'.

2.6.3 Site inspection report

Assessors may ask others to complete the site inspection on their behalf, in which case the assessor will be responsible for ensuring that their representative is competent and able to carry out the task.

A 'Site Inspection Report Template' is available from the Code service provider to assist site inspectors during their visit and to clarify the detail that must be provided in the report. The report must include sufficient information to create an audit trail that justifies the conclusions reached, particularly where the site report is the only evidence supplied at post construction stage. A simple statement confirming compliance will not be sufficient. Photographs may be useful as supporting evidence in a report, though it is unlikely that a photograph on its own will demonstrate compliance. The report template allows the assessor to reference photographs should they choose to provide them.

As many issues as possible should be checked during the site inspection. However, it is unlikely that all issues will be checked during one site visit. Different specifications of the dwelling will be completed at different times, so the site inspection will need to be planned during discussion with the client to identify the most appropriate time. At least one site visit must be carried out for every assessment.

2.6.4 *Written Confirmation from the Developer*

At post construction stage, written confirmation from the developer must be in the form of a letter on company headed paper and must be signed by a senior individual who is deemed responsible for the development by the board of directors or equivalent senior management group of that developer. The letter must refer to specific criteria within the issues and explain how the criteria or design stage commitment have been satisfied. The letter must be explicit in terms of the assessment and the site under development.

2.7 Assessment Routes

There are two routes to certification:

1. Complete both the design stage (DS) assessment and the post construction stage (PCS) assessment. An interim certificate will be issued, followed by the final certificate.

2. Complete the post construction stage (PCS) assessment only. Only the final certificate will be issued.

QA audits will cover both the DS and PCS.

Assessors must be aware of the pros and cons of the routes to certification and advise their clients accordingly. Completing both the DS and PCS should be the preferred route to assessment as it offers two significant benefits.

Firstly, where DS assessments have been carried out and the requirements have been fulfilled, completion and QA of the subsequent PCS assessment report should take less time. This is of significant benefit to the client who is likely to need the final certificate as soon as the dwellings are complete.

Secondly, completing the DS assessment will help to identify opportunities for redesign in order to maximise the number of credits achieved. It is much easier to alter designs at the DS than at the PCS when some of the dwellings may already have been built.

Any pre-assessment estimate of the rating a dwelling may achieve should be informed by a licensed Code assessor who understands the full details of the process where this is used to inform business, funding or contractual decisions.

2.8 Certifying Code for Sustainable Homes assessments

All requests for certification (both design stage or interim, and post construction stage or final) are logged on the service provider database under the site registration number. Certificates are issued on behalf of Communities and Local Government. BRE Global's UKAS Accredited Competent Persons Scheme requires that suitable procedures are in place for all service providers to monitor the quality of reports. Currently, this involves:

- A basic administrative check on every report submitted for certification
- A technical audit of assessments and assessors on a regular basis.

3 Keeping This Guide up to Date

This technical guide will be updated at intervals if standards change or are introduced, or if technologies or processes change.

The Communities and Local Government website will always contain the latest version at www.communities.gov.uk/thecode

Organisations delivering the Code for Sustainable Homes

The Code for Sustainable Homes service provision is managed by BRE Global under contract to Communities and Local Government. Under these arrangements, all Code assessments are carried out under licence by a wide range of organisations. The role of BRE Global is to ensure that Communities and Local Government's requirements are met through the provision of:

- Assessor training

- Registration and monitoring

- Quality assurance of assessments

- Certification

- Investigation and resolution of complaints

- Maintenance of records.

BRE Global's operating systems are accredited by UKAS under BS EN 45011 (General Requirements for Bodies Operating Product Certification Systems) and ISO 17024 (General Requirements for Bodies Operating Certification of Persons) to ensure independence, competence, impartiality and confidentiality with transparency in records, complaints procedures, documentation and maintenance of certification.

BRE Global currently does not carry out assessments and provides clear separation between the roles of training and assessor qualifications to avoid potential conflicts of interest. Under the terms of its agreement with Communities and Local Government, BRE Global will licence:

- Independent assessors to conduct assessments to the requirements of the Code for Sustainable Homes, and;

- Other organisations to provide training and certification service provision.

For further information see:

http://www.breeam.org/filelibrary/CSH_Guidance_Notes_for_Prospective_Service_Providers.pdf

This document sets out the basic requirements for organisations wishing to carry out these activities. Any organisation wishing to offer these services would have to operate to the same high standards that BRE Global is required to reach under its contract with Communities and Local Government, and with mechanisms that clearly demonstrate the avoidance of conflicts of interest.

There are two options for organisations wishing to offer some or all of these services:

- A sub-licence agreement to provide an independent certification service covering assessor training and testing; assessor registration; quality assurance, technical support and certification of assessments, or;
- A sub-contract agreement for partial services working within the parameters of BRE Global's existing accredited services.

BRE Global will maintain a central database in which all the assessed dwellings will be registered, regardless of the organisation providing the Code assessment. This will allow statistics to be reported to Communities and Local Government. Sub-licensees will be supplied with the necessary formatting and access rights to lodge their registrations. Where necessary, interfaces with databases in other organisations can be developed. A fee will be charged at BRE Global's commercial rates for time spent on this activity.

Code assessors must be members of an organisation that pays fees covering:

- Management of the system
- A free telephone helpline
- Regular updates
- Access to a private extranet
- Certification of the assessment.

Category 1: Energy and Carbon Dioxide Emissions

Issue ID	Description	No. of Credits Available	Mandatory Elements
Ene 1	Dwelling Emission Rate	10	Yes

Aim

To limit CO_2 emissions arising from the operation of a dwelling and its services in line with current policy on the future direction of regulations.

Assessment Criteria

Criteria		
% Improvement 2010 DER/TER*[1]	Credits*[2]	Mandatory Requirements
≥ 8%	1	
≥ 16%	2	
≥ 25%	**3**	**Level 4**
≥ 36%	4	
≥ 47%	5	
≥ 59%	6	
≥ 72%	7	
≥ 85%	8	
≥ 100%	**9**	**Level 5**
Zero Net CO_2 Emissions	**10**	**Level 6**
Default Cases		
None		

[1] Performance requirements are equivalent to those in previous scheme versions but are now measured using the AD L1A 2010 TER as the baseline.

[2] Up to nine credits are awarded on a sliding scale. The scale is based on increments of 0.1 credits, distributed equally between the benchmarks defined in this table.

Note: A definition of a zero carbon home is omitted from this document as it will be defined by future legislation. The requirements of this issue will be updated to align with this legislation once it is set.

Information Required to Demonstrate Compliance

Schedule of Evidence Required	
Design Stage	**Post Construction Stage**
Detailed documentary evidence confirming the *TER*, *DER* and percentage improvement of DER over TER based on design stage *SAP outputs**	Detailed documentary evidence confirming the TER, DER and percentage improvement of DER over TER based on As Built SAP outputs*
OR	**OR**
Where applicable:	Where applicable:
A copy of calculations as detailed in the assessment methodology based on design stage SAP outputs*	A copy of revised/final calculations as detailed in the assessment methodology based on as built SAP outputs
AND	Confirmation of FEE performance where SAP section 16 allowances have been included in the calculation
Confirmation of FEE performance where SAP section 16 allowances have been included in the calculation	*Dated outputs with *accredited energy assessor* name and registration number, assessment status, plot number and development address.
*Dated outputs with *accredited energy assessor* name and registration number, assessment status, plot number and development address.	If not produced by an accredited energy assessor additional verification is required as detailed in the assessment methodology.
If not produced by an accredited energy assessor additional verification is required as detailed in the assessment methodology.	

Definitions

Accredited Energy Assessor

A person registered with an accredited energy assessment scheme provider. The scheme provider will be licensed by Communities and Local Government to accredit competent persons to assess the CO_2 emission rates of domestic buildings for the purposes of demonstrating compliance with *Building Regulations*.

Additional Allowable Electricity Generation

Site-wide electricity generation from the following technologies not included in the DER calculation:

- Wind generators

- Photovoltaic panels
- Hydro-electric generators,

These installations can be located on/off-site provided that the connection arrangements meet the requirements defined in Appendix M of *SAP*.

Additional allowable electricity can be utilised to reduce dwelling CO_2 emissions and achieve the mandatory Ene 1 requirements set at all Code levels. For additional allowable electricity to be included in the Ene 1 calculation, the dwelling(s) must at least meet the minimum FEE standard required to achieve 5 credits.

CO_2 emissions reductions from additional allowable electricity must be calculated in accordance with the methodology defined in table Cat 1.1.

(AD L1A) Approved Document L1A

The Building Regulations for England and Wales Approved Document L1A: Conservation of Fuel and Power in New Dwellings (2010 Edition).

Building Control Body

This is the body responsible for ensuring that construction works are according to plan and compliant with applicable requirements through periodic inspection.

Building Regulations

Building Regulations apply in England and Wales and promote:

- Standards for most aspects of a building's construction, including structure, fire safety, sound insulation, drainage, ventilation and electrical safety
- Energy efficiency
- The needs of all people, including those with disabilities, in accessing and moving around buildings.

(DER) Dwelling Emission Rate

The DER is the estimated CO_2 emissions per m^2 per year ($KgCO_2/m^2/year$) for the dwelling as designed. It accounts for energy used in heating, fixed cooling, hot water and lighting.

Energy Averaging

Where a building contains multiple dwellings, it is acceptable to assess this issue based on the average energy performance of all dwellings within the building. The area weighted average DER and TER and must be calculated in accordance with the block averaging methodology defined in clauses 4.6 and 4.14 of *AD L1A*.

(EPC) Energy Performance Certificate

This is a certificate that confirms the energy rating of the dwelling from A to G, where A is the most efficient and G is the least efficient. The better the rating, the more energy efficient the dwelling is, and the lower the fuel bills are likely to be. The energy performance of the building is shown as a carbon dioxide (CO_2) based index. EPCs are generated using approved software by accredited energy assessors.

Where energy averaging is carried out for the purposes of a Code assessment, it is possible to use better fabric and systems performance in some dwellings to offset worse performance in others. This is not possible for the purposes of the EPC calculation and as such Code energy performance may differ from that indicated on the EPC.

Where energy averaging has been used, performance against the requirements of this issue is not indicative of individual dwelling performance or running costs.

(FEE) Fabric Energy Efficiency

Energy demand for space heating and cooling expressed in kilowatt-hours of energy demand per square metre per year ($kWh/m^2/year$).

Fabric energy efficiency is calculated according to the conditions defined in Section 11 of SAP.

See Ene 2.

Net CO_2 Emissions

The annual dwelling CO_2 emissions ($KgCO_2/m^2/year$) from space heating and cooling, water heating, ventilation and lighting, and those associated with appliances and cooking.

To achieve Code level 6, net CO_2 emissions must be zero when calculated according to the methodology defined in table Cat 1.1.

Residual CO_2 Emissions Offset from Biofuel CHP

Where community biofuel CHP systems are specified it is possible for SAP to calculate negative total CO_2 emissions associated with the system. For the purposes of the DER calculation SAP does not account for the negative figure. Instead, it defaults to a value of zero and the benefit is omitted.

Residual CO_2 emissions offsets from biofuel CHP can be utilised to reduce dwelling CO_2 emissions and achieve the mandatory Ene 1 requirements set at all Code levels. For the offset to be included in the Ene 1 calculation, the dwelling(s) must at least meet the minimum FEE standard required to achieve 5 credits.

CO_2 emissions offsets from biofuel CHP must be calculated according to the methodology defined in table Cat 1.1.

SAP Output (design & as built stage)

This is a dated output from accredited SAP software produced by an *accredited energy assessor*. The output must summarise the data necessary to determine performance against the requirements of this issue and include the name and registration number of the accredited energy assessor, the assessment status, plot number and development address. It is not necessary to produce individual SAP outputs for identical dwellings for the purposes of a Code assessment.

The output will be based on either design stage information or on the dwelling as constructed. Design stage outputs must be used when assessing design stage Code performance and as built outputs for post construction Code assessments.

Where SAP outputs are not produced by an accredited energy assessor they must be verified by either an accredited energy assessor or a member of the *building control body* responsible for assessing the dwelling for compliance with Part L of the Building Regulations.

For the purposes of assessing this issue the applicable SAP outputs are:

- SAP DER Worksheet
- AD L1A Building Regulations Compliance Checklist

(SAP) Standard Assessment Procedure for Energy Rating of Dwellings

The Government's approved methodology for assessing the energy performance of new dwellings. The current version is SAP 2009 version 9.90, dated March 2010, rev October 2010. The procedure accounts for energy used in:

- Space heating and cooling
- Hot water provision
- Fixed lighting.

The indicators of energy performance are energy consumption per unit floor area, energy cost rating (SAP rating), environmental impact rating based on CO_2 emissions (EI rating) and dwelling CO_2 emission rate (DER). They are used in the production of energy performance certificates (*EPCs*) and to demonstrate compliance with AD L1A and the Code for Sustainable Homes.

To contribute to reducing CO_2 emissions as calculated by SAP, heat and power must be generated either on or in the home, on the development or through other local community arrangements (including district heat and power).

Stamp Duty Land Tax (Zero Carbon Homes Relief) Regulations 2007

Regulations defining the conditions to be met for a dwelling to achieve exemption from the applicability of Stamp Duty Land Tax (S.I. 2007 No. 3437).

The conditions imposed by the regulations do not apply to dwellings seeking a Code rating alone. For this reason, Code level 6 dwellings will not necessarily be exempt from Stamp Duty Land Tax. Where Stamp Duty Land Tax exemption is sought in addition to a Code rating, the additional conditions defined in the regulations must also be met.

(TER) Target Emission Rate

The target emission rate is the maximum allowable CO_2 emissions per m^2 ($KgCO_2/m^2/year$) arising from energy used in heating, cooling, hot water and lighting which would demonstrate compliance with Criterion 1 of AD L1A.

The TER is calculated using the SAP methodology according to the requirements defined in AD L1A.

Assessment Methodology

The assessment criteria should be read with the methodology and the definitions in this section. Mandatory requirements are met and credits are awarded where the performance requirements (set out in the assessment criteria table) have been met.

Design Stage

Confirm that the SAP output for each dwelling being assessed meets the criteria set out in the definitions section.

For Code Levels 1–5:

- Calculate the percentage improvement in DER over TER for each dwelling being assessed.

For Code Level 6:

- Calculate net CO_2 emissions.

In all cases where additional allowable electricity or residual emissions offsets from biofuel CHP are included in the calculation ensure the minimum FEE performance requirement has been achieved in accordance with the criteria set out in the definitions section.

In the case of a building containing multiple dwellings, it is acceptable to award credits based on the average percentage improvement of DER over TER for all dwellings. Energy averaging must be calculated in accordance with the criteria set out in the definitions section.

Post Construction Stage

Either:

- Confirm that no changes have been made to the design during construction that impact on energy performance.

Or, where changes have been made during construction:

- As for design stage, but based on as built SAP outputs.

Calculation Procedures

For Code Levels 1–5 the percentage improvement in DER over TER must be calculated according to the methodology defined in table Cat 1.1.

For Code level 6, net CO_2 emissions must be calculated according to the methodology defined in table Cat 1.1.

Table Cat 1.1: Dwelling Emission Rate			
Value Required	Data Source Guidance (See note [1])	Unit Required	Value
Levels 1–5			
(1) DER	SAP Worksheet: [**SAP box 273** for systems assessed under **section a**] [**SAP box 384** for systems assessed under **section b**] OR AD L1A Building Regulations Compliance Checklist	+/– $KgCO_2/m^2/yr$	
(2) TER	AD L1A Building Regulations Compliance Checklist	+ $KgCO_2/m^2/yr$	
(3) CO_2 emissions offset from *additional allowable electricity generation* See notes [3] and [4]	SAP Section 16: [**SAP box ZC7**]	– $KgCO_2/m^2/yr$	
(4) *Residual CO_2 emissions offset from biofuel CHP* See notes [3] and [4]	SAP Section 16: [**SAP box ZC5**]	– $KgCO_2/m^2/yr$	
(5) Total CO_2 emissions offset from SAP Section 16 allowances	Value at step **(3)** + Value at step **(4)**	– $KgCO_2/m^2/yr$	
(6) DER accounting for SAP Section 16 allowances	Value at step **(1)** + Value at step **(5)**	+/– $KgCO_2/m^2/yr$	
(7) % improvement DER/TER See note [5]	$100 \times (1-($Value at step **(6)** $\div$ Value at step **(2)**$))$	+ %	
Level 6 Only			
(8) Net CO_2 emissions See notes [2] and [4]	SAP Section 16: [**SAP box ZC8**]	+/– $KgCO_2/m^2/yr$	

Notes to table Cat 1.1:

[1]   The data sources in this calculation correspond with SAP and are intended as supplementary guidance to assist in identifying the values required. It is the responsibility of the assessor to ensure that the correct value is identified and entered into the calculation as the data source may vary dependant on the type of accredited SAP software used to assess energy performance.

[2]   Section 16 of SAP extends the calculation to account for CO_2 emissions from appliances and cooking and to allow for site-wide electricity generating technologies. Follow the procedure set out in Section 16 of SAP 2009 to calculate Net CO_2 emissions for the dwelling.

To achieve the mandatory Ene 1 requirement at Code level 6, no specific conditions are imposed that preclude the use of Section 16 of SAP to calculate net CO_2 emissions apart from those detailed in note [3]. However, it should be noted that to achieve an overall rating of Code level 6 the dwelling(s) must also meet the minimum FEE performance requirement at the 7 credit benchmark.

[3]   The allowances included in Section 16 of SAP for site-wide electricity generating technologies and CO_2 emissions offsets from biofuel CHP systems can be applied to achieve the mandatory Ene 1 requirements set at all Code levels. For the associated emissions offsets to be included in the Ene 1 calculation, the dwelling(s) must meet the minimum FEE performance requirement at the 5 credit benchmark.

For details of acceptable technologies, configurations, output calculations and of how to apportion the output to individual dwellings, refer to Appendix M and Section 16 of SAP.

[4]   Where centralised energy supply infrastructure is in place that services other users (e.g. mixed use developments) the output must be allocated between all users in relation to their proportional net floor area.

[5]   The calculated percentage reduction must rounded to 1 decimal place e.g. 94.8750% becomes 94.9%. This figure is then used to determine the number of credits and mandatory level achieved for Code level 1 – 5 dwellings, in line with the performance requirements defined in the assessment criteria table.

Checklists and Tables

None.

Common Cases of Non-Compliance

Green tariffs cannot be used to offset CO_2 emissions. They do not guarantee increased renewable capacity in line with the increased demand arising from new development and are also not legally binding on occupiers.

Special Cases

None.

Issue ID	Description	No. of Credits Available	Mandatory Elements
Ene 2	Fabric Energy Efficiency	9	Yes

Aim

To improve fabric energy efficiency performance thus future-proofing reductions in CO_2 for the life of the dwelling.

Assessment Criteria

Criteria			
Dwelling Type*[1]			
Apartment Blocks, Mid-Terrace	End Terrace, Semi-Detached & Detached		
Fabric Energy Efficiency kWh/m²/year		Credits*[2]	Mandatory Levels
≤ 48	≤ 60	3	
≤ 45	≤ 55	4	
≤ 43	≤ 52	5*[3]	
≤ 41	≤ 49	6	
≤ 39	**≤ 46**	**7**	**Levels 5 & 6**
≤ 35	≤ 42	8	
≤ 32	≤ 38	9	
Default Cases			
None			

*[1] To determine the applicable performance scale the dwelling type under assessment must be accurately defined according to the guidance at www.zerocarbonhub.org

*[2] Credits are awarded on a sliding scale. The scale is based on increments of 0.1 credits, distributed equally between the benchmarks defined in this table.

*[3] This is the level being considered for Part L of the Building Regulations in 2013 on which a public consultation is expected in late 2011/early 2012.

Ene

Information Required to Demonstrate Compliance

Schedule of Evidence Required	
Design Stage	Post Construction Stage
Detailed documentary evidence confirming fabric energy efficiency based on Design Stage *SAP outputs*	Detailed documentary evidence confirming fabric energy efficiency based on as built SAP 2009 outputs
OR	**OR**
Where applicable:	Where applicable:
A copy of calculations as detailed in the assessment methodology based on design stage SAP outputs	A copy of calculations as detailed in the assessment methodology based on as built SAP outputs
*Dated outputs with *accredited energy assessor* name and registration number, assessment status, plot number and development address.	*Dated outputs with *accredited energy assessor* name and registration number, assessment status, plot number and development address.
If not produced by an accredited energy assessor additional verification is required as detailed in the assessment methodology.	If not produced by an accredited energy assessor additional verification is required as detailed in the assessment methodology.

Definitions

Accredited energy assessor

A person registered with an accredited energy assessment scheme provider. The scheme provider will be licensed by Communities and Local Government to accredit competent persons to assess the CO_2 emission rates of domestic buildings for the purposes of demonstrating compliance with *Building Regulations*.

(AD L1A) Approved Document L1A

The Building Regulations for England and Wales Approved Document L1A: Conservation of Fuel and Power in New Dwellings (2010 Edition).

Building Control Body

This is the body responsible for ensuring construction works are according to plan and compliant with applicable requirements through periodic inspection

Building Regulations

Building Regulations apply in England and Wales and promote:

- Standards for most aspects of a building's construction, including structure, fire safety, sound insulation, drainage, ventilation and electrical safety
- Energy efficiency
- The needs of all people, including those with disabilities, in accessing and moving around buildings.

Dwelling Type

The type of dwelling under assessment determines the applicable FEE and credit scale. To define the dwelling type under assessment refer to www.zerocarbonhub.org

The FEE scale of ≤48 kWh/m^2/year to ≤32 kWh/m^2/year is applicable to:

- Apartment blocks*
- Mid-terrace houses / bungalows**

* For some apartment blocks the FEE scale of ≤60 kWh/m^2/year to ≤38 kWh/m^2/year applies. To define the dwelling type under assessment refer to: www.zerocarbonhub.org

**For stepped and staggered terraced houses/bungalows and houses with an internal garage or drive through, refer to special cases.

The FEE scale of ≤60 kWh/m^2/year to ≤38 kWh/m^2/year is applicable to:

- End terrace houses / bungalows
- Semi-detached houses / bungalows
- Detached houses / bungalows.

Energy averaging

For all apartment blocks, it is acceptable to assess this issue based on the area weighted average FEE performance of all dwellings within the building. The area weighted average FEE performance must be calculated in accordance with methodology defined in clause 4.6 of *AD L1A*.

Use of energy averaging to assess performance against this issue is at the discretion of the developer and assessor.

(EPC) Energy Performance Certificate

This is a certificate that confirms the energy rating of the dwelling from A to G, where A is the most efficient and G is the least efficient. The better the rating, the more energy efficient the dwelling is, and the lower the fuel bills are likely to be. The energy performance of the building is shown as a carbon dioxide (CO_2) based index. EPCs are generated using approved software by accredited energy assessors.

Where energy averaging is carried out for the purposes of a Code assessment, it is possible to use better fabric and systems performance in some dwellings to offset worse performance in others. This is not possible for the purposes of the EPC calculation and as such Code energy performance may differ from that indicated on the EPC.

Where energy averaging has been used, performance against the requirements of this issue is not indicative of individual dwelling performance or running costs.

(FEE) Fabric Energy Efficiency

Energy demand for space heating and cooling expressed in kilowatt-hours of energy demand per square metre per year ($kWh/m^2/year$).

Fabric energy efficiency is calculated according to the conditions defined in Section 11 of SAP. The outputs from FEE calculations should be rounded to 1 decimal place prior to determining the number of credits to award.

SAP Output (design & as built stage)

This is a dated output from accredited SAP software produced by an *accredited energy assessor*. The output must summarise the data necessary to determine performance against the requirements of this issue and include the name and registration number of the accredited energy assessor, the assessment status, plot number and development address. It is not necessary to produce individual SAP outputs for identical dwellings for the purposes of a Code assessment.

The output will be based on either design stage information or on the dwelling as constructed. Design stage outputs must be used when assessing design stage Code performance and as built outputs for post construction Code assessments.

Where SAP outputs are not produced by an accredited energy assessor they must be verified by either an accredited energy assessor or a member of the *building control body* responsible for assessing the dwelling for compliance with Part L of the Building Regulations.

For the purposes of assessing this issue the applicable SAP outputs are:

- SAP DER Worksheet

(SAP) Standard Assessment Procedure for Energy Rating of Dwellings

The Government's approved methodology for assessing the energy performance of new dwellings. The current version is SAP 2009 version 9.90, dated March 2010, rev October 2010. The procedure accounts for energy used in:

- Space heating and cooling
- Hot water provision
- Fixed lighting.

The indicators of energy performance are energy consumption per unit floor area, energy cost rating (SAP rating), environmental impact rating based on CO_2 emissions (EI rating) and dwelling CO_2 emission rate (DER). They are used in the production of energy performance certificates (*EPCs*) and to demonstrate compliance with *AD L1A* and the Code for Sustainable Homes.

To contribute to reducing CO_2 emissions as calculated by SAP, heat and power must be generated either on or in the home, on the development or through other local community arrangements (including district heat and power).

Assessment Methodology

The assessment criteria should be read with the methodology and the definitions in this section. Mandatory requirements are met and credits are awarded where the performance requirements (set out in the assessment criteria table) have been met.

Design Stage

Confirm the *dwelling type* and *FEE* scale to apply to the dwelling being assessed

Confirm that the SAP output for the dwelling being assessed meets the criteria set out in the definitions section.

Identify the FEE performance of the dwelling under assessment.

For all apartment blocks, it is acceptable to award credits based on the area weighted average FEE for all dwellings in the building. *Energy averaging* must be calculated in accordance with the criteria set out in the definitions section.

Post Construction Stage

Either:

- Confirm that no changes have been made to the design during construction that impact on FEE performance.

Or, where changes have been made during construction:

- As for design stage, but based on as built SAP outputs.

Calculation Procedures

None.

Checklists and Tables

None.

Common Cases of Non-Compliance

None.

Special Cases

Terraces of houses/bungalows are often stepped or staggered to account for factors such as site topography or local planning requirements. Where this is the case, the side walls of mid terrace dwellings become partially exposed, increasing heat loss and energy demand.

As the area of exposed side wall increases, the energy performance characteristics of a mid-terrace dwelling become more akin to those of an end terrace dwelling. To account for this, and to maintain the logic behind separate FEE targets for mid and end terrace dwellings, the standard mid terrace FEE performance requirements i.e. those defined in the assessment criteria table, can be reduced for stepped or staggered mid terrace dwellings/bungalows and houses with an internal garage or drive through.

Where these dwelling types are under assessment, the following formula can be applied to adjust the standard mid terrace FEE performance requirements set at each credit level; this includes the mandatory Code level 5 and 6 requirements:

$$\text{Revised FEE Performance Benchmark} = B_{MT} + (2 \times (B_{ET} - B_{MT}) \times R)$$

Where:

B_{MT} = Standard mid-terrace FEE performance benchmark

B_{ET} = Corresponding standard end terrace performance benchmark

R = Ratio of exposed/semi exposed side wall to total wall area

Note: This formula is only applicable where $0 < R < 0.5$. Where $R \geq 0.5$ standard end terrace performance benchmarks apply.

To calculate R:

$$R = \frac{\text{Exposed Side Wall Area m}^2 + \text{Semi-exposed side wall Area m}^2}{\text{Total Side Wall Area m}^2}$$

R should be rounded to 2 decimal places.

For guidance on determining the exposed side wall and semi-exposed side wall area refer to www.zerocarbonhub.org

Ene

Issue ID	Description	No. of Credits Available	Mandatory Elements
Ene 3	Energy Display Devices	2	No

Aim

To promote the specification of equipment to display energy consumption data, thus empowering dwelling occupants to reduce energy use.

Assessment Criteria

Criteria	Credits
Where current electricity **OR** *primary heating fuel* consumption data are displayed to occupants by a *correctly specified energy display device*.	1
Where current electricity **AND** primary heating fuel consumption data are displayed to occupants by a correctly specified energy display device.	2
Default Cases	
Where electricity is the primary heating fuel and current electricity consumption data are displayed to occupants by a correctly specified energy display device.	2

Information Required to Demonstrate Compliance

Schedule of Evidence Required	
Design Stage	Post Construction Stage
Detailed documentary evidence confirming: That the correctly specified energy display device is dedicated to the dwelling **AND** The consumption data displayed by the correctly specified energy display device	For post construction stage only assessments, provide detailed documentary evidence (as listed for the design stage) representing the dwellings as built **OR** Provide written confirmation from the developer that the energy display device has been installed as specified in the design stage detailed documentary evidence **OR** Where only a specification/letter of instruction is provided at the design stage, provide detailed documentary evidence (as listed for the design stage) representing the dwellings as built **OR** Where different from the design stage, provide detailed documentary evidence (as listed for the design stage) representing the dwellings as built **OR** Provide a *site inspection report* confirming compliance
Where detailed documentary evidence cannot be produced at this stage: A specification can be allowed as evidence of intent to meet specific requirements **OR** A letter of instruction to a contractor/supplier or a formal letter from the developer giving the specific undertaking can be allowed	

Definitions

Correctly Specified Energy Display Device

This is a system comprising a self-charging sensor(s) fixed to the incoming mains supply/supplies, to measure and transmit energy consumption data to a visual display unit. As a minimum the visual display unit must be capable of displaying the following information:

- Local time

- Current mains energy consumption (kilowatts and kilowatt hours)
- Current emissions (g/kg CO_2)
- Current tariff
- Current cost (in pounds and pence). For pre-payment customers this should be 'real time' data and for 'credit' paying customers cost should be displayed on a monthly basis
- Display accurate account balance information (amount in credit or debit)
- Visual presentation of data (i.e. non-numeric) to allow consumers to easily identify high and low level of usage
- Historical consumption data so that consumers can compare their current and previous usage in a meaningful way. This should include cumulative consumption data in any of the following forms day/week/month/billing period.

Primary Heating Fuel

The fuel used to provide the majority of heat to the dwelling under assessment.

Site Inspection Report

This is a report prepared by the Code assessor during a post construction stage assessment and issued as evidence with the assessment.

Assessment Methodology

The assessment criteria should be read with the methodology and the definitions in this section. Credits are awarded where the performance requirements (set out in the assessment criteria table) have been met.

Design Stage

- Confirm whether a correctly specified energy display device has been provided.
- Confirm whether the specified device displays electricity consumption data and/ or primary heating fuel consumption data.

Post Construction Stage

Either:

- Confirm that no changes have been made to the design during construction that impact on the energy display device specification.

Or, where changes have been made during construction:

- As for the design stage, but based on as built information.

Calculation Procedures

None.

Checklists and Tables

None.

Common Cases of Non-Compliance

None.

Special Cases

None.

Issue ID	Description	No. of Credits Available	Mandatory Elements
Ene 4	Drying Space	1	No

Aim

To promote a reduced energy means of drying clothes.

Assessment Criteria

Criteria	Credits
Where space and equipment are provided for drying clothes: • For 1 – 2 bedroom dwellings, the drying equipment must be capable of holding 4m+ of drying line • For 3+ bedroom dwellings, the drying equipment must be capable of holding 6m+ of drying line The *drying space* (internal or external) must be *secure*	1
Default Cases None	

Information Required to Demonstrate Compliance

Schedule of Evidence Required	
Design Stage	**Post Construction Stage**
For internal drying space, detailed documentary evidence confirming: • The location of drying fixings • Details/location of ventilation provided • The length of drying line • Details of the lock provided (for communal drying space only)	For post construction stage only assessments, provide detailed documentary evidence (as listed for the design stage) representing the dwellings as built **OR** Written confirmation from the developer that the fittings have been installed as specified in the design stage detailed documentary evidence **OR** Where only a specification/letter of instruction is provided at the design stage, provide detailed documentary evidence (as listed for the design stage) representing the dwellings as built **OR** Where different from the design stage, provide detailed documentary evidence (as listed for the design stage) representing the dwellings as built **OR** A *site inspection report* confirming compliance
For external drying space, detailed documentary evidence confirming: • The location of fixings/footings or posts • The length of drying line • Details of the lock provided (for communal drying space only)	
Where detailed documentary evidence cannot be produced at this stage: A specification can be allowed as evidence of intent to meet specific requirements **OR** A letter of instruction to a contractor/supplier or a formal letter from the developer giving the specific undertaking	

Definitions

(AD F) Approved Document F1

The Building Regulations for England and Wales Approved Document F1: Means of Ventilation (2010 Edition).

Ene

Drying space

A heated space with controlled intermittent extract ventilation. Extract ventilation must achieve a minimum extract rate of 30l/s and be controlled according to the requirements for intermittent extract ventilation defined in AD F.

OR

An unheated outbuilding may also be acceptable, where calculations by an appropriate member of the Chartered Institution of Building Services Engineers (CIBSE), or equivalent professional, confirms that ventilation is adequate to allow drying in normal climatic conditions and to prevent condensation/mould growth.

OR

An external secure space with access restricted to occupants of the dwelling(s). The space should be accessed directly from an external door.

Any fixings/fittings must be a permanent feature of the room or space.

Secure entrance lock

A permanent mortice deadlock or mortice sash lock that conforms to BS 3621:2007.

Secure space

This is an enclosed space accessible only to the residents of an individual dwelling. For dwellings with communal drying space, this is an enclosed space with a secure entrance lock, accessible only to the residents of the dwellings.

Site Inspection Report

A report prepared by the Code assessor during a post construction stage assessment and provided as evidence with the assessment.

Assessment Methodology

The assessment criteria should be read with the methodology and the definitions in this section. Credits are awarded where the performance requirements (set out in the assessment criteria table) have been met.

Design Stage

- Confirm whether internal or external drying space will be provided and whether it is of adequate and secure provision.
- Confirm whether adequate drying equipment will be provided and that it is located appropriately.

Post Construction Stage

Either:

- Confirm that no changes have been made to the dwelling design during construction that impact on the specification of drying facilities.

Or, where changes have been made during construction:

- As for the design stage, but based on as-built information.

Calculation Procedures

None.

Checklists and Tables

None.

Common Cases of Non-Compliance

Internal drying spaces are not allowed in living rooms, kitchens, dining rooms, main halls or bedrooms.

Special Cases

None.

Issue ID	Description	No. of Credits Available	Mandatory Elements
Ene 5	Energy Labelled White Goods	2	No

Aim

To promote the provision or purchase of energy efficient white goods, thus reducing the CO_2 emissions from appliance use in the dwelling.

Assessment Criteria

Criteria	Credits
Where the following appliances are provided and have an **A+** rating under the *EU Energy Efficiency Labelling Scheme*: • Fridges and freezers or fridge-freezers	1
Where the following appliances are provided and have an **A** rating under the EU Energy Efficiency Labelling Scheme: • Washing machines and dishwashers **AND EITHER** • Tumble dryers or washer dryers have a **B** rating (where a washer dryer is provided, it is not necessary to also provide a washing machine) **OR** • *EU Energy Efficiency Labelling Scheme Information* is provided to each dwelling in place of a tumble dryer or a washer dryer	1
Where no white goods are provided but EU Energy Efficiency Labelling Scheme Information is provided to each dwelling Note: To obtain this credit, any white goods available to purchase from the developer must be compliant with the above criteria.	1
Default Cases None	

Information Required to Demonstrate Compliance

Schedule of Evidence Required	
Design Stage	**Post Construction Stage**
If any white goods are to be provided, detailed documentary evidence confirming: The appliances to be provided with their applicable ratings under the EU Energy Efficiency Labelling Scheme	For post construction stage only assessments, provide detailed documentary evidence (as listed for the design stage) representing the dwellings as built **OR**
Where washer dryers or tumble dryers will not be provided and the second credit is sought, provide detailed documentary evidence as follows: • A copy of the EU Energy Efficiency Labelling Scheme Information **AND** • Confirmation that the information will be provided to all dwellings	Written confirmation from the developer that the appliances/fittings have been installed as specified in the design stage detailed documentary evidence **OR**
If no white goods are provided, detailed documentary evidence as follows: • A copy of the information that will be provided on the EU Energy Efficiency Labelling Scheme **AND** • Confirmation that the information will be provided to all dwellings **AND** • Confirmation that all appliances available for purchase with the dwelling are compliant with the assessment criteria	Where only a letter of instruction is provided at the design stage, provide detailed documentary evidence (as listed for the design stage) representing the dwellings as built **OR** Where different from the design stage, provide detailed documentary evidence (as listed for the design stage) representing the dwellings as built
Where details cannot be produced at this stage: • A formal letter from the developer giving the specific undertaking	

Definitions

EU Energy Efficiency Labelling Scheme

The EU energy label rates products from A (the most efficient) to G (the least efficient). For refrigeration, the scale now extends to A++. It is a legal requirement for the label to be shown on all refrigeration and laundry appliances, dishwashers, electric ovens and light bulb packaging at point of sale.

EU Energy Efficiency Labelling Scheme information

An information leaflet explaining the EU Energy Efficiency Labelling Scheme and the benefits of purchasing appliances with higher ratings.

Assessment Methodology

The assessment criteria should be read with the methodology and the definitions in this section. Credits are awarded where the performance requirements (set out in the assessment criteria table) have been met.

Design Stage

- Confirm the EU Energy Efficiency Labelling Scheme rating for specified appliances covered by the assessment criteria.

- Where appliances are not being provided, confirm that EU Energy Efficiency Labelling Scheme Information will be provided.

Post Construction Stage

Either:

- Confirm that no changes have been made to the dwelling design during construction that impact on the appliances' specification.

Or, where changes have been made during construction:

- As for the design stage, but based on as-built information.

Calculation Procedures

None.

Checklists and Tables

None.

Common Cases of Non-Compliance

None.

Special Cases

Where appliances included in the assessment criteria for this issue are not covered by the EU Energy Efficiency Labelling Scheme (e.g. gas-powered tumble dryers), recognition under the Energy Saving Trust's Energy Saving Recommended scheme (http://www.energysavingtrust.org.uk/business/Business/Energy-Saving-Trust-Recommended) is deemed to demonstrate compliance. Evidence should be provided confirming that the make and model of the appliance meets the requirements of the scheme and is permitted to display the Energy Saving Recommended logo. The evidence must be dated to show that the endorsement is current.

Issue ID	Description	No. of Credits Available	Mandatory Elements
Ene 6	External Lighting	2	No

Aim

To promote the provision of energy efficient external lighting, thus reducing CO_2 emissions associated with the dwelling.

Assessment Criteria

Criteria	Credits
Space Lighting Where all external *space lighting*, including lighting in common areas, is provided by *dedicated energy efficient fittings* with appropriate *control systems*. Note: *Statutory safety lighting* is not covered by this requirement	1
Security Lighting Where all *security lighting* is designed for energy efficiency and is adequately controlled such that: All burglar security lights have: • A maximum wattage of 150 W AND • *Movement detecting control devices (PIR)* AND • *Daylight cut-off sensors* All other *security lighting*: • Is provided by *dedicated energy efficient fittings* AND • Is fitted with *daylight cut-off sensors* OR a *time switch*	1
Default Cases If no security lighting is installed, the security lighting credit can be awarded by default, provided all of the requirements related to the specification of space lighting have been met. Dual lamp luminaires with both space and security lamps can be awarded both credits provided they meet the above criteria for energy efficiency	1

Information Required to Demonstrate Compliance

Schedule of Evidence Required	
Design Stage	**Post Construction Stage**
Relevant drawings clearly showing the location of all external light fittings **AND** Detailed documentary evidence confirming: • The types of light fitting and efficacy, in lumens per circuit watt, for all lamps • The control systems applicable to each light fitting or group of fittings	For post construction stage only assessments, provide drawings and detailed documentary evidence (as listed for the design stage) representing the dwellings as built **OR** Written confirmation from the developer that the external light fittings have been installed as specified in drawings and the design stage detailed documentary evidence **OR** Where only a letter of instruction is provided at the design stage, provide calculations and detailed documentary evidence (as listed for the design stage) representing the dwellings as built **OR** Where different from the design stage, provide revised drawings and detailed documentary evidence (as listed for the design stage) representing the dwellings as built **OR** A *site inspection report* confirming compliance
Where detailed information is not available at this stage: A letter of instruction to a contractor/ supplier or a formal letter from the developer giving the specific undertaking	

Definitions

Control systems

A method for controlling the external lighting to ensure that it will not operate unnecessarily, e.g. during daylight hours or when a space is unoccupied. Control systems that can be considered are passive infra red (PIR), 'dusk to dawn' daylight sensors and time switches.

Daylight sensors (dusk to dawn)

A type of sensor that detects daylight and switches lighting on at dusk and off at dawn.

Dedicated energy efficient light fittings

Fittings that comprise the lamp, base, control gear and an appropriate housing, reflector, shade or diffuser. The fitting must be dedicated in that it must be capable of only accepting lamps having a luminous efficacy greater than 40 lumens per circuit watt. A light fitting may contain one or more lamps.

Tubular fluorescent and compact fluorescent light fittings would typically meet this requirement. Light fittings for GLS tungsten lamps with bayonet cap or Edison screw bases, or tungsten halogen lamps would not comply.

Dual-level lighting

Artificial lighting, specified with appropriate control systems, which operates at different levels of illuminance to provide an adequate maintained level of lighting to internal spaces.

Dual-level lighting must be specified to reduce levels of illuminance when spaces are less likely to be occupied, in accordance with the minimum maintained illuminance levels defined in CIBSE LG9: 1997 Lighting for Communal Residential Buildings.

Movement detecting control devices (PIR)

A type of motion detector that uses infra red radiation to detect movement and switches lighting on.

Pin-based compact fluorescent lamp (CFL)

A type of fluorescent lamp that plugs into a small dedicated lighting fixture. CFLs have a longer rated life and use less electricity than conventional incandescent light bulbs. Conventional bayonet or screw (Edison) CFL fittings are not acceptable under the Code.

Security lighting

Security lighting is provided to protect property. There are two types of security lighting commonly used in dwellings – high wattage intruder lights that are operated via PIR sensors which only switch on for a short time, and low wattage lighting that is controlled by time switches and daylight sensors.

Site Inspection Report

A report prepared by the Code assessor during a post construction stage assessment and provided as evidence with the assessment.

Space lighting

The normal lighting required to illuminate a space when in use. It can be used outside the entrance to the home, in outbuildings such as garages and cycle stores, and for external spaces such as paths, patios, decks, porches, steps and verandas.

Space lighting must be designed with appropriate control systems to ensure it is switched off during daylight hours.

Statutory safety lighting

Safety lighting is usually provided in multi-residential buildings such as blocks of flats to illuminate stairwells and exit routes when the main lighting system fails. Its design is specified by regulation (BS 5266) and is therefore outside the scope of the Code.

Time switch

A switch with an in-built clock which will allow lighting to be switched on and off at programmed times.

Tubular fluorescent and compact fluorescent lamp (TFL/CFL)

A type of fluorescent lamp that is named after its shape. These lamps have their own range of dedicated fittings, and have a longer rated life and use less electricity than conventional incandescent light bulbs.

Assessment Methodology

The assessment criteria should be read with the methodology and the definitions in this section. Credits are awarded where the performance requirements (set out in the assessment criteria table) have been met.

Design Stage

- Confirm whether the external space and security lighting specification meets the requirements set out in the assessment criteria.

- For houses, fittings serving the following areas should be included in the assessment: external door, front porch, steps/pathways, patio, garage, garden, carports and any other outbuildings.

- For flats, fittings serving the following areas should be included in the assessment: external steps and pathways, main external entrances and all communal internal spaces.

Post Construction Stage

Either:

- Confirm that no changes have been made to the dwelling design during construction that impact on the external space and security lighting specification.

Or, where changes have been made during construction:

- As for the design stage, but based on as-built information.

Calculation Procedures

None.

Checklists and Tables

None.

Common Cases of Non-Compliance

Credits cannot be awarded by default if no space lighting is installed, even in cases where all security lighting requirements are met.

Special Cases

On a privately managed site, external lighting managed by a Local Authority may be excluded from this issue.

Where a site is redeveloped and existing external lighting remains, the lighting that is retained has to comply with the requirements of the issue. Replacement of the fittings may be necessary.

Any fitting that consumes less than 5 W may be excluded from the requirements set out in this issue. This is to allow for the specification of innovative light sources, such as LEDs.

Where permanent space lighting is required for safety reasons, or for the purpose of meeting other applicable design standards (normally in internal communal corridors or stairwells that receive no daylight), *dual-level lighting* is acceptable.

Issue ID	Description	No. of Credits Available	Mandatory Elements
Ene 7	Low and Zero Carbon Technologies	2	No

Aim

To limit CO_2 emissions and running costs arising from the operation of a dwelling and its services by encouraging the specification of low and zero carbon energy sources to supply a significant proportion of energy demand.

Assessment Criteria

Criteria	Credits
Where energy is supplied by *low or zero carbon technologies* **AND** There is a 10% reduction in CO_2 emissions as a result	1
OR There is a 15% reduction in CO_2 emissions as a result	2
Default Cases None	

Ene

Information Required to Demonstrate Compliance

Schedule of Evidence Required	
Design Stage	Post Construction Stage
A copy of calculations as detailed in the assessment methodology based on design stage *SAP outputs*	A copy of calculations as detailed in the assessment methodology based on as built SAP outputs
AND	**AND**
Detailed documentary evidence confirming that the specified low or zero carbon technologies:	Detailed documentary evidence confirming that the specified low or zero carbon technologies:
• Meet any additional requirements defined in Directive 2009/28/EC as applicable.	• Meet any additional requirements defined in Directive 2009/28/EC as applicable.
And are:	And are:
• Certified under the Microgeneration Certification Scheme*	• Certified under the Microgeneration Certification Scheme*
OR	**OR**
• Certified under the CHPQA standard*	• Certified under the CHPQA standard*
*As applicable.	*As applicable.

Definitions

Accredited energy assessor

A person registered with an accredited energy assessment scheme provider. The scheme provider will be licensed by Communities and Local Government to accredit competent persons to assess the CO_2 emission rates of domestic buildings for the purposes of demonstrating compliance with *Building Regulations*.

Accredited External Renewables

These are renewable energy installations located off site which:

- Are Renewable Energy Guarantee of Origin (REGO) certified.
- Create new installed generation capacity designed to meet the demand of the dwelling.
- Are additional to capacity already required under the Renewables Obligation.

Ene

Actual Case CO_2 Emissions

CO_2 emissions from the dwelling (Kg $CO_2/m^2/year$) accounting for the input from specified/installed low and zero carbon technologies.

The standard case dwelling model must be used as the basis for the calculation of actual case emissions. However, where eligible low or zero carbon technologies are specified in the dwelling they can replace the standard systems assumptions from table Cat 1.2 for the purposes of the actual case calculation.

Actual case CO_2 emissions must be calculated in accordance with the methodology defined in table Cat 1.3.

(AD L1A) Approved Document L1A

The Building Regulations for England and Wales Approved Document L1A: Conservation of Fuel and Power in New Dwellings (2010 Edition).

Building Control Body

The body responsible for ensuring that construction works are according to plan and compliant with applicable requirements through periodic inspection.

Building Regulations

Building Regulations apply in England and Wales and promote:

- Standards for most aspects of a building's construction, including structure, fire safety, sound insulation, drainage, ventilation and electrical safety
- Energy efficiency
- The needs of all people, including those with disabilities, in accessing and moving around buildings.

Direct Supply

The carbon benefit of energy generated by low or zero carbon technologies can only be allocated to dwellings that are directly supplied by the installation via dedicated supplies.

Where electricity is generated which is surplus to the instantaneous demand of the dwelling(s), it may be fed back to the National Grid. The carbon benefit of any electricity fed back to the grid can be allocated as if it were consumed in the dwelling(s) when assessing performance against the requirements of this issue.

For communal PV arrays in buildings with multiple dwellings, the obligations of this definition are satisfied where the requirements of Appendix M of *SAP* are met.

Low and Zero Carbon Technologies

Technologies eligible to contribute to achieving the requirements of this issue must produce energy from renewable sources and meet all other ancillary requirements as defined by Directive 2009/28/EC of the European Parliament and of the Council of

23 April 2009 on the promotion of the use of energy from renewable sources and amending and subsequently repealing Directives 2001/77/EC and 2003/30/EC.

The following requirements must also be met:

- Where not provided by accredited external renewables there must be a *direct supply* of energy produced to the dwelling under assessment.

- Where covered by the *Microgeneration Certification Scheme (MCS)*, technologies under 50kWe or 300kWth must be certified.

- Combined Heat and Power (CHP) schemes above 50kWe must be certified under the CHPQA standard.

- All technologies must be accounted for by SAP.

CHP schemes fuelled by mains gas are eligible to contribute to performance against this issue. Where these schemes are above 50kWe they must be certified under the CHPQA.

(MCS) Microgeneration Certification Scheme

The Microgeneration Certification Scheme (MCS) is an independent scheme that certifies microgeneration products and installers in accordance with consistent standards. It is designed to evaluate microgeneration products and installers against robust criteria, and provides consumers with an independent indication of the reliability of products, assurance that the installation will be carried out to the appropriate standard and a route for complaints should there be any issues.

The MCS is a United Kingdom Accreditation Service (UKAS) accredited certification scheme covering all microgeneration products and services. It has support from the Department of Energy and Climate Change (DECC), industry and non-governmental groups as a prime method for making a substantial contribution to cutting the UK's dependency on fossil fuels and carbon dioxide emissions.

SAP output (design & as built stage)

This is a dated output from accredited SAP software produced by an *accredited energy assessor*. The output must summarise the data necessary to determine performance against the requirements of this issue and include the name and registration number of the accredited energy assessor, the assessment status, plot number and development address. It is not necessary to produce individual SAP outputs for identical dwellings for the purposes of a Code assessment.

The output will be based on either design stage information or on the dwelling as constructed. Design stage outputs are normally used when assessing design stage Code performance and as built outputs for post construction Code assessments. However, for the purposes of assessment against the requirements of this issue 'draft' SAP outputs are acceptable.

Where SAP Outputs are not produced by an accredited energy assessor they must be verified by either an accredited energy assessor or a member of the *building control body* responsible for assessing the dwelling for compliance with Part L of the Building Regulations.

For the purposes of assessing this issue the applicable SAP outputs are:

- SAP DER worksheet

(SAP) Standard Assessment Procedure for Energy Rating of Dwellings

The Government's approved methodology for assessing the energy performance of new dwellings. The current version is SAP 2009 version 9.90, dated March 2010, rev October 2010. The procedure accounts for energy used in:

- Space heating and cooling
- Hot water provision
- Fixed lighting.

The indicators of energy performance are energy consumption per unit floor area, energy cost rating (SAP rating), environmental impact rating based on CO_2 emissions (EI rating) and dwelling CO_2 emission rate (DER). They are used in the production of energy performance certificates (EPCs) and to demonstrate compliance with *AD L1A* and the Code for Sustainable Homes.

To contribute to reducing CO_2 emissions as calculated by SAP, heat and power must be generated either on or in the home, on the development or through other local community arrangements (including district heat and power).

Standard Case CO_2 Emissions

CO_2 emissions from the dwelling (Kg CO_2/m^2/year) assuming a standard systems specification, based on the Domestic Building Services Compliance Guide 2010 Edition.

Standard case CO_2 emissions create the baseline against which the contribution of low and zero carbon technologies is measured. They represent the common scenario where a gas boiler is installed and ensure a 'level playing field' to allow a fair comparison of the contribution of low and zero carbon technologies, regardless of the carbon intensity of the actual heating fuel specified.

The assumptions to be included in the calculation of standard case CO_2 emissions are included in table Cat 1.2.

Standard case CO_2 emissions must be calculated in accordance with the methodology defined in table Cat 1.3.

Assessment Methodology

The assessment criteria should be read with the methodology and the definitions in this section. Credits are awarded where the performance requirements (set out in the assessment criteria table) have been met.

Design Stage

Confirm that the SAP output for each dwelling being assessed meets the criteria set out in the definitions section.

Calculate the *standard case CO$_2$ emissions*.

Calculate the *actual case CO$_2$ emissions*.

Calculate the reduction in actual case CO$_2$ emissions compared to standard case CO$_2$ emissions.

Post Construction Stage

Either:

- Confirm that no changes have been made to the dwelling design during construction that impact on the low and zero carbon technologies specification.

Or, where changes have been made during construction:

- As for design stage, but based on as built SAP outputs.

Calculation Procedures

1. Standard Case CO$_2$ Emissions:

Standard case CO$_2$ emissions must be calculated according to the methodology defined in table Cat 1.3.

The specification assumptions included in table Cat 1.2 must replace those of the actual dwelling in the calculation of standard case CO$_2$ emissions.

Where elements or systems are not listed in table Cat 1.2 they should be included in the calculation of standard case CO$_2$ emissions as specified/constructed.

Table Cat 1.2: Standard CO_2 Emissions Calculation - Specification Assumptions		
Element or System		**Value**
[1]	Main heating fuel (space and water)	Mains gas
[2]	Main heating system (and second main heating system where specified)	Boiler and radiators Fully pumped circulation Water pump in heated space
[2a]	Boiler	SEDBUK (2009) 88% Room-sealed Fanned Flue On/off burner control
[2b]	Heating system controls	Programmer Room thermostats TRVs Boiler interlock
[3]	Secondary heating fuel *(where secondary heating is specified)*	Electricity
[3a]	Secondary heating system *(where secondary heating is specified)*	Panel, convector or radiant heaters
[4]	Hot water system	Stored hot water, heated by boiler only Separate time control for space and water heating
[4a]	Hot water storage	150 litre cylinder insulated with 35mm of factory applied foam
[4b]	Primary water heating losses	Primary pipework insulated Cylinder temperature controlled by thermostat
[4c]	Technologies covered by Appendix H of SAP	None specified
[5]	Technologies covered by Appendix M of SAP	None specified

2. Actual Case CO_2 Emissions:

Actual case CO_2 emissions must be calculated according to the methodology defined in table Cat 1.3.

The standard case dwelling model must be used as the basis for the calculation of actual case emissions. However, where eligible low or zero carbon technologies are specified in the dwelling they can replace the standard systems assumptions from table Cat 1.2 for the purposes of the actual case emissions calculation.

The reduction in CO_2 emissions as a result of the specification of low and zero carbon technologies must be calculated according to the methodology defined in table Cat 1.3.

Ene

Table Cat 1.3: Reduction in CO$_2$ Emissions				
Value Required		Data Source Guidance (See note [1])	Unit Required	Value
(1)	Standard Case CO$_2$ emissions See notes [2] and [4]	SAP Section 16: **[SAP box ZC8]**	+ KgCO$_2$/m^2/yr	
(2)	Actual Case CO$_2$ emissions See notes [2], [3] and [4]	SAP Section 16: **[SAP box ZC8]**	+/– KgCO$_2$/m^2/yr	
(3)	Reduction in CO$_2$ emissions See note [5]	$100 \times (1-($Value at step **(2)** ÷ Value at step **(1)**$))$	+/– %	

Notes to table Cat 1.3:

[1]   The data sources in this calculation correspond with SAP and are intended as supplementary guidance to assist in identifying the values required. It is the responsibility of the assessor to ensure that the correct value is identified and entered into the calculation, as the data source may vary dependant on the type of accredited SAP software used to assess energy performance.

[2]   Section 16 of SAP extends the calculation to account for CO$_2$ emissions from appliances and cooking and to allow for site-wide electricity generating technologies. Follow the procedure set out in Section 16 of SAP 2009 to calculate standard case CO$_2$ emissions and actual case CO$_2$ emissions for the dwelling under assessment. There are no specific conditions imposed that preclude the use of section 16 of SAP to calculate standard or actual emissions.

[3]   In the calculation of actual case CO$_2$ emissions, there are no specific conditions that preclude consideration of the allowances included in Section 16 of SAP for site-wide electricity generating technologies and CO$_2$ emissions offsets from biofuel CHP systems. For details of acceptable technologies, configurations, output calculations and of how to apportion the output to individual dwellings, refer to Appendix M and Section 16 of SAP.

[4]   Where centralised energy supply infrastructure is in place that services other users (e.g. mixed use developments) the output must be allocated between all users in relation to their proportional net floor area.

[5]   The calculated percentage reduction must be truncated (not rounded down) to an integer percentage e.g. 9.8750% becomes 9%. This figure is then used to determine the number of credits achieved, in line with the performance requirements defined in the assessment criteria table.

Checklists and Tables

None.

Common Cases of Non-Compliance

Energy supplied from remote sources through the National Grid is not eligible to contribute towards achieving the requirements set out in this issue. This includes electricity procured through 'green tariffs'.

Special Cases

None.

Issue ID	Description	No. of Credits Available	Mandatory Elements
Ene 8	Cycle Storage	2	No

Aim

To promote the wider use of bicycles as transport by providing adequate and secure cycle storage facilities, thus reducing the need for short car journeys and the associated CO_2 emissions.

Assessment Criteria

Criteria	Credits
Where individual or communal cycle storage is provided, that is *adequately sized, secure* and *convenient*, for the following number of cycles:	
Studios or 1 bedroom dwellings – storage for 1 cycle for every two dwellings	1
2 and 3 bedroom dwellings –- storage for 1 cycle per dwelling	
4 bedrooms and above –- storage for 2 cycles per dwelling	
OR	
Studios or 1 bedroom dwellings – storage for 1 cycle per dwelling	2
2 and 3 bedroom dwellings – storage for 2 cycles per dwelling	
4 bedrooms and above – storage for 4 cycles per dwelling	
Note: The requirements for secure cycle storage are met where compliance with clause 35 of Secured by Design (SBD) New Homes 2010 is achieved.	
Default Cases	
None	

Information Required to Demonstrate Compliance

Schedule of Evidence Required	
Design Stage	**Post Construction Stage**
Detailed documentary evidence showing: • The number of bedrooms and the corresponding number of cycle storage spaces per dwelling • Location, type and size of storage • Convenient access to cycle storage • Any security measures • Details of the proprietary system (if applicable) • How the requirements of clause 35 of Secured by Design – New Homes 2010 will be met (if applicable) Where detailed information is not available at this stage: A letter of instruction to a contractor/ supplier or a formal letter from the developer giving the specific undertaking	For post construction stage only assessments, provide detailed documentary evidence (as listed for the design stage) representing the dwellings as built **OR** Written confirmation from the developer that the cycle storage facilities have been installed as specified in the design stage detailed documentary evidence **OR** Where only a letter of instruction is provided at the design stage, provide detailed documentary evidence (as listed for the design stage) representing the dwellings as built **OR** Where different from the design stage, provide detailed documentary evidence (as listed for the design stage) representing the dwellings as built **OR** A *site inspection report* confirming compliance

Definitions

Adequately Sized Cycle Storage

The minimum storage area required to store cycles on the floor, defined by the *New Metric Handbook*, which includes space to allow the cycles to be moved independently.

- 1 cycle: 2 m long × 0.75 m wide
- 2 cycles: 2 m long × 1.5 m wide
- 4 cycles: 2 m long × 2.5 m wide

OR

Where a proprietary storage or hanging system is provided, the space requirements are flexible but the system must allow each cycle to be removed independently and meet all other criteria.

Where cycle storage is provided in a shed, a minimum of 1 m^2 is required for garden tools (in addition to the above dimensions). The shed must be set on a concrete foundation and secure fixing needs to be provided.

Where cycle storage is provided in a garage, adequate space must be provided to store both the bicycle(s) and the car(s) at the same time.

For double garages, it must be assumed that each garage space is occupied by a car. Storage areas above must be added to the typical minimum garage sizes below:

- 2.4 m × 4.9 m for a single garage
- 5 m × 5.2 m for a double garage

Convenient Cycle Storage

Easy and direct access from/to the dwelling(s) and from/to the cycle store to a public right of way.

Access from the store to a public right of way through the dwelling is not acceptable, e.g. where cycles are stored in a shed in the back garden of a mid-terraced home and there is no direct access from the garden to a public right of way.

Communal cycle store(s) must be located within 100 m of the front door or the main entrance to a block of flats.

If, for strategic reasons outside the control of the developer, the store cannot be located within the required distance, exceptions to the rule may be allowed. Full details must be provided and the Code service provider consulted prior to awarding credits.

Lighting in communal cycle stores must comply with the requirements for space lighting defined in Ene 6 – External Lighting.

Cycle storage

Cycles may be stored in any of the following:

- Garage or shed
- External or internal communal cycle store
- Proprietary system.

Ene

Secure entrance lock

A permanent mortice deadlock or mortice sash lock that conforms to BS 3621:2007 can be used where the door is at least 44mm thick and is locked to the doorframe. Alternatively a 'sold secure' Silver Standard padlock with a hasp and staple that are coach bolted through the structure is deemed compliant.

Where communal cycle storage will be provided within a block of flats, the entrance must be a secure doorset and meet the requirements of clauses 21.2 to 21.6 and 21.8 to 21.13 of the 'Secured by Design New Homes 2010' document. Note that this room should have no windows.

Secure fixing

A ground anchor certificated to 'Sold Secure' Silver Standard.

Where a communal cycle store will be used, a stand must be provided to support the bike, and a secure ground anchor point for each cycle space (certificated to 'Sold Secure' Silver Standard). Alternatively a *secure stand* can be provided.

Secure Stand

A stand which allows both wheel and frame to be locked and must, as a minimum, be of galvanised steel bar construction (with a minimum thickness of 3mm) and have a minimum foundation depth of 300mm with a welded anchor T-bar set in concrete to prevent it being easily removed from the ground.

Secure storage

A fully enclosed structure with a *secure entrance lock* and/or *secure fixings* or *secure stands* depending on the situation and solution.

In individual dwellings:

- For solid enclosed structures: secure entrance lock or secure fixing(s)
- For non-solid structures: secure entrance lock and secure fixing(s)

Blocks of flats and multi-dwellings with communal storage areas:

- Communal halls and solid enclosed structures: secure entrance lock and secure fixing(s) for all cycles
- For non-solid structures: secure entrance lock and secure fixing(s)

Where an external container specifically designed for the secure storage of cycles will be provided, it must be certified to LPS 1175 SR 1.

Site Inspection Report

This is a report prepared by the Code assessor during a post construction stage assessment and provided as evidence with the assessment.

Ene

Assessment Methodology

The assessment criteria should be read with the methodology and the definitions in this section. Credits are awarded where the performance requirements (set out in the assessment criteria table) have been met.

Design Stage

- Confirm whether cycle storage is to be provided.
- Confirm whether any proposed cycle storage is adequately sized, has convenient access and is secure.

Post Construction Stage

Either:

- Confirm that no changes have been made to the design during construction that impact on the cycle storage specification.

Or, where changes have been made during construction:

- As for the design stage, but based on as-built information.

Calculation Procedures

None.

Checklists and Tables

None.

Common Cases of Non-Compliance

Where cycles are to be stored inside the dwelling, credits cannot be achieved (unless within a porch including adequate storage space as defined above).

Provision by the developer of a folding cycle to be stored in the dwelling does not meet the requirements of this issue or warrant a reduction in the adequate size requirements.

Special Cases

None.

Issue ID	Description	No. of Credits Available	Mandatory Elements
Ene 9	Home Office	1	No

Aim

To promote working from home by providing occupants with the necessary space and services thus reducing the need to commute.

Assessment Criteria

Criteria	Credits
Where *sufficient space* and *services* have been provided which allow occupants to set up a home office in a *suitable room*. The space dedicated for use as a home office must have *adequate ventilation* and achieve an *average daylight factor* of 1.5%.	1
Default Cases	
None	

Information Required to Demonstrate Compliance

Schedule of Evidence Required	
Design Stage	**Post Construction Review Stage**

Detailed documentary evidence showing:
 	
• Location of and sufficient space for the home office
 	
• Location and number of sockets
 	
• Location of telephone points
 	
• That adequate ventilation will be provided
 	
• That an average daylight factor of at least 1.5% is achieved
 	
• Confirmation of one of the following:
 	
  – cable connection
 	
  – that broadband is available at the site level (not for individual dwellings), i.e. a letter from the developer confirming that they have checked that broadband is available
 	
  – two telephone points (or double telephone point)
	For post construction stage only assessments, provide detailed documentary evidence (as listed for the design stage) representing the dwellings as built
	
	OR
	
	Written confirmation from the developer that the home office and related services have been provided as specified in the design stage detailed documentary evidence
	
	OR
	
	Where only a letter of instruction is provided at the design stage, provide detailed documentary evidence (as listed for the design stage) representing the dwellings as built
	
	OR
	
	Where different from the design stage, provide detailed documentary evidence (as listed for the design stage) representing the dwellings as built
	
	OR
	
	A *site inspection report* confirming compliance

Where detailed information is not available at this stage: A letter of instruction to a contractor/supplier or a formal letter from the developer giving the specific undertaking	

Definitions

Adequate ventilation

In all cases the room must have an openable window or alternative ventilation e.g. passive stack. Where the room has a window, the minimum openable casement must be 0.5 m². A room with only an external door does not meet the minimum requirements for adequate ventilation.

Average daylight factor

The average daylight factor is the average indoor illuminance (from daylight) on the working plane within a room, expressed as a percentage of the simultaneous outdoor illuminance on a horizontal plane under an unobstructed CIE 'standard overcast sky'. The average daylight factor can be calculated using the following equation:

$$DF = \frac{MWuT}{A(1 - R^2)}$$

Where:

W = total glazed area of windows or roof lights

A = total area of all the room surfaces (ceiling, floor, walls and windows)

R = area-weighted average reflectance of the room surfaces

M = a correction factor for dirt

T = glass transmission factor

u = angle of visible sky

Guide values for a typical dwelling with light-coloured walls are as follows (for more accurate values, refer to CIBSE Lighting Guide 10):

R	=	0.5
M	=	1.0 (vertical glazing that can be cleaned easily)
		0.8 (sloping glazing)
		0.7 (horizontal glazing)
T	=	0.7 (double glazing)
		0.6 (double glazing with low emissivity coating)
		0.6 (triple glazing)
u	=	65° (vertical glazing)

It is advised that this default figure for the angle of visible sky is used with caution; the methodology detailed in the angle of visible sky definition must be preferred for more accuracy.

Sufficient services

The following services must be provided in the suitable room intended as a home office:

- Two double power sockets

- Two telephone points (or double telephone point), or one telephone point where cable or broadband is available.
- A window (Note: The room chosen to be the nominated home office must have a daylight factor of at least 1.5%)
- Adequate ventilation.

Sufficient space

This is defined as the minimum size (1.8 m wall length) to allow a desk, chair and filing cabinet or bookshelf to be installed, with space to move around the front and side of the desk, use the chair appropriately and operate the filing cabinet safely (the 1.8 m wall size requirement can, in some circumstances, be altered if drawings can prove that a desk can be fitted in any other type of arrangement, i.e. alcove or similar, fulfilling all the above criteria).

Suitable room

For dwellings with three or more bedrooms, a suitable room is a room other than the kitchen, living room, master bedroom or bathroom.

For dwellings with one or two bedrooms or studio homes, a suitable room is the living room, one of the bedrooms or any other suitable area in the home such as a large hall or dining area (provided the minimum service requirements defined above are met).

In all cases, the room must be large enough to allow the intended use of that room, e.g. if a home office is to be set up in the main bedroom, that room also needs to be able to fit in a double bed and other necessary furnishing.

Site Inspection Report

This is a report prepared by the Code assessor during a post construction stage assessment and provided as evidence with the assessment.

Assessment Methodology

The assessment criteria should be read with the methodology and the definitions in this section. Credits are awarded where the performance requirements (set out in the assessment criteria table) have been met.

Design Stage

- Confirm whether sufficient space for a home office is to be provided in a suitable room.
- Confirm whether the location for the proposed home office has adequate ventilation and is specified with sufficient services.
- Confirm that the space dedicated for use as a home office achieves a daylight factor of at least 1.5%.

Post Construction Stage

Either:

- Confirm that no changes have been made to the design during construction that impact on the home office specification.

Or, where changes have been made during construction:

- As for the design stage, but based on as-built information.

Calculation Procedures

None.

Checklists and Tables

None.

Common Cases of Non-Compliance

None.

Special Cases

None.

Category 2: Water

Issue ID	Description	No. of Credits Available	Mandatory Elements
Wat 1	Indoor water use	5	Yes

Aim

To reduce the consumption of *potable water* in the home from all sources, including borehole well water, through the use of water efficient fittings, appliances and water recycling systems.

Assessment Criteria

Criteria		
Water consumption (litres/person/day)	**Credits**	**Mandatory Levels**
≤ 120 l/p/day	1	Levels 1 and 2
≤ 110 l/p/day	2	
≤ 105 l/p/day	3	Levels 3 and 4
≤ 90 l/p/day	4	
≤ 80 l/p/day	5	Levels 5 and 6
Default Cases		
None		

Information Required to Demonstrate Compliance

Schedule of Evidence Required	
Design Stage	**Post Construction Stage**
Completed *Water Efficiency Calculator for New Dwellings* internal potable water use for each dwelling which has a different specification **AND** Detailed documentary evidence showing: • Location, details and type of appliances/ fittings that use water in the dwelling including any specific *water reduction equipment* with the capacity / flow rate of equipment. • Location, size and details of any *rainwater* and *greywater* collection systems provided for use in the dwelling Where detailed documentary evidence is not available at this stage; Completed Water Efficiency Calculator for New Dwellings internal potable water use for each dwelling which has a different specification **AND** A letter of instruction to a contractor/ supplier or a formal letter from the developer giving a specific undertaking, providing sufficient information to allow the water calculations to be completed	For post construction stage only assessments, provide Water Efficiency Calculator for New Dwellings and detailed documentary evidence (as listed for design stage) representing the dwellings as built **OR** Written confirmation from the developer that the appliances/fittings have been installed as specified in the design stage detailed documentary evidence **OR** Where only a letter of instruction is provided with calculations at design stage provide revised calculations and detailed documentary evidence (as listed for design stage) representing the dwellings as built **OR** Where different from design stage, provide revised Water Efficiency Calculator for New Dwellings and detailed documentary evidence (as listed for design stage) representing the dwellings as built

Definitions

Delayed inlet valves

Delayed inlet valves prevent water entering the WC cistern until it has completely emptied, enabling a precise volume of water to be discharged independent of water pressure.

Flow restrictors

Flow restrictors contain precision-made holes or filters to restrict water flow and reduce the outlet flow and pressure. They are typically fitted within the console of the tap or shower heads, in pipework or at the mains inlet to the dwelling.

Grey-water recycling

The appropriate collection, treatment and storage of used shower, bath and tap water for use instead of potable water in WCs and/or washing machines. Grey-water recycling systems normally collect used shower, bath and tap water and recycle it for toilet flushing.

Ion exchange water softeners

Ion exchange water softeners remove the agents causing hard water by passing water from the mains through a resin. The resin must be regenerated regularly. Regeneration may occur either at set time intervals, or when a given volume of water has passed through the resin. The water consumed during regeneration depends on the hardness of the water (this varies geographically) and the efficiency of the water softener.

Low flush WCs

Low flush WCs are specifically designed to reduce the volume of water consumed during flushing. There are various systems that can be specified to achieve a reduction in flush volume, such as low single flush cisterns, delayed action water inlet valves, and dual-flush cisterns which provide a part flush for liquids and a full flush for solids. Such systems must be matched to suitable WC pans and must pass the discharge performance requirements of BS EN 997:2003 for Class 2 WC suites.

Mains potable water

Drinking quality water taken from a connection to the mains water supply.

Potable water

Drinking quality water that is taken from a connection to the mains water supply in the dwelling, which may be from the public water supply or a private supply such as from groundwater via a borehole.

Rainwater recycling

The appropriate collection and storage of rain from hard outdoor surfaces for use instead of potable water in WCs and/or washing machines. In some cases, rainwater could also be used to contribute towards Wat 2 for irrigation and possibly large water-consuming fittings such as hot tubs or swimming pools. In such cases, reference should be made to the relevant definition for sufficient size, as set out in Wat 2.

Water Efficiency Calculator for New Dwellings

The Water Efficiency Calculator for New Dwellings is the Government's national calculation method for the assessment of water efficiency in new dwellings in support of Building Regulations Part G 2009 and the Code for Sustainable Homes, May 2009 and subsequent versions. The calculator assesses the contribution that each internal water fitting (micro component) has on the water consumption of the whole house, measured in litres per person per day based on research into typical water use.

Water reduction equipment

Fittings such as flow restrictors may be fitted in taps and showers and delayed inlet valves may be fitted in WCs.

Assessment Methodology

The assessment criteria should be read with the methodology and the definitions in this section. Mandatory requirements are met and credits are awarded where the performance requirements (set out in the assessment criteria table) have been met.

Design Stage

- Calculate the water consumption for each dwelling using the methodology set out in the Water Efficiency Calculator for New Dwellings.

- In all cases, a risk assessment of microbial contamination (i.e. *Legionella*) must be carried out on the hot and cold water systems. Action must be taken to avoid any risks of contamination (e.g. through location and labelling of pipes). This is particularly important where rainwater and greywater are to be used. The risk assessment and action taken should be in accordance with guidance from HSE ACoP and/or CIBSE TM13. While these guidance documents refer to non-domestic situations, similar principles apply to domestic use.

- If water is extracted locally from a borehole, it should be treated as potable water from the mains supply because using water from a borehole well will not reduce the burden on drainage and treatment systems.

- Swimming pools or other large water consuming features (where the water is replaced over a greater time interval), whether internal or external, are assessed in the following issue, Wat 2. An internal hot tub should be assessed as a bath.

- Where an instantaneous water heater is specified/intended, problems may occur when low flow rate taps are fitted as such systems vary in their trigger flow rates. In such cases, confirmation should be sought that the specified fittings are compatible.

Post Construction Stage

- Confirm which specifications and evidence provided at the design stage are still valid.

- Assess all the new specifications and evidence provided at the post construction stage.

Calculation Procedures

The calculation procedures must be carried out in line with the Water Efficiency Calculator for New Dwellings:
www.communities.gov.uk/publications/planningandbuilding/watercalculator

Checklists and Tables

None.

Common Cases of Non-Compliance

- The credit will not be awarded where requirements for provision of better than typical practice white goods have only been set within tenancy agreements. It is unlikely such a requirement would be enforced.

- The Code recognises only fixed fittings and fixtures such as low-flush WCs and *flow restrictors*. Devices that can be retrofitted to WCs, such as cistern displacement and flushing reduction, are not recognised by the Code. Such devices may provide reduced water use in existing dwellings, but can be easily removed.

Special Cases

None.

Issue ID	Description	No. of Credits Available	Mandatory Elements
Wat 2	External Water Use	1	No

Aim

To promote the recycling of rainwater and reduce the amount of mains potable water used for external water uses.

Assessment Criteria

Criteria	Credits
Where a *correctly specified* and *sufficient sized system to collect rainwater* for external/internal irrigation/use has been provided to a dwelling with a garden, patio or communal garden space (examples of such systems include *rainwater butts* and *central rainwater collection systems*)	1
Default Cases If no individual or communal *garden* spaces are specified or if only balconies are provided, the credit can be awarded by default	1

Information Required to Demonstrate Compliance

Schedule of Evidence Required	
Design Stage	**Post Construction stage**
Detailed documentary evidence stating type, size and location of any rainwater collection systems	For post construction stage only assessments, provide detailed documentary evidence (as listed for design stage) representing the dwellings as built
Where detailed documentary evidence is not available; A letter of instruction to a contractor / supplier or a formal letter from the developer giving a specific undertaking	
	OR
	Written confirmation from the developer that the rainwater collection system has been installed as specified in the design stage detailed documentary evidence
	OR
	Where only a letter of instruction is provided at design stage provide detailed documentary evidence (as listed for design stage) representing the dwellings as built
	OR
	Where different from design stage, provide detailed documentary evidence (as listed for design stage) representing the dwellings as built
	OR
	Site Inspection Report confirming compliance

Definitions

Central rainwater collection system

A system which will collect and store rainwater for use across the development. This could be a large storage tank or other form of surface water system.

Correctly specified

The specification of the rainwater collector must meet the following criteria:

- No open access at the top of the collector (a child-proof lid is allowed)
- Provision of a tap or other arrangement for drawing off water
- Connection to the rainwater downpipes with an automatic overflow into the conventional rainwater drainage system
- A means of detaching the rainwater downpipe and access provision to enable the interior to be cleaned
- Where the collection system is to be sited outside, and not buried, it must be stable and adequately supported; the material used for the container shall be durable and opaque to sunlight
- Where the system is part of a rainwater collection system providing internal water, water for external use may be provided in a separate tank to water required for internal use. This could be an overflow pipe leading from the main tank to a correctly specified water butt for external water use.

Garden

An area where irrigation is required which is normally an external space but may be an internal atrium. This may be a private or communal space.

Rainwater butt

A large cask or barrel which is set up on end to collect and store rainwater for external irrigation/watering.

Site Inspection Report

This is a report prepared by the Code assessor during a post construction stage assessment and provided as evidence with the assessment.

Sufficient size

Storage volume requirements for homes with individual gardens, patios and terraces:

- Terraces and patios – 100 litres minimum
- 1 – 2 bedroom home with private garden – 150 litres minimum
- 3+ bedroom home with private garden – 200 litres minimum

The above volume requirements can be halved if there is no planting provided and the whole of the external space is covered by a hard surface.

For houses with front and rear gardens, a rainwater collector is required only in the main (i.e. larger) garden but must meet the capacity requirements above.

Size requirements for communal gardens:

- 1 litre/m^2 of land allocated to the dwelling with a minimum of 200 litres per communal garden. Where the communal garden is allocated to more than six dwellings, a maximum of 30 litres per dwelling can be applied. The allocated land can be planted (including grass) or left as unplanted soil, and can be split into plots or communally maintained

- Where planting requiring little water has been specified (following the recommendations from a suitably qualified ecologist, see Eco 1 and 2), the above requirements can be halved subject to written confirmation from the suitably qualified ecologist stating that this is acceptable.

Where the rainwater collection system is providing internal demand for Wat 1 and also for irrigation to achieve credit under this issue, the system can only qualify for external use where:

- The Water Efficiency Calculator for New Dwellings indicates that the demand of internal fittings to be supplied with rainwater has been met and where an excess volume of water is being collected to meet external water use of 5 litres per person per day* (in line with the external water consumption assigned in the Water Efficiency Calculator for New Dwellings for compliance with Building Regulations Part G).

*Where gardens are covered entirely by hard landscaping, the above requirement can be halved.

Where a swimming pool or other large water-consuming feature is present, this must be provided with 100 per cent rainwater or grey water. The water must comply with appropriate EU bathing water standards.

System to collect rainwater

Equipment to collect and store rain from hard surfaces (typically roofs) to replace the use of potable mains water for external irrigation/watering.

Assessment Methodology

The assessment criteria should be read with the methodology and the definitions in this section. Credits are awarded where the performance requirements (set out in the assessment criteria table) have been met.

Design Stage

- Check that the specifications and capacity of storage comply with the assessment criteria.

Post Construction Stage

- Confirm which specifications and evidence provided at the design stage are still valid.
- Assess all the new specifications and evidence provided at the post construction Stage.

Calculation Procedures

- Where rainwater is collected for irrigation for individual gardens, the size requirements are calculated based on the number of bedrooms as defined above in the definition of sufficient size. Once this has been determined, it should then be confirmed whether the garden provided is made up entirely of hard spaces or is provided as a terrace or patio. The size required may then be adjusted and this should be in compliance with the definition of sufficient size defined above.

- Where rainwater is collected for irrigation in communal gardens, the size requirements are based on the size of the communal gardens provided in m^2, as detailed in the definition of sufficient size. The size requirements can be adjusted where the garden comprises hard landscaping or where the planting requires minimal water, as defined in the definition of sufficient size.

- Where rainwater is collected for both internal and external use, the Water Efficiency Calculator for New Dwellings must be used to determine whether sufficient volume has been collected for external use. Sufficient volume to meet the requirements of this issue can be demonstrated where the demand of internal fittings, which are to use rainwater, is met and where the excess water collected for external use is of sufficient volume (as defined in the definition of sufficient size).

Checklists and Tables

None.

Common Cases of Non-Compliance

Pools, hot tubs or other large water-using features which are fed by mains water will automatically mean that credits cannot be awarded for this issue. This rule applies whether it is an internal or external feature, with the exception of internal hot tubs which should be assessed as a bath under the previous issue, Wat 1. Where such water features are present, credits can be awarded only where they use appropriately treated water from 100% rainwater or 100% greywater and all other criteria for this issue are met.

Special Cases

None.

Category 3: Materials

Issue ID	Description	No. of Credits Available	Mandatory Elements
Mat 1	Environmental Impact of Materials	15	Yes

Aim

To specify materials with lower environmental impacts over their life-cycle.

Assessment Criteria

Criteria	Credits	Mandatory Levels
Where at least three of the following five key elements of the *building envelope* achieve a rating of A+ to D in the 2008 version of *The Green Guide*: • Roof • External walls • Internal walls (including separating walls) • Upper and ground floors (including separating floors) • Windows		All Levels
Where the *Code Mat 1 Calculator Tool* is used to assess the number of credits awarded for the five key elements described above	1 – 15	
Default Cases None		

Information Required to Demonstrate Compliance

Schedule of Evidence Required	
Design Stage	**Post Construction Stage**
Completed Code Mat 1 Calculator Tool, showing building elements at the design stage with the relevant *Green Guide element numbers* AND References stating the design or specification documentation used to complete the tool	For post construction stage only assessments, provide; • The Code Mat 1 Calculator Tool, showing building elements as built with the relevant Green Guide element numbers • References stating the source of data used to complete the tool **OR** Written confirmation from the developer that the building envelope has been constructed as specified in the Mat 1 Calculator Tool and references provided at design stage **OR** Where different from design stage, provide; • The revised Code Mat 1 Calculator Tool, showing building elements as built with the relevant Green Guide element numbers • Revised references stating the source of data used to complete the tool

Definitions

Building envelope

For the purpose of issue Mat 1, the building envelope is defined as the overall superstructure of the particular building. Each building envelope may contain single or multiple dwellings.

Where multiple dwellings are contained within a single envelope, Green Guide specifications do not need to be applied to the individual dwellings. In this case, the percentages of all individual Green Guide specifications throughout the entire building must be included, even where significantly differing construction methods are used for different parts of the building.

The same specification may also be applied in the case where there are several identical buildings with identical building envelopes. In this case, there is no need to assess the identical buildings separately. For the building envelopes to be identical, they must be of the same size and share the same percentages of elements with the same Green Guide specifications.

Code Mat 1 Calculator Tool

A spreadsheet-based tool designed to simplify assessment of this issue, available to assessors from the Code service provider.

Green Guide Element Number

A unique BRE Global reference number given to a Green Guide rating for any particular building element type specification. Both standard Green Guide ratings and those calculated using the Online Green Guide Calculator will have an element number.

Online Green Guide Calculator Tool

BRE Global have created the Green Guide Calculator tool to enable BREEAM and Code assessors to quickly and efficiently generate Green Guide ratings for a significant proportion of specifications not listed in the Green Guide Online. The Green Guide Calculator database is based on the components currently used to create specifications within the Green Guide Online. These components can be selected and combined to generate instant Green Guide ratings for a multitude of different specifications.

To access the Green Guide Calculator, you must be a licensed BREEAM/EcoHomes/Code assessor.

The Green Guide to Specification

The Green Guide to Specification is an easy to use comprehensive reference website and electronic tool, providing guidance for specifiers, designers and their clients on the relative environmental impacts for a range of different building elemental specifications. The ratings within the Guide are based on Life Cycle Assessment, using the Environmental Profile Methodology.

The Green Guide categorises ratings by building type and element. When using the Green Guide online, (www.thegreenguide.co.uk), the main page asks the user to select a building type. To obtain the appropriate ratings for the assessed building elements, select the corresponding building type for this scheme.

Assessment Methodology

The assessment criteria should be read with the methodology and the definitions in this section. Mandatory requirements are met and credits are awarded where the performance requirements (set out in the assessment criteria table) have been met.

Design Stage

- Confirm that at least three mandatory building elements have achieved a Green Guide rating of A+ to D for each building envelope. The mandatory requirement applies to 100% of the area for each element.

- Where an exact match to a specification cannot be found in the Green Guide, it is necessary to find a similar specification.

- For specifications that address a function which is not typical for the element, e.g. security, severe exposure, unusual loading or structural conditions, refer to the Code Service Provider. If in doubt, or if no similar specification is available, the assessor should contact the Code service provider for a bespoke rating.

- Where credits are sought, performance must be calculated using the method described in the calculation procedures.

Post Construction Stage

- Verify that the evidence provided at the design stage is still valid and that no changes have occurred during construction. Where changes have occurred, the assessor should reassess the issue as set out for design stage.

Calculation Procedures

Design Stage

Credits are awarded on the basis of the rating in the Green Guide as follows:

Green Guide Rating	Credits
A+ Rating	3
A Rating	2
B Rating	1
C Rating	0.5
D Rating	0.25
E Rating	0

Where there is more than one specification for an element (e.g. more than one type of external wall), Mat 1 performance is calculated based on the area weighted Green Guide rating of each specification. For the purpose of this issue, any doors with a large expanse of glazing, such as patio doors, should be assessed as windows. Similarly, glazed areas of conservatories and rooflights should be assessed as windows.

The Code Mat 1 Calculator Tool allows up to four different specification types per element.

Where there is a close match to a specification in the Green Guide, enter details of the specification and its associated Green Guide rating in the appropriate columns.

Where a specification does not have a close Green Guide match, the assessor should contact the Code service provider for a bespoke rating or use the *Online Green Guide Calculator* to generate a rating. A description of the specification and the bespoke rating must then be entered into the Code Mat 1 Calculator Tool and a note made in the assessment report to indicate the source of the bespoke rating.

Calculate and enter the percentage area of each specification type for each element in the 'Percentage' column. The Green Guide rating for each assessed element must also be entered into the Code Mat 1 Calculator Tool. The total credits awarded will then be calculated automatically.

Post Construction Stage

Confirm that the final building construction matches that specified at design stage. Where any design changes have occurred, reassess the element.

Ensure that the documentary evidence provided meets the requirements as stated in the post-construction section of Information Required to Demonstrate Compliance.

Checklists and Tables

None.

Common Cases of Non-Compliance

None.

Special Cases

For mixed use developments, contact the Code Service Provider for advice on how to proceed. The following principles will form the basis of guidance given:

- Where dwellings are located over non-domestic accommodation (e.g. retail space or car parking), the lowest residential floor should be assessed as the 'ground floor' using the 'upper floor' ratings in the Green Guide.

- If the external walls, internal walls and/or windows are located over non-domestic accommodation, only those that relate to the dwellings need to be included in the assessment.

- Where non-domestic accommodation is located between the dwellings and the roof, the roof must be assessed as it is protecting the dwellings below. If the roof is directly above a commercial use property (e.g. a restaurant or office), the equivalent commercial rating for the roof must be used as opposed to the ratings for domestic roofs. Roof areas to parts of the building not containing dwellings can be omitted from the assessment.

Issue ID	Description	No. of Credits Available	Mandatory Elements
Mat 2	Responsible Sourcing of Materials – Basic Building Elements	6	No

Aim

To promote the specification of responsibly sourced materials for the basic building elements.

Assessment Criteria

Criteria	Credits
Where 80% of the *assessed materials* in the following *Building Elements* are responsibly sourced: a) Frame b) Ground floor c) Upper floors (including separating floors) d) Roof e) External walls f) Internal walls (including separating walls) g) Foundation/substructure (excluding sub-base materials) h) Staircase Additionally, 100% of any timber in these elements must be legally sourced	1–6 *1
Default Cases	
None	

Note: These criteria are assessed at the building envelope level.

*1 See table Cat 3.3 for credit rewards structure

Mat

Information Required to Demonstrate Compliance

Schedule of Evidence Required	
Design Stage	**Post Construction Stage**
Completed *Code Mat 2 Calculator Tool*, showing building elements at the design stage **AND** Detailed documentary evidence stating the materials specified in each element	For post construction stage only assessments, provide Code Mat 2 Calculator Tool and detailed documentary evidence (as listed for design stage) representing the dwellings as built **OR** Written confirmation from the developer that the materials specified in the Code Mat 2 Calculator Tool and the detailed documentary evidence provided at design stage have been used as specified **OR** If different from design stage, provide revised Code Mat 2 Calculator Tool and detailed documentary evidence (as listed for design stage) representing the dwellings as built
Where materials are *re-used* the following evidence will be required: Documentation* stating specific materials to be re-used *Supplier information or a letter from the developer is acceptable	Where materials were re-used the following evidence will be required: Documentation* demonstrating which particular materials have been re-used *A receipt or letter from the supplier, which includes material quantities, is acceptable
Where materials are recycled the following evidence will be required: Documentation stating specific recycled materials **AND** A letter of intent to use suppliers who can provide an EMS certificate (or equivalent) for the recycling process	Where materials are recycled the following evidence will be required: Documentation stating the particular recycled materials used in the development **AND** Documentary evidence confirming the key process is certified by EMS

Mat

Where certified materials will be used following evidence will be required:

A letter of intent from the developer or other detailed documentary evidence confirming the product shall be sourced from suppliers capable of providing certification to the level required for the particular tier claimed.

OR

A copy of the relevant certificate(s) as appropriate;

- A copy of the timber scheme certificate (including *CoC*)

- *BES6001* certificate (or compliant sector standard certificate)

- *EMAS* certificate

- ISO14001 certificate.

- For small companies, (see Definitions) confirmation that the company EMS is structured in compliance with BS 8555 2003 (or equivalent) and the EMS has completed phase audits one to four as outlined in BS 8555. This can be found in company documentation demonstrating the process and typical outputs from phase four audits such as an EMS manual/ paperwork and guidance to staff. Where independent certification exists to demonstrate these phases, it can be used as evidence

Green Dragon Environmental Standard ® 2006 (Safon Amgylcheddol Y Ddraig Werdd ®) completed up to and including Level 4. Confirmation is taken from a Green Dragon Standard certificate stating the company's achievement of Level 4. As company's achieving Level 4 will normally be required to undertake annual audits, this certification should be dated within 1 year at the point of the last purchase made from the company.

Where certified materials were used the following evidence will be required (where applicable):

All relevant certificates

Mat

Mat

For smaller companies with low environmental impacts, a renewal date of within 2 years is acceptable.	
Where any non-certified timber is used, written confirmation from the supplier/s confirming that: • All timber will come from a legal source • All timber species and sources to be used in the development are not listed on any of the *CITES* appendices for endangered or threatened species (Appendix I, II, or III*). * Or in the case of Appendix III of the CITES list, it will not be sourced from the country seeking to protect this species as listed in Appendix III.	Where any non-certified timber is used, written confirmation from the supplier(s) confirming that: • All timber comes from a legal source. • All timber species and sources used in the development are not listed on any of the CITES appendices for endangered or threatened species (Appendix I, II, or III*). * Or in the case of Appendix III of the CITES list, it has not been sourced from the country seeking to protect this species as listed in Appendix III. Where any non-certified timber is used, written confirmation from the supplier/s confirming that: • All timber comes from a legal source • All timber species and sources used in the development are not listed on any of the CITES appendices for endangered or threatened species (Appendix I, II, or III) • Or in the case of Appendix III of the CITES list, it has not been sourced from the country seeking to protect this species as listed in Appendix III.

Definitions

Assessed materials

The following materials are assessed in the calculation of points:

- Brick (including clay tiles and other ceramics)

- Resin-based *composite materials* (including GRP and polymeric render, but excluding composite which incorporates timber)
- Concrete (including in situ and pre-cast concrete, blocks, tiles, mortars, cementitious renders, etc)
- Glass
- Plastics and rubbers (including *EPDM, TPO, PVC, VET,* roofing membranes and polymeric render)
- Metals (steel, aluminium etc)
- Dressed or building stone including slate
- Timber, wood panel products and wood-based composites (including cement bonded particle board, laminated veneered lumber, glulam)
- Plasterboard and plaster
- Bituminous materials, such as roofing membranes and asphalt
- Other mineral-based materials, including fibre cement and calcium silicate
- Products with recycled content.

Note: Insulation materials, fixings, adhesives and additives are excluded from the assessment. For any other materials which do not fit into the assessed materials or the exclusions, please refer to the Code service provider who will identify the relevant *key processes* and supply chain process or processes.

Basic building elements

Basic building elements are defined as follows:

a) *Frame*

b) Ground floor

c) Upper floors (including separating floors)

d) Roof (structure and cladding, including any loft boarding)

e) External walls (including external cladding)

f) Internal walls (including internal partitions and separating walls)

g) Foundation/substructure

h) Staircase (includes the tread, risers and stringers).

BES 6001:2008 Framework Standard for Responsible Sourcing of Construction Products

BES 6001:2008 is a BRE Global standard that provides a framework for the assessment of responsible sourcing schemes and provides a route to certification of construction products.

The framework comprises a number of criteria setting out the criteria of an organisation in managing the supply of construction products in accordance with a set of agreed principles of sustainability. To comply with the standard, a product must meet a number of mandatory criteria, where a product demonstrates compliance beyond the mandatory levels, higher levels of performance can be achieved. The standard's performance ratings range from Pass to Good, Very Good and Excellent,

The development of this standard and subsequent certification schemes will, it is envisaged, provide construction products, not wholly covered under current recognised standards, a means for demonstrating their responsibility sourced credentials. In turn this will allow clients, developers and design teams to specify responsibly sourced construction products with greater assurance and provide a means of demonstrating compliance with the assessment criteria for this BREEAM issue.

To view a list of products approved to BES 6001:2008 please visit www.greenbooklive.com/page.jsp?id=169

For further information about BES6001:2008, including a copy of the standard itself visit: www.greenbooklive.com/page.jsp?id=153

Chain of custody (CoC)

This is a process used to maintain and document the chronological history of the evidence/path for products from forests to consumers. Wood must be tracked from the certified forest to the finished product. All the steps, from the transportation of wood from the forest to a sawmill until it reaches the customer, must maintain adequate inventory control systems that allow for separation and identification of the certified product. Chain of custody certification ensures that a facility has procedures in place to track wood from certified forests and avoid confusion with non-certified wood. Chain of custody is established and audited according to the rules of relevant forest certification systems.

CITES

The Convention on International Trade in Endangered Species of Wild Fauna and Flora.

Code Mat 2 Calculator Tool

A spreadsheet-based tool designed to simplify assessment of this issue, available to assessors from the Code service provider.

Composite materials

Composite material can be defined as an engineered material made from two or more constituent materials with significantly different physical or chemical properties, and which remain separate and distinct on a macroscopic level within the finished structure. Resin-based composites (such as GRP and polymeric render) and timber composites (such as chipboard/particle board, *MDF*, *OSB*, plywood, hardboard, laminated veneered lumber, glulam and cement bonded particle board) are required to be assessed for responsible sourcing within the Code for Sustainable Homes.

CPET

Central Point of Expertise on Timber.

CSA

Canadian Standards Association.

EMS

Environmental management system.

EMAS

Eco-Management and Audit Scheme.

EPDM

Ethylene propylene diene monomer.

Frame

The frame is any of the main structural elements that are not included in the roof, external walls and floors. For example, timber or metal studwork within a plasterboard partition would be included within the internal walls, and timber joists would be included within the floor construction.

Where a concrete or steel frame is used, this would be treated as the frame as it would not be integral to the internal walls for example.

Green Dragon Environmental Standard® (Safon Amgylcheddol Y Ddraig Werdd®)

A stepped standard used to accredit compliance with the Green Dragon environmental management scheme. Depending on the content of the EMS being assessed, a level of 1, 2, 3, 4 or 5 may be achieved. At level 4 and above, the Green Dragon Environmental Standard® can be used as evidence of a compliant EMS for small companies being considered under the Mat 2 and Mat 3 issues.

Green Guide Element Number

See Mat 1

Key processes

These are the final major aspects of processing that are carried out. There may be a single process or multiple processes requiring assessment, depending on the end product. The requirements for each of the assessed materials are detailed in table Cat 3.2: EMS Requirements.

Legally sourced timber

The definition of legally sourced timber follows the UK Government's definition of legally sourced timber, according to the *CPET* 2nd Edition report on UK Government timber procurement policy. The report states that legal timber and wood derived products are those which originate from a forest where the following criteria are met:

1. The forest owner/manager holds legal use rights to the forest

2. There is compliance by both the forest management organisation and any contractors with local and national legal criteria including those relevant to:

    a. Forest management

    b. Environment

    c. Labour and Welfare

    d. Health and safety

    e. Other parties' tenure and use rights

3. All relevant royalties and taxes are paid

4. There is compliance with the criteria of CITES

Relevant documentation demonstrating the above must be provided or made available on request subject to the availability of such materials in the country concerned. Certification against any of the timber certification schemes identified in tiers 1, 2 and 4 demonstrates that timber has been legally sourced.

MDF

Medium density fibreboard.

MTCC

Malaysian Timber Certification Council.

OSB

Oriented strand board.

PEFC

Programme for the Endorsement of Forest Certification Schemes.

Post-consumer waste stream

Waste material generated by households or by commercial, industrial and institutional facilities in their role as end-users of the product, which can no longer be used for its intended purpose. This includes returns of material from the distribution chain.

Pre-consumer waste stream

Waste material generated during manufacturing processes. Excluded is reutilisation of materials such as rework, regrind or scrap generated in a process and capable of being reclaimed within the same process that generated it.

PVC

Polyvinyl chloride.

Recycled material

Materials diverted from the pre-consumer and/or post-consumer waste streams that require significant processing before they can be used again. For further information refer to *calculating and declaring recycled content in construction products*, 'Rules of Thumb' Guide (WRAP, 2008).

Responsible sourcing

This is demonstrated through auditable third-party certification schemes.

Re-used materials

Materials diverted from the waste stream and used again without further processing, or with minor processing that does not alter the nature of the material (e.g. cleaning, cutting, fixing to other materials).

SFI

Sustainable Forestry Initiative.

SGS

Société Générale de Surveillance. This is a Swiss-based private monitoring company.

Small company

A company is defined as 'small' if it satisfies at least two of the following criteria:

    a. A turnover of not more than £5.6 million

    b. A balance sheet total of not more than £2.8 million

    c. 50 employees or fewer.

This is based on the definition stated in the Companies Act of 1985.

Supply Chain EMS

This covers all the major aspects of processing and extraction involved in the supply chain for the end product. Note: *Recycled materials* are not required to demonstrate a supply chain EMS. If EMS certification is provided for the key processes for recycled materials, this is assumed by default.

TFT

The Forest Trust.

Tier levels

The tier levels are graded on a scale to reflect the rigour of the certification scheme used to demonstrate responsible sourcing, forming the basis for awarding points (all as detailed in table Cat 3.1).

TPO

Thermoplastic olefin.

Verified

'Verified' is a scheme produced by SmartWood.

VET

(Mat 2 and 3)

Vinyl ethylene terpolymer.

Assessment Methodology

The assessment criteria should be read with the methodology and the definitions in this section. Credits are awarded where the performance requirements (set out in the assessment criteria table) have been met.

Design Stage

- Where a construction make-up is not specified within the Code Mat 2 Calculator Tool, confirm the construction details of elements using the specification and drawings, or similar (see Information Required to Demonstrate Compliance). Obtain a breakdown of volumes and/or percentages of materials for each element present.

- Obtain the relevant confirmation of *tier* certification for all* materials, from all sources/suppliers.

  * The following exclusions apply:

  Material groups not included in the list in Definitions (e.g. insulation materials, fixings, adhesives, additives).

  Materials that account for less than 10% by volume of an element may also be excluded (e.g. screws). However, if certification has been provided for materials in this category, it may be beneficial to include them in the calculation (e.g. if a material type accounting for 9% is placed in a higher tier than other materials used to make up the element).

- Assign a tier level to each material based on the level of certification provided (see table: Cat 3.1: Tier Levels, and Compliance and Information Required to Demonstrate Compliance).

- Follow the calculation procedures outlined below. It is recommended that the Code Mat 2 Calculator Tool is used to assess the number of points and credits to be awarded.

- Ensure that all timber is *legally sourced* and none of the species to be used is identified on the CITES list.

Notes:

1. For any other materials which do not fit into the assessed materials or the exclusion, please refer back to the Code service provider who will identify the relevant key processes and supply chain process(es).

2. MDF, chipboard, OSB and cement bonded particle board are all considered as timber and therefore must be assessed as timber material.

3. Where a mix of virgin and recycled timber is used, only the virgin timber needs to be assessed. Credits can then be awarded based on the certification schemes it is under.

4. Slate is classed as stone and is therefore considered as an assessed material.

Post Construction Stage

- Confirm that the final building construction matches that specified at design stage. Where any design changes have occurred, reassess the certification tier for each element according to the methodology set out for design stage.

Calculation Procedures

Points and credits for this issue should be calculated using the Code Mat 2 Calculator Tool. The tool will calculate the total number of points awarded to each element taking into account the scenarios mentioned above. It will also state the associated number of credits.

Elements should be entered as present or not present and the tool will calculate the range of points required to achieve a number of credits in accordance with table: Cat 3.3. **A minimum of five elements must be assessed**. This is the minimum number of elements assumed by the calculator tool. Where fewer are indicated, the calculator will award **zero** credits and flag an error message, as it does at other stages if there is non-compliance with any of the criteria.

A minimum of 80% of each material assessed must comply with tiers 1 to 4 (excluding materials not assessed).

If 80% of an assessed element is compliant with a single tier, the full score available for that tier will apply.

If 80% of an element is compliant over a number of tiers, the calculator will first review the percentage compliant with the highest tier and apportion a score to that. If less than 80% is compliant, it will review the percentage of the element in the next highest tier and apportion a score to that. This will continue until the 80% requirement has been met.

Consequently, it may be beneficial to include even small percentages of materials that are in the higher tiers if the majority of the rest of the element would otherwise be allocated to a lower tier level.

Checklists and Tables

Table: Cat 3.1 Tier Levels				
Tier Level	Issue Assessed	Points Available per Element	Evidence / Measure Assessed	Examples of Compliant Schemes
1	Legality & *Responsible Sourcing*	3	Certification Scheme	FSC, *CSA*, *SFI* with CoC, *PEFC*, Reused Materials, Schemes compliant with BES6001:200861 (or similar) Excellent* and Very Good* Performance Ratings (Note; the EMS required to achieve these ratings must be independently certified**)
2a	Legality & Responsible Sourcing	2.5	Certification Scheme	Schemes compliant with BES6001:2008 (or similar) 'Good' Performance Rating (Note: the EMS required to achieve this rating must be independently certified**).
2b	Legality & Responsible Sourcing	2	Certification Scheme	Schemes compliant with BES6001:2008 (or similar) 'Pass' Performance Rating (Note: the EMS required to achieve this rating must be independently certified).
3	Legality & Responsible Sourcing	1.5	Certification Scheme / EMS	Timber: *MTCC***, *Verified****, *SGS*, *TFT* Other materials: Certified EMS for the *Key Process* and *Supply Chain* Recycled materials with certified EMS for the *Key Process*
4	Legality & Responsible Sourcing	1	Certification Scheme / EMS	Certified EMS for the *Key Process*

Notes to table Cat 3.1:

Where any timber is used, it must be legally sourced. Where evidence cannot be provided to demonstrate legal sourcing for any element, no points can be awarded for the Responsible Sourcing Issue.

Where cement and aggregate, or dry mix concrete are mixed on site, (i.e. not concrete previously certified as pre–cast concrete products or wet ready mix concrete), certification must cover the manufacture of the cement as the primary process, and the extraction of the aggregate and limestone used to make the cement as the supply chain process.

* Performance ratings for schemes compliant with BES6001:2008 (or similar) can only be used to demonstrate compliance with the assessment criteria for this issue where certification covers the key process and supply chain processes for the material being assessed.

** In BES6001:2008 to achieve a 'Pass', level 'a' must, as a minimum, be achieved for clauses 3.3.1, 3.3.2 and 3.3.3. Under clause 3.3.2 level 'a' requires a documented EMS system following the principles of ISO14001, but not formal certification. To achieve higher ratings such as 'Good', 'Very Good' and Excellent a minimum number of points from a combination of clauses 3.3.1, 3.3.2 and 3.3.3 must be achieved. It is possible therefore to get a 'Good' or 'Very good' rating by only complying with level 'a' for clause 3.3.2 and levels 'c' and 'd' for the other two clauses without necessarily having in place a formal independently certified EMS (as required above). In conducting BES6001 assessment, if the assessor confirms full compliance with clause 3.3.2 level 'a' the requirement for an independently certified EMS has been met.

*** PEFC International has recently endorsed the Malaysian MTCS scheme, as a result any MTCC timber certified against the new PEFC endorsed scheme documents can be classified as tier 1 for the purposes of the BREEAM assessment. The PEFC endorsement only covers certificates issued against the latest MTCC scheme documents, it must be stressed therefore that any holders of certifications against the previous MTCC scheme documents, including the forest management standard MC&I 2001 or any parts thereof, are NOT PEFC endorsed and this timber must still be classified as Tier 3.

When seeking the higher tier level for MTCC certified timber the assessor will need to verify the above via the scope of the supplier's certificate.

For further information and guidance please visit the PEFC website: http://www.pefc.org/internet/html/members_schemes/4_1120_59/5_1246_320/5_1123_1887.htm

*** "Verified" is the name of a scheme produced by SmartWood.

Table: Cat 3.2 Environmental Management System (EMS) Requirements		
Material	**Key Process**	**Supply Chain Processes**
Brick (including clay tiles and other ceramics)	Product manufacture	Clay extraction
Resin-based composite materials (including GRP and polymeric render, but excluding composite using timber)	Composite product manufacture	• Glass fibre production (or other principal reinforcement material if used) • Polymer production (or other principal matrix material if used)
In situ concrete (including ready mix and cementitious mortars and renders)	Ready mixed concrete plant	• Cement production • Aggregate extraction and production
Precast concrete and other concrete products (including blocks, cladding, precast flooring, concrete or cementitious roof tiles)	Concrete product manufacture	• Cement production • Aggregate extraction and production
Glass	Glass production	• Sand extraction • Soda ash production or extraction
Plastics and rubbers (including polymeric renders, EPDM, TPO, PVC and VET roofing membranes)	Plastic/rubber product manufacture	Main polymer production
Metals (steel, aluminium, etc)	Metal product manufacture – e.g. cladding production, steel section production	Metal production: • Steel: electric arc furnace or basic oxygen furnace process • Aluminium: ingot production • Copper: ingot or cathode production
Dressed or building stone (including slate)	Stone product manufacture	Stone extraction
Plasterboard and plaster	Plasterboard or plaster manufacture	• Gypsum extraction • Synthetic gypsum (from flue gas desulphurisation) by default (recycled content)
Virgin timber and timber products such as laminated veneered lumber, glulam, etc	Timber from certified sources	• Timber from certified sources
Cement bonded particle board	Key supply chain process for the production of cement bonded particle board and the associated timber certification(s) are required.	• Cement production • Timber from certified sources
Wood panel products such as oriented strand board, plywood, chipboard/particle board, etc)	Wood panel products, including those with recycled content, can only use the timber certification route	

continued

Mat

Table: Cat 3.2 Environmental Management System (EMS) Requirements		
Material	**Key Process**	**Supply Chain Processes**
Bituminous materials, such as roofing membranes and asphalt	Product manufacture	• Bitumen production • Aggregate extraction and production
Other mineral-based materials, including fibre cement and calcium silicate	Product manufacture	• Cement production • Lime production • Other mineral extraction and production
Products with 100% recycled content	Product manufacture	Recycled input by default
Products with lower percentage of recycled content	Product manufacture	• Supply chain process(es) for any virgin material in the relevant product type above • Recycled input by default
Any other product	Key process is likely to be product manufacture	One or two main inputs with significant production or extraction impacts should be identified
Excluded products: insulation materials, fixings, adhesives, additives	N/A	N/A

Table: Cat 3.3 Credit Structure				
Number of Elements	**Credits Available**			
	6	4	3	2
	Range of Points			
8	≥ 18	≥ 12	≥ 9	≥ 6
7	≥ 15.75	≥ 10.25	≥ 7.87	≥ 5.25
6	≥ 13.5	≥ 9	≥ 6.75	≥ 4.5
5	≥ 11.25	≥ 7.5	≥ 5.625	≥ 3.75

Common Cases of Non-Compliance

Timber and Environmental Management Schemes (EMS)

Where an environmental management scheme is used to assess products made from recycled timber, 100% of the timber content must be recycled or sourced from one of the recognised timber certification schemes in table: Cat 3.1. A timber product with 50% recycled timber and 50% legally sourced timber will not comply with the criteria and will not be awarded any points.

Using an EMS for new timber does not demonstrate timber certification and therefore does not qualify for points.

A statement of intent from a product manufacturer and/or supplier does not meet the requirements for this issue.

Special Cases

If an element is made up primarily of a material not specified in this issue (e.g. straw bales), please contact the Code service provider for guidance on how to proceed.

For mixed use buildings, please refer to special cases in issue Mat 1.

Mat

Issue ID	Description	No. of Credits Available	Mandatory Elements
Mat 3	Responsible Sourcing of Materials – Finishing Elements	3	No

Aim

To promote the specification of responsibly sourced materials for the finishing elements.

Assessment Criteria

Criteria	Credits
Where 80% of the *assessed materials* in the following *Finishing Elements* are responsibly sourced: a) Staircase b) Windows c) External & internal doors d) Skirting e) Panelling f) Furniture g) Fascias h) Any other significant use Additionally, 100% of any timber in these elements must be *legally sourced*	1–3
Default Cases None	

Information Required to Demonstrate Compliance

Schedule of Evidence Required	
Design Stage	**Post Construction Stage**
Completed Code Mat 3 Calculator Tool, showing building elements at the design stage

AND

Detailed documentary evidence stating the materials specified in each element | For post construction stage only assessments, provide Code Mat 3 Calculator Tool and detailed documentary evidence (as listed for design stage) representing the dwellings as built

OR

Written confirmation from the developer that the materials specified in the Code Mat 3 Calculator Tool and the detailed documentary evidence provided at design stage have been used as specified

OR

Where different from design stage, provide revised Code Mat 3 Calculator Tool and detailed documentary evidence (as listed for design stage) representing the dwellings as built |
| Where materials are re-used the following evidence will be required:

Documentation* stating specific materials to be re-used

*Supplier information or a letter from the developer is acceptable | Where materials were re-used the following evidence will be required:

Documentation* demonstrating which particular materials have been re-used

*A receipt or letter from the supplier, which includes material quantities, is acceptable |
| Where materials are recycled the following evidence will be required:

Documentation stating specific *recycled materials*

AND

A letter of intent to use suppliers who can provide an *EMS* certificate (or equivalent) for the recycling process | Where materials were recycled the following evidence will be required:

Documentation stating the particular recycled materials used in the development

AND

Documentary evidence confirming the key process is certified by EMS |

Where certified materials will be used following evidence will be required:

A letter of intent from the developer or other detailed documentary evidence confirming the product shall be sourced from suppliers capable of providing certification to the level required for the particular tier claimed.

OR

A copy of the relevant certificate(s) as appropriate;

- A copy of the timber scheme certificate (including *CoC*)

- *BES6001* certificate (or compliant sector standard certificate)

- *EMAS* certificate

- ISO14001 certificate.

- For small companies, (see Relevant Definitions) confirmation that the company EMS is structured in compliance with BS 8555 2003 (or equivalent) and the EMS has completed phase audits one to four as outlined in BS 8555. This can be found in company documentation demonstrating the process and typical outputs from phase four audits such as an EMS manual/ paperwork and guidance to staff. Where independent certification exists to demonstrate these phases, it can be used as evidence

Green Dragon Environmental Standard ® 2006 (Safon Amgylcheddol Y Ddraig Werdd ®) completed up to and including Level 4. Confirmation is taken from a Green Dragon Standard certificate stating the company's achievement of Level 4. As company's achieving Level 4 will normally be required to undertake annual audits, this certification should be dated within

Where certified materials were used the following evidence will be required (where applicable):

All relevant certificates

Mat

1 year at the point of the last purchase made from the company. For smaller companies with low environmental impacts, a renewal date of within 2 years is acceptable.	
Where any non-certified timber is used, written confirmation from the supplier/s confirming that: • All timber will come from a legal source • All timber species and sources to be used in the development are not listed on any of the *CITES* appendices for endangered or threatened species (Appendix I, II, or III*). * Or in the case of Appendix III of the CITES list, it will not be sourced from the country seeking to protect this species as listed in Appendix III.	Where any non-certified timber is used, written confirmation from the supplier(s) confirming that: • All timber comes from a legal source. • All timber species and sources used in the development are not listed on any of the CITES appendices for endangered or threatened species (Appendix I, II, or III*). * Or in the case of Appendix III of the CITES list, it has not been sourced from the country seeking to protect this species as listed in Appendix III. Where any non-certified timber is used, written confirmation from the supplier/s confirming that: • All timber comes from a legal source • All timber species and sources used in the development are not listed on any of the CITES appendices for endangered or threatened species (Appendix I, II, or III) • Or in the case of Appendix III of the CITES list, it has not been sourced from the country seeking to protect this species as listed in Appendix III.

Definitions

Assessed materials

The following materials are assessed in the calculation of points:

• Brick (including clay tiles and other ceramics)

- Resin-based *composite materials* (including GRP and polymeric render, but excluding composite which incorporates timber)

- Concrete (including in situ and pre-cast concrete, blocks, tiles, mortars, cementitious renders, etc)

- Glass

- Plastics and rubbers (including *EPDM*, TPO, *PVC*, VET, roofing membranes and polymeric render)

- Metals (steel, aluminium etc)

- Dressed or building stone including slate

- Timber, wood panel products and wood-based composites (including cement bonded particle board, laminated veneered lumber, glulam)

- Plasterboard and plaster

- Bituminous materials, such as roofing membranes and asphalt

- Other mineral-based materials, including fibre cement and calcium silicate

- Products with recycled content.

Note: Insulation materials, fixings, adhesives and additives are excluded from the assessment. For any other materials which do not fit into the assessed materials or the exclusions, please refer to the Code service provider who will identify the relevant *key processes* and supply chain process or processes.

BES 6001:2008 Framework Standard for Responsible Sourcing of Construction Products

BES 6001:2008 is a BRE Global standard that provides a framework for the assessment of responsible sourcing schemes and provides a route to certification of construction products.

The framework comprises a number of criteria setting out the criteria of an organisation in managing the supply of construction products in accordance with a set of agreed principles of sustainability. To comply with the standard, a product must meet a number of mandatory criteria, where a product demonstrates compliance beyond the mandatory levels, higher levels of performance can be achieved. The standard's performance ratings range from Pass to Good, Very Good and Excellent,

The development of this standard and subsequent certification schemes will, it is envisaged, provide construction products, not wholly covered under current recognised standards, a means for demonstrating their responsibility sourced credentials. In turn this will allow clients, developers and design teams to specify responsibly sourced construction products with greater assurance and provide a means of demonstrating compliance with the assessment criteria for this BREEAM issue.

To view a list of products approved to BES 6001:2008 please visit www.greenbooklive.com/page.jsp?id=169

Mat

For further information about BES6001:2008, including a copy of the standard itself visit: www.greenbooklive.com/page.jsp?id=153

Chain of custody (CoC)

This is a process used to maintain and document the chronological history of the evidence/path for products from forests to consumers. Wood must be tracked from the certified forest to the finished product. All the steps, from the transportation of wood from the forest to a sawmill until it reaches the customer, must maintain adequate inventory control systems that allow for separation and identification of the certified product. Chain of custody certification ensures that a facility has procedures in place to track wood from certified forests and avoid confusion with non-certified wood. Chain of custody is established and audited according to the rules of relevant forest certification systems.

CITES

The Convention on International Trade in Endangered Species of Wild Fauna and Flora.

Composite materials

Composite material can be defined as an engineered material made from two or more constituent materials with significantly different physical or chemical properties, and which remain separate and distinct on a macroscopic level within the finished structure. Resin-based composites (such as GRP and polymeric render) and timber composites (such as chipboard/particle board, MDF, OSB, plywood, hardboard, laminated veneered lumber, glulam and cement bonded particle board) are required to be assessed for responsible sourcing within the Code for Sustainable Homes.

CPET

Central Point of Expertise on Timber.

CSA

Canadian Standards Association.

EMS

Environmental management system.

EMAS

Eco-Management and Audit Scheme.

EPDM

Ethylene propylene diene monomer.

Finishing elements

For the purpose of this issue, the assessed finishing elements are defined below:

a) Stair (including handrails, balustrades, banisters, other guarding/rails, excluding staircase)

b) Window (including sub-frames, boards, sills)

c) External and internal door (including sub-frames, frames, linings, door)

d) Skirting (including architrave, skirting board and rails)

e) Panelling (including any other trim)

f) Furniture (including fitted kitchen, bedroom and bathroom units)

g) Fascias (soffit boards, bargeboards, gutter boards, others)

h) Any other significant use.

FSC

Forest Stewardship Council.

Green Dragon Environmental Standard® (Safon Amgylcheddol Y Ddraig Werdd®)

A stepped standard used to accredit compliance with the Green Dragon environmental management scheme. Depending on the content of the EMS being assessed, a level of 1, 2, 3, 4 or 5 may be achieved. At level 4 and above, the Green Dragon Environmental Standard® can be used as evidence of a compliant EMS for small companies being considered under the Mat 2 and Mat 3 issues.

Green Guide Element Number

See Mat 1

Key processes

These are the final major aspects of processing that are carried out. There may be a single process or multiple processes requiring assessment, depending on the end product. The requirements for each of the assessed materials are detailed in table Cat 3.2: EMS Requirements.

Legally sourced timber

The definition of legally sourced timber follows the UK Government's definition of legally sourced timber, according to the *CPET* 2nd Edition report on UK Government timber procurement policy. The report states that legal timber and wood derived products are those which originate from a forest where the following criteria are met:

1. The forest owner/manager holds legal use rights to the forest

2. There is compliance by both the forest management organisation and any contractors with local and national legal criteria including those relevant to:

   a. Forest management

   b. Environment

   c. Labour and Welfare

   d. Health and safety

   e. Other parties' tenure and use rights

3. All relevant royalties and taxes are paid

4. There is compliance with the criteria of CITES

Relevant documentation demonstrating the above must be provided or made available on request subject to the availability of such materials in the country concerned. Certification against any of the timber certification schemes identified in tiers 1, 2 and 4 demonstrates that timber has been legally sourced.

MDF

Medium density fibreboard.

MTCC

Malaysian Timber Certification Council.

OSB

Oriented strand board.

PEFC

Programme for the Endorsement of Forest Certification Schemes.

Post-consumer waste stream

Waste material generated by households or by commercial, industrial and institutional facilities in their role as end-users of the product, which can no longer be used for its intended purpose. This includes returns of material from the distribution chain.

Pre-consumer waste stream

Waste material generated during manufacturing processes. Excluded is reutilisation of materials such as rework, regrind or scrap generated in a process and capable of being reclaimed within the same process that generated it.

PVC

Polyvinyl chloride.

Recycled material

Materials diverted from the pre-consumer and/or post-consumer waste streams that require significant processing before they can be used again. For further information please see *Calculating and declaring recycled content in construction products*, 'Rules of Thumb' Guide (WRAP, 2008).

Assessment Methodology

The assessment criteria should be read with the methodology and the definitions in this section. Credits are awarded where the performance requirements (set out in the assessment criteria table) have been met.

Design Stage

- Where a construction make-up is not specified within the Code Mat 3 Calculator Tool, confirm the construction details of elements using the specification and drawings, or similar (see Information Required to Demonstrate Compliance). Obtain a breakdown of volumes and/or percentages of materials for each element present.

- Obtain the relevant confirmation of tier certification for design stage (see Information Required to Demonstrate Compliance) for all* materials, from all sources/suppliers.

  * The following exclusions apply:

  Material groups not included in the list in Definitions (e.g. insulation materials, fixings, adhesives, additives).

  Materials that account for less than 10% by volume of an element may also be excluded (e.g. screws). However, if certification has been provided for materials in this category, it may be beneficial to include them in the calculation (e.g. if a material type accounting for 9% is placed in a higher tier than other materials used to make up the element).

- Assign a tier level to each material based on the level of certification provided (see table Cat 3.1: Tier Levels, and Compliance and Information Required to Demonstrate Compliance).

- Follow the calculation procedures outlined below. Ensure that all timber is legally sourced and none of the species to be used is identified on the CITES list.

Notes:

1. For any other materials which do not fit into the assessed materials or the exclusion, please refer back to the Code service provider who will identify the relevant key processes and supply chain process(es).

2. MDF, chipboard, OSB and cement bonded particle board are all considered as timber and therefore must be assessed as timber material.

Mat

3. Where a mix of virgin and recycled timber is used, only the virgin timber needs to be assessed. Credits can then be awarded based on the certification schemes it is under.

4. Slate is classed as stone and is therefore considered as an assessed material.

Post Construction Stage

- Confirm that the final building construction matches that specified at design stage. Where any design changes have occurred, reassess the certification tier for each element according to the methodology set out above.

Calculation Procedures

Credits for this issue should be calculated using the Code Mat 3 Calculator Tool. The tool will calculate the total number of points awarded to each element taking into account the scenarios mentioned above. It will also state the associated number of credits. A copy of the tool should be included with the assessment report.

Elements should be entered as present or not present and the tool will calculate the range of points required to achieve a number of credits in accordance with table Cat 3.3. The calculator is programmed to flag up error messages at stages where there is non-compliance with the criteria, which should assist with assessing this issue.

A minimum of 80% of each material assessed must comply with tiers 1 to 4 (excluding materials not assessed).

If 80% of an assessed element is compliant with a single tier, the full score available for that tier will apply.

If 80% of an element is compliant over a number if tiers, the calculator will first review the percentage compliant with the highest tier and apportion a score to that. If less than 80% is compliant, it will review the percentage of the element in the next highest tier and apportion a score to that. This will continue until the 80% requirement has been met.

Consequently, it may be beneficial to include even small percentages of materials that are in the higher tiers if the majority of the rest of the element would otherwise be allocated a lower tier level.

Mat

Checklists and Tables

Refer to Mat 2 for Tier Levels and EMS requirements.

Table Cat 3.4: Credit Structure			
	Credits Available		
	3	2	1
No. of Elements Present	Points Range		
8	= 18	≥ 12	≥ 6
7	≥ 15.75	≥ 10.25	≥ 5.25
6	≥ 13.5	≥ 9	≥ 4.5
5	≥ 11.25	≥ 7.5	≥ 3.75

Common Cases of Non-Compliance

Timber and EMS Schemes

Where an EMS scheme is used to assess products made from recycled timber, 100% of the timber content must be recycled or sourced from one of the recognised timber certification schemes in table Cat 3.1. A timber product with 50% recycled timber and 50% legally sourced timber will not comply with the criteria and will not be awarded any points.

Using an EMS scheme for new timber does not demonstrate timber certification and therefore does not qualify for any points.

A statement of intent from a product manufacturer and/or supplier does not meet the requirements for this issue.

Special Cases

If an element being considered is made up primarily of a material not specified in this issue, please contact the Code service provider for further guidance.

For mixed use buildings refer to special cases in Mat 1.

Category 4: Surface Water Run-off

Issue ID	Description	No. of Credits Available	Mandatory Elements
Sur 1	Management of Surface Water Run-off from Developments	2	Yes

Aim

To design surface water drainage for housing developments which avoid, reduce and delay the discharge of rainfall run-off to *watercourses and public sewers* using SuDS techniques. This will protect receiving waters from pollution and minimise the risk of flooding and other environmental damage in watercourses.

> Note: This section will be revised when the National Standards for Sustainable Drainage and associated regulations come into force.

Assessment Criteria*

Criteria		
	Credits	Mandatory Elements
Hydraulic Control Criteria The *SuDS Management Train* should be used as a guide to achieve the following: *1) Peak Rate of Run-off* If there is no increase in the man-made impermeable area as a result of the new development, then the peak rate of run-off criterion does not apply. Where there is an increase in impermeable area, ensure that the peak rate of run-off over the development lifetime, allowing for climate change, will be no greater for the developed site than it was for the *pre-development* site. This should comply at the 1 year[1] and 100 year[2] return period events (see Calculation Procedures). Where the pre-development peak rate of run-off for the site would result in a requirement for the post-development flow rate (referred to as the *limiting discharge*) to be less than 5 l/s at a *discharge point*, a flow rate of up to 5 l/s may be used where required to reduce the risk of blockage. *Note: If as a result of the new development, there is an increase in the volume of run-off discharged for the 100 year 6 hour event and section 2A cannot be met (see section 2 below), these run-off rates do not apply.*	None	All Levels *continued*

continued

---

* Supplementary guidance will be published by the Welsh Assembly Government to reflect planning policy and practice in Wales. The guidance which will not materially affect the aims and objectives of the Surface Water Run Off requirements of the Code, will be based on Technical Advice Note 15 (TAN 15) which supplements Planning Policy Wales, and surface management techniques currently in force in Wales.

[1] This can also be referred to as the 1 in 1, 1:1 or 100% probability of an event occurring in any year.

[2] This can also be referred to as the 1 in 100, 1:100 or 1% probability of an event occurring in any year.

Criteria		
	Credits	Mandatory Elements

2) Volume of Run-off
 	
 If there is no increase in the man-made impermeable area as a result of the new development, then the volume of run-off criteria does not apply.
 	
 If the developed site would otherwise discharge, over the development lifetime allowing for climate change, a greater volume of rainwater run-off than the pre-development site for the 100 year 6 hour event, (see Calculation Procedures) then criterion A applies. If A cannot be satisfied then B applies.
 	
     A: Ensure that the post development volume of run-off, allowing for climate change over the development lifetime, is no greater than it would have been before the development.
 	
     The additional predicted volume of run-off for the 100 year 6 hour event must be prevented from leaving the site by using infiltration or other *SuDS techniques* (see Definitions).
 	
 OR
 	
     B: If A cannot be satisfied (full justification must be provided) then reduce the post development peak rate of run-off to the limiting discharge.
 	
     The limiting discharge is the pre-development flow rate equivalent to the 1-year peak flow rate, mean annual flood flow rate (Qbar) or 2 l/s/ha, whichever is the highest flow rate.
 	
     For the 1-year peak flow rate the 1 year return period event criterion in section 1 above, applies. For all other events up to the 100 year return period event, the peak rate of run-off for the developed site must not exceed the limiting discharge.
 	
     Where the limiting discharge flow rate would require a flow rate of less than 5 l/s at a discharge point, a flow rate of up to 5 l/s may be used where required to reduce the risk of blockage.
 	
 Note: Criterion B generally results in more storage than compliance with criterion A.
 	
 3) Designing for local drainage system failure.
 	
 Demonstrate that the flooding of property would not occur in the event of local drainage system failure (caused either by extreme rainfall or a lack of maintenance).
 	
 Note: Where the run-off is being discharged into an existing drainage system, the responsible body may stipulate a more stringent set of hydraulic flow rate criterion which will therefore take precedence.		

Water Quality Criteria 1. One credit can be awarded by ensuring there is no discharge from the developed site for rainfall depths up to 5 mm (see Calculation Procedures). 2. One credit can be awarded by ensuring that: • The run-off from all hard surfaces shall receive an appropriate *level of treatment* in accordance with The SuDS Manual to minimise the risk of pollution. *Note: The SuDS Manual best practice recommendations should be followed where there is a risk to groundwater from infiltration (for example contaminated land, developments with high risk of pollution incidents)*	1 1	
Default Cases: The mandatory criteria can be deemed to be met by default if the site discharges rainwater directly to a *tidal estuary* or the sea. Credits cannot be awarded unless the relevant water quality criteria are met.		

Sur

Information Required to Demonstrate Compliance

Schedule of Evidence Required	
Design Stage	**Post Construction Stage**
Mandatory Elements:	Mandatory Elements:

Statement from the *appropriately qualified professional* confirming that they are qualified in line with the Code definition. **AND** The appropriately qualified professional's report containing all information necessary to demonstrate compliance with the peak rate of run-off and volume of run-off requirements. The report should include: • Areas of permeable and impermeable surfaces on the site pre- and post- development Where the impermeable area has increased post development the report should also include: • Details of the permeability characteristics of the site pre- and post-development (e.g. infiltration tests etc where appropriate) • Peak rates of run-off (l/s) calculations for the 1 year and 100 year events, pre- and post-development, including an allowance for climate change over the development lifetime • Detailed documentary evidence showing the methods used to reduce the peak rate of run-off to pre-development rates • The pre- development volume of run-off (m³) for the 100 year 6 hour event • The additional volume of run-off (m³) for the 100 year 6 hour event caused by the development without mitigation measures • The additional volume of run-off (m³) with the proposed mitigation	Written confirmation from the developer or *appropriately qualified professional* that the solutions designed have been implemented as specified in the design stage evidence **OR** Where different from the design stage, provide the evidence as listed for the design stage but representing the development as built **OR** For post construction stage only assessments, provide evidence as listed for the design stage but representing the development as built Evidence must be provided at post construction to confirm that maintenance responsibilities have been defined for any SuDS solutions installed. *For information: Where SuDS have been implemented, the location and brief explanation of their purpose should be included in the Home User Guide (in Code Category 8: Man 1) where supplied.* Where more than five years have passed since the Flood Risk Assessment was carried out: • Confirmation that the basis of the Flood Risk Assessment has not changed.

- Information to demonstrate that the hierarchical approach to reducing the additional volume of run-off was followed

- Information on the calculation methods used, as well as summary results

AND

A *Flood Risk Assessment* confirming the risk of flooding from all *sources of flooding* (this may be contained within the appropriately qualified professional's report)

AND

Drawings showing the pre-development drainage for the site (natural or constructed)

AND

Drawings showing the proposed drainage solution, system failure flood flow routes, potential flood ponding levels and ground floor levels

AND

Confirmation from the appropriately qualified professional that local drainage system failure would not cause an increase in the risk of flooding within dwellings either on or off site

Where credits are sought: The appropriately qualified professional's report detailing the design specifications, calculations and drawings to support the awarding of the credit(s)	Where credits are sought: Written confirmation from the developer or appropriately qualified professional that the solutions designed have been implemented as specified in the design stage evidence **OR** Where different from the design stage, provide the evidence as listed for the design stage but representing the development as built

	OR
	For post construction stage only assessments, provide evidence as listed for the design stage but representing the development as built

Definitions

Annual flood probability

The estimated probability of a flood of given magnitude occurring or being exceeded in any year. Expressed as a 1 in x year event. This is the equivalent to 1-in-x, 1:x or x% chance of a flood event occurring in any one year.

Annual flow rate probability

The estimated probability of a flow rate of given magnitude occurring or being exceeded in any year. Expressed as a 1 in x year event. This is the equivalent to 1-in-x, 1:x or x % chance of the flow rate being exceeded in any one year.

Appropriately qualified professional

A professional or team of professionals with the skills and experience to champion the use of SuDS within the overall design of the development at an early stage.

The professional or team of professionals must be capable of understanding the site's particular surface water management needs and opportunities. In addition, they must have knowledge and experience in using SuDS-based solutions to influence the holistic design of a development's drainage system and provide the robust hydraulic design calculations referred to in key guidance documents such as *The SuDS manual* (CIRIA C697, 2007) and *Preliminary rainfall runoff management for developments* (EA/DEFRA, 2007).

Suitable professionals may be found in a variety of disciplines, such as engineering, landscape design or hydrology or a combination.

Geotechnical advisers or specialists may be required for SuDS techniques that allow infiltration.

Brownfield site

Land which is or was occupied by a permanent structure, including the curtilage of the developed land and any associated hard surfaces.

Catchment

The area contributing surface water flow to a drainage point or a point on a watercourse. It can be divided into sub-catchments.

Control devices

Any drainage structure or unit designed to control the runoff of stormwater.

Examples of SuDS control devices are check dams within swales and basins, and combined weir/orifice controls for ponds. Examples of traditional control devices are throttles constructed with pipes and vortex controls. The control devices must be capable of regular inspection and maintenance, and the system should be fail-safe so that upstream flooding does not result from blockage or other malfunction. For guidance on control devices, refer to *The SuDS manual* (CIRIA C697, 2007) and other best practice guidelines.

Discharge point

The point of discharge into watercourses and sewers (see definition of 'Watercourses and sewers')

Flood probability

The estimated probability of a flood of given magnitude occurring or being exceeded in any specified time period. For example, the 100-year flood has a 1-in-100 or 1% chance of occurring in any given year.

Flood risk

An expression of the combination of flood probability and the magnitude of the potential consequences of the flood.

Flood Risk Assessment (FRA)

A study to assess the risk of a site flooding and the impact that any changes or development on the site will have on flood risk on the site and elsewhere. A flood risk assessment must be prepared according to good practice guidance as outlined in PPS25 *Development and Flood Risk: Practice Guide* (available from www.communities.gov.uk). For developments of less than 1 ha (10,000 m²), the level of detail required in an acceptable FRA (for Sur 1) will depend on the size and density of build. This will range from a brief report for small, low-density developments, to a more detailed assessment for a high-density development of 2000–10,000 m². For example, for very small developments (2000 m² and less), an acceptable FRA could be a brief report carried out by the contractor's engineer confirming the risk of flooding from all *sources of flooding*, including information obtained from the Environment Agency, water company/sewerage undertaker, other relevant statutory authorities, site investigation and local knowledge.

Flood risk management hierarchy

The hierarchy of flood risk management measures and the role of the planning process in reducing flood risk (see PPS25 as applicable).

Flood storage

The temporary storage of excess run-off or river flow in ponds, basins, reservoirs or on a flood plain during a flood.

Greenfield land

Land that has not been previously developed.

Greenfield run-off rate

The rate of run-off that would occur from the site in its undeveloped state.

Impermeable surfaces

Often referred to as impervious or hard surfaces, these are surfaces which do not allow water to pass into the ground.

Infiltration techniques

Techniques which allow the passage of water into the ground. Techniques used purely for infiltration purposes would typically involve soakaways or pervious paving. Other SuDS techniques, such as swales and filter strips, will also achieve a level of infiltration but, unlike soakaways, they also normally function as a conveyance mechanism for transporting run-off.

Level of Treatment

When used in the context of one, two or three levels of treatment for surface water, treatment level should be regarded as the number of SuDS components in series through which run-off passes from the originating surface on which rainfall fell to the site discharge point.

Where a SuDS component has more than one treatment process, it might be considered to provide more than one level of treatment. In these circumstances advice should be sought from the Code service provider.

Limiting discharge

The limiting discharge is based upon the calculated pre-development flow rate at a discharge point, but may be increased to 5 l/s.

Peak rate of run-off

Referred to as Q_p [m³/sec], this is the highest rate of flow from a defined catchment area assuming that rainfall is uniformly distributed over the drainage area, considering the entire drainage area as a single unit and estimation of flow at the most downstream point only.

Pervious paving

Also referred to as porous and permeable paving. Pervious pavements are SuDS structures and provide a pavement suitable for pedestrian and/or vehicular traffic, while allowing rainwater to infiltrate through the surface and into the underlying layers. The water may be temporarily stored before infiltration into the ground, re-use or discharge to a watercourse or other drainage system (see CIRIA C697 *The SuDS manual* for additional information).

The design of the pervious pavement will depend on its drained area, climate and local geological and hydrological conditions.

For example, a block paved surface on a permeable sub-base on permeable ground, will store the water temporarily and allow it to seep into the soil.

For less permeable soils, more storage volume may be needed to compensate for reduced infiltration rates. For very low permeability areas (e.g. less than 1×10^{-6}m/s) water may be discharged to a conveyance system, with the pervious paving providing attenuation and water treatment.

Pre-development

The site's condition immediately before project commencement, i.e. brownfield or greenfield.

Probability of flooding – Low (Zone 1)

Probability of river and sea flooding, but does not take into account other sources of flooding or defences. These are defined in PPS25.

Low annual probability of flooding is an area where the chance of both river and sea flooding each year is <0.1% (1 in 1000) or less.

Probability of flooding – Medium (Zone 2)

An area where the chance of river flooding in any year is 1% (1 in 100) or less but greater than 0.1% (1 in 1000), and the chance of flooding from the sea is 0.5% – 0.1% (between 1 in 200 and 1 in 1000).

Probability of flooding – High (Zone 3a)

An area where the chance of river flooding in any year is >1% (1 in 100) and the chance of flooding from the sea is >0.5% (1 in 200) or greater.

Probability of flooding – Functional flood plan (zone 3b)

The land where water flows or is stored in times of flood.

Qbar

An estimation of the mean annual flood flow rate from a catchment (see Report IH124 *Flood estimations for small catchments*).

Rainfall intensity

Depth of rain falling in a period of time, e.g. mm/hour, sometimes given in l/s/m^2.

Rainwater discharge

Rainwater discharge is the rainwater which flows from the development site to watercourses and sewers. It is also referred to as run-off.

Relevant statutory body

In England and Wales this will in most cases be the Environment Agency, and for Northern Ireland will be the Rivers Agency.

Run-off rate

The rate of flow of water from a surface.

Sewerage undertaker

This is a Body with statutory responsibility for the disposal of foul wastewater and also surface water from roofs and hard surfaces.

Sewers for Adoption

A guide agreed between sewerage undertakers and developers (through the Home Builders Federation) specifying the standards to which private sewers must be constructed to facilitate adoption.

Soakaway

Underground structure designed to permit infiltration into permeable/slightly permeable ground. They can be grouped and linked together to drain large areas including highways.

Sources of flooding and flood risk

Streams and Rivers: Flooding that can take place from flows that are not contained within the channel due to high levels of rainfall in the catchment.

Coastal or Estuarine: Flooding that can occur from the sea due to a particularly high tide or surge, or combination of both.

Groundwater: Where the water table rises to such a height where flooding occurs. Most common in low-lying areas underlain by permeable ground (aquifers), usually due to extended periods of wet weather.

Sewers and highway drains: Combined, foul or surface water sewers and highway drains that are temporarily over-loaded due to excessive rainfall or due to blockage.

Surface water: The net rainfall falling on a surface (on or off the site) which acts as runoff which has not infiltrated into the ground or entered into a drainage system.

Infrastructure failure: canals, reservoirs, industrial processes, burst water mains, blocked sewers or failed pumping stations.

SuDS

As defined in the SuDS manual, sustainable drainage systems are an approach to surface water management that combines a sequence of management practices and control structures designed to drain surface water in a more sustainable fashion than some conventional techniques.

These systems infiltrate, store, convey and partially treat surface water runoff, which minimises environmental impact and maximises environmental opportunities. SuDS should aim to maximise the use of on-the-surface techniques for operational and maintenance reasons.

SuDS Management Train

An approach to drainage design that combines a sequence of appropriate surface water drainage structures using SuDS systems for management of the runoff to treat the flow, reduce runoff volume and restrain the runoff rate in order to minimise man's impact on the environment. Additional benefits associated with operation and maintenance, ecology and amenity are aspects which are considered when designing a management system. The management train incorporates a hierarchy of techniques:

1. Source control. Examples of SuDS techniques include:
   - Soakaways
   - Porous/pervious paving
   - Roof water directed to garden (rather than piped drains)
   - Rainwater re-use/harvesting
   - Green roofs
   - Other surface infiltration, attenuation and conveyance techniques that deal with run-off at source.

2. Site/local control. Examples of SuDS techniques include:
   - Swales
   - Pond
   - Infiltration basins
   - Detention Basin
   - Larger soakaways
   - Pervious (porous or permeable) paving.

3. Regional control. Examples of techniques include:
   - Balancing ponds
   - Wetlands
   - Large detention basin

SuDS techniques

One or more components built to manage surface water run-off to prevent flooding and pollution, including:

- Wet ponds
- Infiltration basins
- Detention basins
- Swales
- Reed beds
- Pervious (porous or permeable) paving
- Soakaways
- Rainwater harvesting
- Filter strips
- Filter drains and trenches with or without perforated pipes
- Green roofs
- Underground Attenuation storage.

For more information refer to *The SuDS manual* (CIRIA C697, 2007)

Surface water run-off

Rainfall that flows off the catchment.

Tidal estuary

A semi-enclosed coastal body of water which has a free connection with the open sea and within which seawater is measurably diluted with fresh water derived from land drainage.

Tidal rivers (i.e. where no measurable seawater content is present during normal tidal movements) cannot be included as part of the estuary.

Treatment

Improving the quality of water by physical, chemical and/or biological means.

Volume of run-off

The volume of run-off that is generated by rainfall occurring on the site. This is typically measured in cubic metres.

Additional predicted volume of run-off is the difference between the volumes of run-off pre- and post-development, usually calculated for a specific rainfall event.

Watercourses and sewers

A term that includes rivers, streams, ditches, drains, cuts, culverts, dykes, sluices, sewers and passages through which water flows.

Assessment Methodology

The assessment criteria should be read with the methodology and the definitions in this section. Mandatory requirements are met and credits are awarded where the performance requirements (set out in the assessment criteria table) have been met.

Design Stage

- Owing to the nature of Issue Sur1, it is critical in all cases that compliance with the criteria is clearly demonstrated at this stage.

- The assessor is not required to perform any calculations. These must be provided, with all the necessary supporting information, by the appropriately qualified professional.

Mandatory requirements:

- Check that an appropriately qualified professional has been appointed

- Check that an appropriate Flood Risk Assessment (FRA) has been carried out

- Check that allowances have been made for climate change over the lifetime of the development in all post-development calculations

- Where the impermeable area draining to watercourses or sewers has increased, check that the appropriately qualified professional's report contains the following:

  Peak rate of run-off calculations:

  – Calculations for the 1 year and 100 year return periods for both pre- and post-development, including an allowance for climate change for the post-development state.

  – Check that the calculation methodology used complies with the requirements in the Calculation Procedures.

  Volume of run-off calculations:

  – The additional volume of run-off for the 100 year 6 hour event including an allowance for climate change for the post-development state. The additional volume with and without mitigation measures should be provided.

  – Check that the appropriately qualified professional's report demonstrates that the hierarchy specified has been followed and the additional volume of run-off is zero in line with criterion A or, if this cannot be satisfied, then evidence to demonstrate criterion B has been met and full justification has been provided.

  – Check that the route of water over ground in the event of a local drainage system failure (system failure flood flow routes), for whatever reason have been demonstrated, and the possible consequences have been evaluated, ensuring that there is no increased risk of flooding to properties either on or off site.

Note: Site drainage design should drain using gravity based systems in preference to those which require the use of pumping stations.

Credits:

- Where credits are sought, check that the report contains the information needed to allow the credit(s) to be awarded.

Post Construction Stage

- If a design stage assessment was carried out, the appropriately qualified professional should confirm that the design stage solutions have been implemented or, if designs have changed, evidence should be supplied showing the as-built design and construction.

- If a design stage assessment was not carried out, follow the Assessment Methodology guidance for the design stage to document the post construction evidence representing the development as built.

- Check the time elapsed since the FRA was carried out. Where this is significant, for example, more than five years (or less if major surface water regulation changes have occurred during this period), or it does not include an allowance for climate change, ask the appropriately qualified professional to confirm that the design basis of the surface water system is still valid.

- Confirm that the maintenance responsibilities have been defined for any SuDS components present, including all necessary control devices, and that maintenance regimes have been put in place.

Calculation Procedures

Assessors are not required to carry out calculations. The information below is for the appropriately qualified professional to use when completing calculations. It will also be helpful to guide assessors when checking that sufficient evidence has been provided to demonstrate compliance.

- Key publications that should be referred to for guidance include:
    - *The SuDS Manual*, CIRIA C697 (2007) – Useful Link: http://www.ciria.org.uk/suds/publications.htm

    - *Preliminary rainfall run-off management for developments*, W5-074/A/TR/1 Revision D, EA/DEFRA (September 2005) – Useful Link: http://www.defra.gov.uk/environment/flooding/documents/research/sc030219.pdf

    - *Development and Flood Risk*, Planning Policy Statement 25. Communities and Local Government (2006 as revised 2010), along with the latest version of the practice guide. Useful Link: http://www.communities.gov.uk/documents/planningandbuilding/pdf/planningpolicystatement25.pdf

Peak rate of run-off:

The peak rate of run-off calculations must be carried out as follows:

- Climate change

  An allowance for climate change must be made for all sites in accordance with current best planning guidance. The climate change allowance must be added to the post-development run-off rate and volume calculations only. Information regarding the percentage allowance can be found in PPS25 as applicable.

- Greenfield sites of less than 50 ha

  The calculation of greenfield run-off rates must be in accordance with IH Report 124, *Flood estimation for small catchments* (Marshall and Bayliss, 1994). The pro-rata method on the size of *catchment* detailed in Table 4.2 in *The SuDS Manual*, CIRIA C697 (2007) must be followed.

- Greenfield sites of 50 ha to 200 ha

  The calculation of greenfield run-off rates must be in accordance with IH Report 124, *Flood estimation for small catchments* (Marshall and Bayliss, 1994). FEH can be used for these sites as an alternative, where there is a preference to do so, but only if the catchment is considered to be suitable for its application.

- Greenfield sites of more than 200 ha

  The calculation of greenfield run-off rates must be in accordance with the *Flood Estimation Handbook* (Centre for Ecology & Hydrology, 1999) and any subsequent updates. Where the *Flood Estimation Handbook* is not considered appropriate for the development IH Report 124 can be used.

- *Brownfield sites*

  The calculation of brownfield run-off rates should be as follows:

  a) If the existing drainage is known then it should be modelled using best practice simulation modelling, to determine the 1 year and 100 year peak flow rates at discharge points (without allowing surcharge of the system above cover levels to drive greater flow rates through the discharge points).

  b) If the system is not known, then the Brownfield run-off should be calculated using the greenfield run-off models described above but with a Soil Type 5.

- Limiting discharge rate

  The limiting discharge for each discharge point should be calculated as the flow rates from the pre-developed site, as detailed in the calculation procedures above. The calculation should include the total flow rate from the total area of site feeding into the discharge point (this should include both Code and non-Code parts of the development, if applicable). The discharge point is defined as the point of discharge into the watercourse/sewers (including rivers, streams, ditches, drains, cuts, culverts, dykes, sluices, public sewers and passages through which water flows, see Definitions). Where this calculation results in a peak flow rate of less than 5 l/s, the limiting discharge rate may be increased up to a level of no more than 5 l/s at the point of discharge from the site to reduce the risk of blockage.

For example, if the flow rate for the 1 year and 100 year events were 4 l/s and 7 l/s respectively, then the limiting discharges would be 5 l/s and 7 l/s. Similarly, if it was calculated to be 2 l/s and 4 l/s, then a maximum of 5 l/s limiting discharge rate could be applied to both discharge points.

Sites should not be subdivided to enable higher overall limiting discharge rates to be claimed. It is, however, recognised that some sites may require more than one discharge point as a result of the local topography or existing surrounding drainage infrastructure, and in such cases the limiting discharge flow rate may be increased to a level no more than 5 l/s at each discharge point. The assessor should seek evidence that the number of discharge points is necessary due to topography and/or infrastructure limitations. Evidence may be in the form of a topographical map and an explanation from the appropriately qualified professional as to why multiple discharge points are required, stating that it is not feasible to have fewer discharge points.

- 100-year peak rate event: Excess volume of run-off

The storage of excess flows from the 100-year event does not necessarily have to be contained within the drainage system or SuDS features (the features designed solely for the purpose of drainage). Where appropriate, storage of some or all of this volume can be achieved using temporary surface flooding of areas such as a playing field. Specific consideration should be given to overland flow routeing. Overland flood flows and temporary storage of flood water on the surface must not be so frequent as to unreasonably inconvenience residents and other users.

Volume of run-off:

The volume of run-off calculations must be carried out as follows:

- Calculation methodology

Refer to Chapter 4, Section 4.5.5 of *The SuDS Manual* (CIRIA C697, 2007) for guidance on calculating the additional volume of run-off caused by the development.

- Allowance for climate change

An allowance for climate change must be made in accordance with current planning guidance. The climate change allowance must be added to the post-development run-off calculation only. Information regarding the percentage allowance can be found in PPS25 as applicable.

- Criterion A or B

If the development causes an additional volume of run-off, meeting criterion A must be preferred to B. If criterion A cannot be met, the appropriately qualified professional must provide evidence within their report to justify the reason(s); criterion B must be met through the use of appropriate SuDS techniques.

- 5 l/s flow rate

Where criterion B is met, the limiting discharge rate at the discharge point(s) may be increased to 5 l/s, as described in the calculation procedures above.

Designing for system failure:

The consequences of system failure caused by extreme rainfall, lack of maintenance, blockage or other causes, should be considered /evaluated fully.

CIRIA publication C635 (2006) *Designing for exceedence in urban drainage – good practice* should be referred to for guidance.

Water Quality Credits:

- Where one credit is sought for preventing discharge from the site for rainfall depths up to 5 mm

  A range of SuDS techniques can be used to prevent discharge from the site for rainfall depths of up to 5 mm, however, end-of-pipe solutions, such as ponds and basins, will only be deemed to comply where the principal run-off control to prevent discharge from the first 5 mm of a rainfall event, is achieved using source control and site control methods.

  Green roofs can be deemed to comply with this requirement for the rain that falls onto their surface. However evidence is still required to demonstrate that the 5 mm rainfall from all other hard surfaces on site is being dealt with, to allow this credit to be awarded.

- Treatment levels

  Where treatment levels are introduced to gain a credit, section 3.3 and chapter 5 of *The SuDS Manual* (CIRIA C697, 2007) should be referred to for guidance. The run-off from hard surfaces must receive treatment before being discharged from the site.

General guidance:

- Using computer software

  Reputable computer drainage software can be used to demonstrate compliance. However, where hydrograph tables are provided as output, the relevant calculations should be highlighted.

- Rainwater harvesting

  BS 8515 *Rainwater harvesting systems: Code of Practice*, Annex A should be followed where rainwater harvesting systems are used for stormwater control. To ensure *flood risk* is not increased if the rainwater harvesting system is, for some reason, not utilised, the exceedance flow route capacity provided in accordance with CIRIA report C635 should ignore the beneficial effect of the rainwater harvesting system.

- Assessing mixed Code and non-Code dwelling developments

  Where Code dwellings are dispersed throughout a larger development of non-Code dwellings, there are a number of options for assessment under Sur 1.

  1. Individual dwellings (as part of a larger site) can only be assessed independently where the run-off is being dealt with on a dwelling by

dwelling basis (i.e. each dwelling has its own dedicated sub-catchment that serves only that dwelling).

2. Where assessing groups of Code dwellings within a larger development, the drainage assessment must incorporate the local sub-catchment serving all of those dwellings.

3. Where assessing the run-off from both Code and non-Code dwellings (or Code and non-domestic buildings) the assessment must take into account the drainage from the local sub-catchment serving all those dwellings/buildings.

   Note that proportioning cannot be used to calculate the percentage of run-off discharging into the local sub-catchment resulting from just the Code dwellings.

4. Alternatively the whole development can be assessed for compliance.

   Whichever approach is taken to demonstrate compliance, it must be consistent when completing both the rate of run-off and volume of run-off calculations.

   Note the special case regarding highways and impermeable areas when assessing a site.

- Contaminated sites

   Drainage designs for sites must take into account legislation relating to contaminated sites, such as the Water Resources Act 1991, the Environmental Protection Act 1990, the Groundwater Directive (2006/118/EC) and, more recently, the Groundwater (England and Wales) Regulations 2009. Where the site risk assessment confirms that infiltration SuDS techniques are not appropriate, SuDS techniques that do not allow infiltration, such as swales lined with an impermeable membrane, can be used. It may be the case that only some areas of the site are contaminated and therefore infiltration SuDS techniques can be used elsewhere on the site. There may also be a requirement to remediate the contaminated soils, creating opportunities for the use of infiltration SuDS post-remediation.

Common Cases of Non-Compliance

Neither the mandatory element nor credits can be awarded where the assessed development has proceeded against the recommendation of the Environment Agency regarding surface water drainage.

Special Cases

Minimum flow rate/maximum storage requirement set by sewerage undertaker (or other statutory body)

Where the statutory authority have exercised their statutory powers and have set specific *minimum* flow rate/*maximum* storage requirements that are less onerous than the specific Sur 1 criterion, the statutory requirements will take precedent over the specific Code criterion. All other criteria will still be applicable. Evidence should be provided to confirm that this is the case and should be formal documentation from the statutory authority. This should include evidence such as planning approvals/ conditions and/or correspondence from a statutory body setting out specific requirements, i.e. sewerage undertaker, Environment Agency etc. The Flood Risk Assessment may contain some of the evidence required to demonstrate compliance.

Note: Where the statutory authority has approved a design on the basis of a minimum discharge rate identified through a FRA, compliance with this minimum standard, will be deemed to meet the mandatory peak rate of run-off requirement, where supported by the documentary evidence. In all other cases, the approval of a specific design feature or the setting of a non-compliant discharge rate will not be sufficient to demonstrate compliance.

Maximum flow rate set by sewerage undertaker (or other statutory body)

If a maximum flow rate is set that can be discharged, the peak rate of run-off requirement within the Code will still apply unless the maximum flow rate set is more rigorous (lower rate) than the Code, in which case compliance with the Sewerage Undertaker's requirements will apply.

Highways and impermeable areas

Where new non-adoptable highways are built, including those for developments with a mixture of Code and non-Code dwellings, all of the new impermeable surfaces must be included in calculations to demonstrate compliance with the peak rate of run-off and volume of run-off criteria.

Where Code dwellings are built beside existing highways or where adoptable highways are built, the impermeable area of the highway does not need to be included in the calculations.

Derelict sites

If the site has been derelict for over five years, the appropriately qualified professional must assess the previous drainage network and make reasonable assumptions to establish probable flow rates and volumes. The Wallingford Procedure Modified Rational Method should be used. To complete the calculations, a site visit prior to development will be required unless accurate data already exist from a previous survey. The resultant professional report can then be used to determine the pre-development volumes and rates of run-off. Without this professional input, the site must be deemed *greenfield* pre-development, assuming Soil Type 5 for the calculation of the pre-development site run-off.

No change or reduction in impermeable area

Where a man-made impermeable surface draining to the watercourse and sewers has decreased or remained unchanged post-development, the peak rate of run-off and volume of run-off requirements will be met by default and run-off calculations will not be required. Instead, drawings clearly showing the man-made impermeable surfaces of the site draining to the watercourse and sewers should be provided for the pre- and post-development scenarios. Figures must also be given (ideally on the drawings as well) to show a comparison between the areas of drained man-made impermeable surfaces pre- and post-development.

Sites with existing infrastructure/planning approval

Some sites may not be in a position to meet the requirements set out in the Code owing to existing or approved infrastructure strategies that pre-date the requirement for a Code rating.

a) For sites where planning approval (covering the *detailed* drainage strategy for the site) has been granted prior to the Code requirement being set for the development, the mandatory element of Sur 1 can be met by default. No credits for water quality can be awarded if the mandatory element is met using this method. Evidence requirements 1, 2 and 3 as listed below.

b) For sites where the assessed dwellings are *directly* connected to existing infrastructure which pre-dates the Code requirement for the site, the mandatory element of Sur 1 can be met by default. No credits for water quality can be awarded if the mandatory element is met using this method. Evidence requirements 3 and 4 as listed below.

Note: The phrase 'directly connected to existing infrastructure' should be interpreted as individual dwellings being directly connected to the existing sewer without any significant shared installation (this Special Case is predominantly only relevant for single dwellings). It does not cover instances where an entire site or new shared system is being connected into the existing main sewer. It should be a simple connection from a dwelling into an existing manhole/sewer rather than a new network being created.

Evidence referred to in a) and b) above is as follows:

1. Planning approvals/conditions.

2. HCA grant approvals or planning conditions which demonstrate the date the Code requirement was enforced.

3. Plans showing coverage of existing and approved drainage designs and the connections to them

4. Flood Risk Assessment – this may contain some of the evidence required in items 1 to 3 above and therefore, if completed in accordance with the Calculation Procedures, may also be provided for any of the above scenarios in support of any of the above evidence.

Issue ID	Description	No. of Credits Available	Mandatory Elements
Sur 2	Flood Risk	2	No

Aim

To promote housing development in low *flood risk* areas, or to take measures to reduce the impact of flooding on houses built in areas with a medium or high risk of flooding.

Assessment Criteria*

Criteria	Credits
EITHER Two credits are available for developments situated in Zone 1 – *low annual probability of flooding* (as defined in PPS25 *Development and Flood Risk*) and where the site-specific *Flood Risk Assessment (FRA)* indicates that there is low risk of flooding from all sources.	2
OR One credit is available for developments situated in Zones 2 and 3a – *medium* and *high annual probability of flooding* where the finished ground floor level of all habitable parts of dwellings and access routes to the ground level and the site, are placed at least 600 mm above the *design flood level* of the *flood zone*. The Flood Risk Assessment accompanying the planning application must demonstrate to the satisfaction of the local planning authority and statutory body that the development is appropriately flood resilient and resistant, including safe access and escape routes where required, and that any *residual risk* can be safely managed.	1
Default Cases None	

---

* Supplementary guidance will be published by the Welsh Assembly Government to reflect planning policy and practice in Wales. The guidance which will not materially affect the aims and objectives of the Surface Water Run Off requirements of the Code, will be based on Technical Advice Note 15 (TAN 15) which supplements Planning Policy Wales, and surface management techniques currently in force in Wales.

Information Required to Demonstrate Compliance

Schedule of Evidence Required	
Design Stage	**Post Construction Stage**
For developments situated in Zone 1: • A Flood Risk Assessment (prepared according to good practice guidance as outlined in PPS25 *Development and Flood Risk*) which shows that there is a low risk of flooding from all sources.	Written confirmation from the developer that the evidence submitted at the design stage has not changed **OR** Where different from the design stage, provide evidence (as listed for the design stage) representing the dwellings as built **OR** When at post construction stage assessment only, provide evidence (as listed for the design stage) representing the dwellings as built.
For medium (Zone 2) or high (Zone 3a) flood risk areas: • A Flood Risk Assessment (prepared according to good practice guidance as outlined in PPS25 *Development and Flood Risk*) which shows there is a medium or high risk of flooding **AND** • Site plans indicating the design flood level, the range of ground levels of the dwellings, car parking areas and site access (lowest to highest), showing that the criteria (finished floor levels of all habitable rooms and access routes being at least 600 mm above the design flood level) are met, along with any notes explaining the function of any areas lying below the design flood level **AND** • Confirmation from the local planning authority that the development complies with PPS25 and is appropriately flood resilient and resistant, and has managed any residual risk safely.	

Where the site is under the protection of flood defences and the flood risk category of the site is reduced:	Where more than five years have passed since the Flood Risk Assessment was carried out:
• Written confirmation from the Environment Agency of the reduction in flood risk category *. *Note: There are many defences, owned by third parties, which, owing to their location, act as a defence by default, e.g. motorway and railway embankments, walls. Confirmation is required that these defences will remain in place for the lifetime of the development if a significant risk is predicted.	• Confirmation that the basis of the Flood Risk Assessment has not changed.

Definitions

Design flood level

The maximum estimated water level during the design storm event. A site's design flood level can be determined through known historical data or modelled for the specific site.

Flood probability

The estimated probability of a flood of given magnitude occurring or being exceeded in any specified time period. For example, the 100-year flood has a 1% chance of occurring in any given year.

Flood protection measures

This covers the range of flood protection measures which can be employed to protect individual dwellings and developments from the effects of flooding.

Flood resilient construction

Buildings that are designed to reduce the consequences of flooding and facilitate recovery from the effects of flooding sooner than conventional buildings.

Flood resistant construction

Buildings that prevent the entry of water or minimise the amount of water that may enter a building where there is flooding outside.

Sur

Flood Risk Assessment (FRA)

A study to assess the risk of a site flooding and the impact that any changes or development on the site will have on flood risk on the site and elsewhere. A flood risk assessment must be prepared according to good practice guidance as outlined in PPS25 *Development and Flood Risk: Practice Guide* (available from www. communities.gov.uk).

For developments of less than 1 ha (10,000 m²), the level of detail required in an acceptable FRA (for Sur 1) will depend on the size and density of build. This will range from a brief report for small, low-density developments, to a more detailed assessment for a high-density development of 2000–10,000 m². For example, for very small developments (2000 m² and less), an acceptable FRA could be a brief report carried out by the contractor's engineer confirming the risk of flooding from all *sources of flooding*, including information obtained from the Environment Agency, water company/sewerage undertaker, other relevant statutory authorities, site investigation and local knowledge.

Flood zones – PPS25

These zones relate to flooding from the sea and rivers only and do not take into account flood defences. These are defined in PPS25.

Zone 1: Low annual probability of flooding

Zone 2: Medium annual probability of flooding

Zone 3a: High annual probability of flooding

Zone 3b: Functional flood plain (where water is stored in times of flood)

Functional flood plain (Zone 3b)

This land is where water flows or is stored in times of flood.

High annual probability of flooding (Zone 3a)

An area where the chance of river flooding in any year is >1% (1 in 100) and the chance of flooding from the sea is >0.5% (1 in 200) or greater.

Low annual probability of flooding (Zone 1)

An area where the chance of both river and sea flooding each year is <0.1% (1 in 1000) or less.

Medium annual probability of flooding (Zone 2)

An area where the chance of river flooding in any year is 1% (1 in 100) or less but greater than 0.1% (1 in 1000), and the chance of flooding from the sea is 0.5% – 0.1% (between 1 in 200 and 1 in 1000).

Residual risk

The risk which remains after all risk avoidance, reduction and mitigation measures have been implemented.

Sources of flooding and flood risk

<u>Streams and Rivers</u>: Flooding that can take place from flows that are not contained within the channel due to high levels of rainfall in the catchment.

<u>Coastal or Estuarine</u>: Flooding that can occur from the sea due to a particularly high tide or surge, or combination of both.

<u>Groundwater</u>: Where the water table rises to such a height where flooding occurs. Most common in low-lying areas underlain by permeable rock (aquifers), usually due to extended periods of wet weather.

<u>Sewers and highway drains</u>: Combined, foul or surface water sewers and highway drains that are temporarily over-loaded due to excessive rainfall or due to blockage.

<u>Surface water</u>: The net rainfall falling on a surface (on or off the site) which acts as runoff which has not infiltrated into the ground or entered into a drainage system.

<u>Infrastructure failure</u>: Canals, reservoirs, industrial processes, burst water mains, blocked sewers or failed pumping stations.

Assessment Methodology

The assessment criteria should be read with the methodology and the definitions in this section. Credits are awarded where the performance requirements (set out in the assessment criteria table) have been met.

Design Stage

- The assessor should confirm that a Flood Risk Assessment has been carried out. This is necessary to ensure that other *sources of flooding* (other than river and sea) are also a low risk. For small developments in low flood risk areas, this will be a relatively brief report.

- If the development is in Zone 1 and the Flood Risk Assessment shows low risk overall, two credits can be awarded. It should be noted that the flood map accessible from the Environment Agency website gives only a rough estimation of flood risk and is not used for planning submission. A Flood Risk Assessment requires contact with the local planning authority to discuss the site, and benefit from the information available.

- If the development is in Zone 2 or 3a, the assessor should check that the Flood Risk Assessment submitted with the planning application has demonstrated to the relevant authorities that the development is appropriately designed, as detailed in the criteria. If the evidence shows that the finished floor levels and

Sur

all access routes comply with the criteria and any residual risks can be safely managed, one credit can be awarded.

Post Construction Stage

- For developments in Zone 1, the assessor should simply check that the Flood Risk Assessment submitted at the design stage (or, if no design stage report was completed, the Flood Risk Assessment used to gain planning consent) still represents an accurate assessment of flood risk. Whilst this can be assumed in most cases, some sites can take 10 years to build out and during this time many factors can change. Where the time lapse since the original report is more than five years, or does not include an allowance for climate change, ask the consultant to confirm that the basis on which the design was completed has not changed.

- For developments in Zones 2 and 3a, the assessor should check the Flood Risk Assessment as above and ensure that the as-built plans confirm the correct levels of the floors and access routes above the design flood levels.

- Where applicable, check that the specified *flood protection measures* have been designed and built according to the consultant's recommendations.

Calculation Procedures

None.

Common Cases of Non-Compliance

Credits cannot be awarded where the assessed development has proceeded against the recommendation of the Environment Agency on the basis that the flooding implications are too great.

Credits will also be withheld if flood defence schemes considered for this issue would reduce the performance of *functional flood plains* elsewhere.

Special Cases

A site's flood risk may be downgraded to a lower flood risk category as a result of flood defence installations. This may occur in the following circumstances:

[1]   Where permanent new flood defences are planned* to minimise the risk of flooding to the site and its locality.

   * Mentioned in formal planning documents with budgets allocated.

OR

[2]   Where the development is located on a site benefiting from existing maintained flood defences.

In these circumstances, flood risk will be downgraded from medium to low flood risk, as defined in PPS25, and two credits can be awarded. The following evidence will be needed to demonstrate compliance:

a) Confirmation from the flood defence agency (e.g. Environment Agency) that the flood risk level for the site will be reduced to less than 0.1% probability of flooding in any one year.

AND

b) Confirmation from the flood defence agency that there are plans to maintain the defences for the lifetime of the development. (For private flood defences, evidence must be provided that there is a contractual agreement to cover the maintenance of the defences for the lifetime of the development.)

AND

c) The Flood Risk Assessment clearly demonstrates that the residual risks have been identified and will be managed appropriately.

Where sites are downgraded from high to medium flood risk as a result of flood defences, they can only achieve a maximum of one credit. To award that credit, the criteria must be met as specified in the criteria table.

Sur

Category 5: Waste

Issue ID	Description	No. of Credits Available	Mandatory Elements
Was 1	Storage of Non-recyclable Waste and Recyclable Household Waste	4	Yes

Aim

To provide adequate internal and external storage space for non-recyclable waste and recyclable household waste.

Assessment Criteria

Criteria	Credits	Mandatory Elements
Storage of household waste An *adequate external space* should be allocated for waste storage and sized to accommodate containers according to the largest of the following two volumes: • The minimum volume recommended by British Standard 5906 (British Standards Institution, 2005) based on a maximum collection frequency of once per week. This volume is 100 litres for a single bedroom dwelling, with a further 70 litres for each additional bedroom. • The total volume of the external waste containers provided by the Local Authority. Storage space must provide *inclusive access and usability* (Checklist IDP). Containers must not be stacked.	None	All Levels
Storage of recyclable household waste Dedicated internal storage for recyclable household waste can be credited where there is no (or insufficient) dedicated external storage capacity for recyclable material, no *Local Authority collection scheme* and where the following criteria are met: At least three internal storage bins: • all located in an *adequate internal space* • with a minimum total capacity of 60 litres.	2	
Storage of recyclable household waste A combination of internal storage capacity provided in an adequate internal space, with either: • a Local Authority collection scheme, or • no Local Authority collection scheme but adequate external storage capacity.	4	

continued

Criteria	Credits	Mandatory Elements
Local Authority collection scheme In addition to a Local Authority collection scheme (with a collection frequency of at least fortnightly), at least one of the following requirements must be met: • Recyclable household waste is sorted **after** collection and a single bin of at least 30 litres is provided in an adequate internal space. • Materials are sorted **before** collection and at least three separate bins are provided with a total capacity of 30 litres. Each bin must have a capacity of at least 7 litres and be located in an adequate internal space. • An *automated waste collection system* which collects at least three different types of recyclable waste. **No Local Authority collection scheme but adequate external storage capacity** For houses and flats there must be at least three identifiably different internal storage bins for recyclable waste located in an adequate internal space: • with a minimum total capacity of 30 litres • with a minimum individual capacity of at least 7 litres. **AND** **For houses**, an adequate external space must be provided for storing at least three external bins for recyclable waste: • with a minimum total capacity of 180 litres • with a minimum individual capacity of 40 litres. **For flats**, a *private recycling scheme operator* must be appointed to maintain bins and collect recyclable waste regularly. Recycling containers must: • be located in an adequate external space • be sized according to the *frequency of collection*, based on guidance from the recycling scheme operator • store at least three types of recyclable waste in identifiably different bins.		
Default Cases None		

Information Required to Demonstrate Compliance

Schedule of Evidence Required	
Design Stage	**Post Construction Stage**
Mandatory element: Provide table: Cat 5.1 – Supplementary Information Sheet for Was 1 and Checklist IDP	Mandatory element: For post construction stage only assessments, provide table: Cat 5.1 Supplementary Information Sheet for Was 1 and Checklist IDP (as listed for design stage) representing the dwellings as built

Was

	OR Written confirmation from the developer that the dwelling has been constructed in accordance with the evidence provided at design stage and that the services outlined at design stage will be provided
Where 2 credits are sought: Detailed documentary evidence stating: • the location of internal storage • the number, types and sizes of internal storage	Where 2 or 4 credits are sought: For post construction stage only assessments, provide detailed documentary evidence (as listed for design stage) representing the dwellings as built
Where 4 credits are sought: Detailed documentary evidence stating: • the location of internal and external storage • the number, types and sizes of internal and external storage **AND** A letter, leaflet, website or other published information from the Local Authority/waste scheme provider* describing; • the types of waste collected • the frequency of collection • if there will be pre or post collection sorting * In the case of an automated collection system, the waste scheme operator will only need to confirm the types of waste collected and if there will be pre or post collection sorting	**OR** Written confirmation from the developer that the dwelling has been constructed in accordance with the evidence provided at design stage and that the services outlined at design stage will be provided **OR** Where different from design stage, provide detailed documentary evidence (as listed for design stage) representing the dwellings as built **OR** *Site Inspection Report* confirming compliance

Was

Definitions

Adequate external space

This refers to the outdoor space supplied for storing non-recyclable waste and recyclable materials. All bins must be located on level hard-standing and be accessed by an inclusive route (Checklist IDP) from the closest external door to the dwelling/ block of flats:

- For flats: external recycling bins must be covered.

- For dwellings other than flats: external recycling bins, if not provided by the local authority, must be *covered*

Adequate internal space

This refers to the indoor space supplied for storing non-recyclable waste and recyclable materials. Internal recycling bins must be located in a dedicated non-obstructive position. This must be in a cupboard in the kitchen, close to the non-recyclable waste bin, or located adjacent (within 10 m) to the kitchen in a utility room or connected garage. Free-standing recycling bins that are placed directly on the floor or in a cupboard do not comply.

Automated waste collection system

Some companies now offer a fully automated underground system for the collection, sorting and transportation of waste. It allows for waste separation at source, for different types of waste and from multiple locations, with enhanced hygiene and occupational health and safety standards. It also reduces the transport of waste by refuse vehicles, reducing nuisance and associated CO_2 emissions.

Covered bins

The requirement for bin storage to be covered can be satisfied either by providing an enclosed structure (four walls, door and a roof) in which the bins would be placed if they do not have lids OR by providing bins with lids.

Frequency of collection

The space required for storage of non-recyclable household waste is determined by the calculation methodology included in BS5906:2005. This calculation is based on a once weekly collection frequency.

For recyclable waste, the frequency of collection is dependent on the volume and nature of the material being collected. Consequently, it is important for the designer to contact the local authority at an early stage regarding the space required to store recyclable waste.

Inclusive access and usability

The purpose of the Code is not to deliver purpose-designed wheelchair housing but rather inclusive general needs housing that caters for the widest possible segment of

Was

the population (including older people), and which can easily be adapted to meet the needs of wheelchair users. The principles of inclusive design are embedded within the Was 1, Was 3, Hea 3 and Hea 4 issues of the Code. They aim to prevent barriers that create undue effort and separation and enable everyone to participate equally, confidently and independently in everyday activities such as taking out rubbish and spending time outside.

Local authority collection scheme

Local authorities are responsible for regular collection of waste from dwellings. This includes the collection of residual waste (waste not intended for recycling or composting) and, in many cases, recyclable household waste.

Private recycling scheme operator

A private recycling scheme operator can be appointed to collect recyclable materials where a local authority collection scheme is not in operation or where a landlord/ occupier elects to go private, e.g. in some apartments. This can be a scheme that either collects from bins or uses automated vacuum pipes linked to an automated waste collection system managed by a private operator.

Recyclable materials

For the purpose of this issue, the space needs to be compatible with the range of recyclable collection provided by the local authority; at least three of the following recyclable waste materials must be collected:

- Paper
- Cardboard
- Glass
- Plastics
- Metals (tins and cans)
- Textiles (clothes and shoes).

Site Inspection Report

This is a report prepared by the Code assessor during a post construction stage assessment and provided as evidence to support the assessment.

Assessment Methodology

The assessment criteria should be read with the methodology and definitions in this section. Credits are awarded where the performance requirements (set out in the assessment criteria table) have been met.

Design Stage

- Calculate external space volume requirements as per BS 5906:2005 and the volume of external containers (for recyclable and non-recyclable waste) provided by the Local Authority.

- Check that external space has been sized to hold the larger of the previous two volumes so that containers will not be stacked and it complies with the definition of adequate external space.

- Check that the space provides inclusive access and usability by meeting the applicable requirements of Checklist IDP.

- Check the minimum capacity required for internal and external waste recycling storage based on the assessment criteria.

- Check the types of recyclable waste, frequency and level of separation in operation for the locality, now and in the medium term.

- Check that a letter, leaflet or other published information about the recycling scheme is provided.

Post Construction Stage

- Confirm which specifications and evidence provided at the design stage are still valid.

- Assess all the new specifications and evidence provided at the post construction stage.

Calculation Procedures

None.

Checklists and Tables

Calculate the storage of non-recyclable waste, which should be at least the minimum recommended by British Standard BS 5906. A Local Authority recycling scheme offering containers equal to or greater than this previous capacity would meet the requirement, providing adequate external space is allocated to accommodate them. If the Local Authority provides less capacity, or if no Local Authority scheme exists, the developer will need to ensure and demonstrate that the minimum recommended capacity is met.

Was

Table: Cat 5.1: Supplementary Information Sheet for Was 1 – Storage of Non-recyclable Waste and Storage of Recyclable Household Waste		
Development name:		
Dwelling reference:		
NUMBER OF BEDROOMS:		
MINIMUM REQUIREMENTS OF BS 5906:2005 (according to assessment criteria):		
Calculation:	TOTAL VOLUME:	
LOCAL AUTHORITY PROVISION or other (according to assessment criteria):		
REFUSE	DIMENSIONS:	VOLUME:
RECYCLING 1	DIMENSIONS:	VOLUME:
RECYCLING 2	DIMENSIONS:	VOLUME:
RECYCLING 3	DIMENSIONS:	VOLUME:
RECYCLING 4	DIMENSIONS:	VOLUME:
TOTAL VOLUME:		
SPACE PROVIDED:		
Demonstrate (through the use of drawings) how the space allowed for waste storage has been sized to accommodate the maximum requirements of either the volume of storage provided by the Local Authority or the minimum from BS 5906.		

Checklist IDP - Inclusive design principles necessary to provide access and usability to amenities recognised under Was 1, Was 3 and Hea 3				
Inclusive access and usability requirement	Specifications and dimensions to meet requirement	Applicability		Tick
		Typology	Issue	
The following guidelines are drawn from BS 8300:2009, BS 5709:2006, BS 1703:2005, Approved Documents Part M and H				
1) The distance of the inclusive access route, taken as the route between the closest external entrance door and the external amenity (the waste storage space, composting facility or private space for which mandatory elements or credits are being awarded), must be kept to a minimum and be level or gently sloping. In all cases, the inclusive access route towards the waste storage/ composting facility/ private space must be from the closest external entrance door and be direct and the shortest possible.	Pathways making up any part of the inclusive access route must preferably be level (no gradient exceeding 1:60 and/ or no crossfall exceeding 1:40) or gently sloping. Where topography prevents this, a 'gently sloping' pathway must be provided. Maximum gradients permitted dependent on the distance are given below: 1:12 on an individual slope up to 2 metres; 1:13 on an individual slope up to 3 metres; 1:14 on an individual slope up to 4 metres; 1:15 on an individual slope up to 5 metres; 1:16 on an individual slope up to 6 metres; 1:17 on an individual slope up to 7 metres; 1:18 on an individual slope up to 8 metres; 1:19 on an individual slope up to 9 metres; 1:20 on an individual slope of 10 metres, or more than 10 m* *Providing there are top, bottom and intermediate landings of not less than 1.2 m excluding the swing of doors and gates for each 10 metre length of slope. Steps specified in accordance with section 6 of Approved Document Part M are only acceptable on an alternative/ secondary route, this secondary route being in addition to the inclusive access route provided to the amenity. Where any part of the inclusive access route is gently sloping (with maximum gradients as set out above), a secondary stepped approach in accordance with section 6 of Approved Document M must also be provided. Note: All dwellings, regardless of site topography, must meet this requirement. Allowance is given for walk-up and basement flats below.	All forms of dwelling – For dwellings with individual entrance doors, an inclusive access route must be provided from the closest entrance door to each amenity (regardless of whether this is a principal or secondary entrance). For blocks of dwellings with communal entrances, this requirement applies to the closest communal entrance door to each amenity (regardless of whether this is a principal or secondary entrance). For walk-up or basement flats with individual external entrances, this requirement applies from the closest external entrance door of the flat to the amenity, regardless of whether the entrance is principal or secondary. In this situation, external stairs are permitted provided they comply with criterion 8.	Was 1, Was 3, Hea 3	
2) The inclusive access route from the closest external entrance door must not exceed: a) 50 m walking distance to the private space.	As a principal aim, both private space and composting facilities must be as close to the dwelling or block as possible. Please note that to comply with Part H of the Building Regulations, storage areas for waste containers and chutes should be sited so that the distance householders are required to carry refuse does not usually	All forms of dwelling – as above.	Hea 3	

continued

Checklist IDP - Inclusive design principles necessary to provide access and usability to amenities recognised under Was 1, Was 3 and Hea 3				
Inclusive access and usability requirement	Specifications and dimensions to meet requirement	Applicability		Tick
		Typology	Issue	
b) 30 m walking distance to composting facilities.	exceed 30 m. It is not the role of the Code assessor to confirm this.			
3) Any pathways making up part of the inclusive access route must be made of a suitable surface. Those within the curtilage of an individual dwelling must have a minimum width of 900 mm. Communal paths must have a minimum width of 1200 mm.	Suitable surfaces must be firm, slip-resistant and reasonably smooth, and must contrast visually against adjacent surfaces. Surfaces in accordance with section 6 of Approved Document Part M can achieve this requirement.	All forms of dwelling.	Was 1, Was 3, Hea 3	
4) Waste containers must be sited on a suitable surface.	As above.	All forms of dwelling.	Was 1	
5) There must be space for turning a wheelchair at the amenity.	A turning circle of 1500 mm diameter or a 1700 mm x 1400 mm ellipse is required. This area must be made of a surface in accordance with criterion 3 above.	All forms of dwelling.	Was 1, Was 3, Hea 3	
6) The closest external entrance door to the amenity must: a) Have level access over the threshold. b) Have a clear opening width of at least 800 mm (including balcony and roof terrace entrances). The minimum clear opening width of any communal entrances along the inclusive access route must be at least 875 mm.	a) If raised, the threshold must be no higher than 15 mm and is to have as few upstands and slopes as practicable; any upstand in excess of 5 mm in height is to be chamfered. b) For details of how to measure the clear opening width of doors please see Figure 11 of BS 8300:2009.	All forms of dwelling. For dwellings with individual entrance doors, this requirement applies to the closest entrance door to each facility. For blocks of dwellings with communal entrances, this requirement applies to the closest communal entrance door to each amenity.	Was 1, Was 3, Hea 3	

continued

Checklist IDP - Inclusive design principles necessary to provide access and usability to amenities recognised under Was 1, Was 3 and Hea 3				
Inclusive access and usability requirement	Specifications and dimensions to meet requirement	Applicability		Tick
		Typology	Issue	
c) Be equipped with door opening furniture specified in accordance with section 6.4 of BS 8300:2009.	c) It must be possible to operate all door opening furniture with one hand, without the need to grasp or twist. Door opening furniture used in conjunction with locks and latches must have a lever action.			
7) Gates positioned along the inclusive access route must: a) Have level access over the threshold. b) Have a clear opening width of at least 900 mm.	a) As 6a above. b) As 6b above. Gates must not be spring loaded and must be operable from both sides. Note: Gates specified in accordance with Secured by Design will achieve requirement 7b by default.	All forms of dwelling.	Was 1, Was 3, Hea 3	
8) Any external stairs that form part of the inclusive access route from walk-up/ basement flats to the amenity must provide easy access.	A stepped approach in accordance with section 6 of Approved Document Part M must be provided. The AD sets out the following requirements for a staircase: 1. Has flights whose unobstructed widths are at least 900 mm; 2. The rise of a flight between landings is not more than 1.8 m; 3. Has a top and bottom and, if necessary to comply with the AD, intermediate landings, each of whose lengths is not less than 900 mm; 4. Has steps with suitable tread nosing profiles (see Diagram 27 of Approved Document Part M) and the rise of each step is uniform and between 75 mm and 150 mm; 5. The going of each step is not less than 280 mm, which for tapered treads, must be measured at a point 270 mm from the 'inside' or the tread; and 6. Where the flight comprises three or more risers, there is a suitable continuous handrail on at least one side of the flight. A suitable handrail should have a grippable profile; be between 850 mm and 1000 mm above the pitch line of the flight; and extend 300 mm beyond the top and bottom nosings.	Walk-up or basement flats (providing accommodation above or below the ground floor of the building and with an individual external entrance accessed by external steps).	Was 1, Was 3, Hea 3	

Was

continued

Checklist IDP - Inclusive design principles necessary to provide access and usability to amenities recognised under Was 1, Was 3 and Hea 3				
Inclusive access and usability requirement	Specifications and dimensions to meet requirement	Applicability		Tick
		Typology	Issue	
9) Communal waste storage and composting facilities must be provided with:		All forms of dwelling – communal bin stores/ composting facilities only.	Was 1, Was 3	
a) Signs and information specified in accordance with section 9.2 of BS 8300:2009.	a) Visual signs must be provided at the communal waste storage and composting facility giving instructions on how to use the facility (identifying different waste types, collection times etc). Signs must comprise simple words, clearly separated from one another, in short sentences. A sans serif typeface with an x height of at least 15 mm to 25 mm (lower case letter height) to capital height must be used. Any symbols or pictograms used on visual signs must be at least 100 mm in overall height. Letters, symbols and pictograms must contrast visually with the signboard. Signboards must contrast visually with their backgrounds.			
b) Lighting specified in accordance with section 9.4 of BS 8300:2009 with adequately controlled dedicated energy efficient fittings.	b) Artificial lighting systems should be designed to maintain a level of illumination that is suitable for blind and partially sighted people and is compatible with electronic and radio frequency installations. Where artificial lighting is provided, it should use high frequency electronic ballasts to avoid any perception of flicker. Space lighting must meet the requirements of the Ene 6 Issue (capable of only accepting lamps having a luminous efficacy greater than 40 lumens per circuit Watt and controlled by push button time switches/PIR sensors or equivalent).			
10) Switches, sockets and service controls must be at a height usable by all.	Any switches, sockets or service controls situated along the inclusive access route or at the amenity must be located so that they are easily reachable and between 450 mm and 1200 mm from the floor.	All forms of dwelling.		
11) Refuse hoppers** must be located at a height usable by all.	Hoppers must be fixed at a height of 750 mm, measured from floor level to the lower edge of the inlet opening.	All forms of dwelling.		
** A fitting into which refuse is placed and from which it passes into a chute or directly into a refuse container. The fitting consists of a fixed frame and hood unit and a hinged or pivoted combined door and receiving unit, as defined in British Standard 1703 (British Standards Institution, 2005).				

Was

Common Cases of Non-Compliance

Bin stores should be positioned so that a level or gently sloping access route, meeting criteria 1 of Checklist IDP, can be provided from the closest external entrance door of the dwelling. Location should be considered before the plot layout is finalised to ensure levels can be managed to achieve this. An exemption for steeply sloping sites cannot be applied as it can be for the Hea 4: Lifetime Homes Issue.

Where Credits in the Security Issue are sought, attention should also be given to the requirements of Secured by Design when locating the bin store.

Special Cases

Credits can be awarded for developments in areas not yet covered by a Local Authority recyclable waste collection scheme, or with collection coverage of only two *recyclable materials*. In these circumstances a written statement from the Local Authority must be provided stating when the collection will commence (this date must be within one year of the completion date of the dwelling), and/or cover all three required recyclable materials.

If no Local Authority collection scheme exists or where the Local Authority does not limit the amount of waste collected weekly, the developer will need to ensure and demonstrate that the storage space is sized to accommodate the minimum volume calculated according to the methodology included in BS 5906:2005.

Was

Issue ID	Description	No. of Credits Available	Mandatory Elements
Was 2	Construction Site Waste Management	3	No

Aim

To promote resource efficiency via the effective and appropriate management of construction site waste.

Assessment Criteria

Criteria	Credits
Minimising Construction Waste Where there is a compliant Site Waste Management Plan (SWMP) that contains: a. Target benchmarks for resource efficiency, i.e. m^3 of waste per 100 m^2 or tonnes of waste per 100 m^2 set in accordance with *best practice* b. Procedures and commitments to minimize non-hazardous construction waste at design stage. Specify waste minimisation actions relating to at least 3 waste groups and support them by appropriate monitoring of waste. c. Procedures for minimising hazardous waste d. Monitoring, measuring and reporting of hazardous and non-hazardous site waste production according to the defined waste groups (according to the waste streams generated by the scope of the works)	1
Diverting Waste from Landfill Where there is a compliant Site Waste Management Plan (SWMP) including procedures and commitments to sort and divert waste from landfill, through either; a. Re-use on site (in situ or for new applications) b. Re-use on other sites c. Salvage/reclaim for re-use d. Return to the supplier via a 'take-back' scheme e. Recovery and recycling using an approved waste management contractor f. Compost according to the defined *waste groups* (in line with the waste streams generated by the scope of the works). **AND** One of the following has been achieved:	
Where at least 50% by weight or by volume of non-hazardous construction waste generated by the project has been diverted from landfill.	2
OR	
Where at least 85% by weight or by volume of non-hazardous construction waste generated by the project has been diverted from landfill.	3

Was

Information Required to Demonstrate Compliance

Schedule of Evidence Required	
Design Stage	**Post Construction Stage**
A copy of the compliant SWMP containing the appropriate benchmarks, commitments and procedures for waste minimisation and diversion from landfill in line with the criteria and with Checklists Was 2a, Was 2b and Was 2c **OR** Confirmation from the developer that the SWMP includes/will include benchmarks, procedures and commitments for minimising and diverting waste from landfill in line with the criteria and with Checklists Was 2a, Was 2b and Was 2c	For post construction stage only assessments, confirmation that the SWMP implemented meets the criteria **OR** Confirmation from the developer that no details specified in the SWMP have changed from the evidence provided at the design stage **OR** Where different from the design stage, provide confirmation from the developer that the SWMP implemented covers all the criteria

Definitions

Best practice

The SWMP should include procedures, commitments for waste minimisation and diversion from landfill, as well as setting target benchmarks for resource efficiency in accordance with guidance from:

- DEFRA (Department for Environment, Food and Rural Affairs)
- BRE (Building Research Establishment)
- Envirowise
- WRAP (Waste & Resources Action Programme)
- Environmental performance indicators and/or key performance indicators (KPI) from Envirowise or Constructing Excellence.

Environmental performance indicators (EPIs)

When operated as part of a measuring-to-manage programme, environmental performance indicators allow companies to track how well they are doing and to identify opportunities to: save money and increase profits; use resources more efficiently; minimise waste (raw materials, product, energy, water, packaging, etc); and prevent pollution. For more information see http://envirowise.wrap.org.uk

Was

Site waste management plans regulations

Powers were included in the Clean Neighbourhoods and Environment Act 2005 for regulations requiring a SWMP for works involving construction or demolition waste. The regulations, which came into force in April 2008, mean that any construction project in England costing over £300,000 will require an SWMP. See www.environment-agency.gov.uk/business and www.defra.gov.uk.

SMARTWaste

This is a software tool for preparing, implementing and reviewing a SWMP. This tool includes an integrated waste measurement tool (SMARTStart which is aligned to defined waste groups). SMARTWaste will manage all aspects of creating SWMPs and measuring waste generated on projects. This is linked to online waste measurement, industry waste benchmarks and a recycling site locator tool (BREMAP). For more information see www.smartwaste.co.uk.

Target benchmarks for waste minimisation

These can be set by using best practice and should be reviewed throughout the construction process as part of implementing an SWMP. Results are reported in the SWMP on completion. Specific quantitative targets are not set within this Technical Guide. It is the responsibility of the client and/or the principal contractor (as defined by the SWMP regulations 2008) to ensure that appropriate targets are set for the site.

Waste groups

In a SWMP, details of the amount of waste produced, reduced, re-used, recycled or otherwise recovered on or off site need to be monitored and reported according to the following list (see also Checklist 2d):

Bricks (170102*)

Concrete (170101*)

Insulation (170604*)

Packaging (15018*)

Timber (170201*)

Electrical and electronic equipment (1602*)

Canteen/office/ad hoc

Asphalt and tar (1703*)

Tiles and ceramics (170103*)

Inert (1705*)

Metals (1704*)

Gypsum (170802*)

Plastics (170203*)

Floor coverings (soft)

Soils (1705*)

Hazardous

Architectural features

Other/Mixed**

* From the European Waste Catalogue, codes for waste type

** Efforts should be made to categorise waste into the above categories wherever possible

Waste hierarchy

This is a general guide to the relative environmental benefits of different waste management options. It is represented by an inverted pyramid – from top to bottom: waste prevention, re-use of material, recycling/composting, recovery, and disposal (see England's Waste Strategy 2007 at www.defra.gov.uk)

Assessment Methodology

The assessment criteria should be read with the methodology and definitions in this section. Credits are awarded where the performance requirements (set out in the assessment criteria table) have been met.

Design Stage

- Use Checklist Was 2a to confirm the criteria to minimise construction waste.
- Use Checklist Was 2b to identify all waste groups to be monitored.
- Use Checklist Was 2c to confirm the criteria to divert waste from landfill.
- Confirm the percentage of non-hazardous waste generated by the project that will be diverted from landfill.

Post Construction Stage

- Verify that if the SWMP was revised during the construction phase, any target deviations from the original SWMP have been recorded.
- Confirm the percentage of non-hazardous waste generated by the project that has been diverted from landfill.

Calculation Procedures

None.

Checklists and Tables

Checklist Was 2a: Minimising Construction Waste Generated on Site			
Criteria	Evidence Demonstrating how Criteria will be Met	Reference	Tick
1) Confirmation that target benchmarks are set to reduce waste generated on site. These should be reported as part of the SWMP implementation and on completion. Waste minimisation targets during the construction process can be set using best practice.			
2) Set procedures and commitments to minimize non-hazardous construction waste at design stage. Specify waste minimisation actions relating to at least 3 waste groups and support them by appropriate monitoring of waste.			
3) Procedures for minimising hazardous waste.			

Checklist Was 2b: Waste Groups					
Actions identified to monitor, reduce, sort and divert from landfill site construction waste (fill in where applicable, i.e. waste groups arising on housing project)					
Codes: (European Waste Catalogue)	Key Group	Examples	All that Apply	As Specified in SWMP	
			Materials to be Monitored	Materials to be Reduced	Materials to be Diverted from Landfill
170102	Bricks	Bricks			
170101	Concrete	Pipes, kerb stones, paving slabs, concrete rubble, precast and in situ			
170604	Insulation	Glass fibre, mineral wool, foamed plastic			
15018	Packaging	Pallets, cardboard, cable drums, wrapping bands, polythene sheets			
170201	Timber	Softwood, hardwood, board products such as plywood, chipboard, medium density fibreboard (MDF)			
1602	Electrical and electronic equipment	Electrical and electronic TVs, fridges, air-conditioning units, lamp equipment			

continued

Checklist Was 2b: Waste Groups					
Actions identified to monitor, reduce, sort and divert from landfill site construction waste (fill in where applicable, i.e. waste groups arising on housing project)					
Codes: (European Waste Catalogue)	Key Group	Examples	All that Apply	As Specified in SWMP	
			Materials to be Monitored	Materials to be Reduced	Materials to be Diverted from Landfill
	Canteen/office	Office waste, canteen waste, vegetation			
1703	Asphalt and tar	Bitumen, coal tars, asphalt			
170103	Tiles and ceramics	Ceramic tiles, clay roof tiles, ceramic sanitary ware			
1705	Inert	Mixed rubble/excavation material, glass			
1704	Metals	Radiators, cables, wires, bars, sheet			
170802	Gypsum	Plasterboard, render, plaster, cement, fibre cement sheets, mortar			
170203	Plastics	Pipes, cladding, frames, non-packaging sheet			
	Floor coverings (soft)	Carpets, vinyl flooring			
1705	Soils	Soils, clays, sand, gravel, natural stone			
	Hazardous	Defined in Environment Agency technical guidance (see www.environment-agency.gov.uk/subjects/waste)			
	Architectural features	Roof tiles, reclaimed bricks, fireplaces			
	Other/Mixed	Try to categorise waste into the above categories wherever possible.			

Was

Checklist Was 2c: Diverting from Landfill Construction Waste Generated on Site			
Criteria	Evidence Demonstrating how Criteria will be Met	Reference	Tick
1) Procedures and commitments to sort and divert waste from landfill, either; a. Re-use on site (in situ or for new applications) b. Re-use on other sites c. Salvage/reclaim for re-use d. Return to the supplier via a 'take-back' scheme e. Recovery and recycling using an approved waste management contractor f. Compost according to the defined waste groups (according to the waste streams generated by the scope of the works).			
2) Confirmation of the percentage of non-hazardous construction waste generated by the project that has been diverted from landfill.			

Common Cases of Non-Compliance

Where the credit for minimising waste has not been achieved, the credits for diversion from landfill cannot be awarded.

Since April 2008, any construction project in England costing over £300,000 requires a SWMP. To achieve any of the construction site waste management credits, the assessed development, regardless of value or locality, must have a SWMP compliant with regulations and best practice.

Hazardous waste should be segregated on site to avoid contaminating non-hazardous waste streams. This is standard practice and therefore no credits for diversion from landfill will be awarded for segregating hazardous waste.

Special Cases

Where space on site is too limited for waste material segregation, a licensed external contractor may be used to separate and process recyclable materials off site or the materials can be returned to the supplier via a take-back scheme. In this case, sufficient documentary evidence must be produced which demonstrates that material segregation is carried out to the correct standards and that materials are re-used/recycled as appropriate.

Issue ID	Description	No. of Credits Available	Mandatory Elements
Was 3	Composting	1	No

Aim

To promote the provision of compost facilities to reduce the amount of household waste send to landfill.

Assessment Criteria

Criteria	Credits
• Individual *home composting facilities*. **OR** • A local *communal or community composting service*, which the Local Authority runs or where there is a management plan in place. **OR** • A Local Authority green/*kitchen waste collection system* (this can include an automated waste collection system). All *facilities* must also: • be in a dedicated position • provide *inclusive access and usability* (Checklist IDP) • have a supporting *information leaflet* provided to each dwelling.	1
Default Cases None	

Was

Information Required to Demonstrate Compliance

Schedule of Evidence Required	
Design Stage	**Post Construction Stage**
Detailed documentary evidence stating: • the location and size of internal and external storage • that an information leaflet will be supplied • distance of storage from dwelling **AND** Completed Checklist IDP	For post construction stage only assessments, provide detailed documentary evidence (as listed for design stage) representing the dwellings as-built **OR** Confirmation that the design stage composting solution has been implemented demonstrated by: • A letter from the developer confirming that the composting facility specified at design stage has been provided **OR** Where only a letter of instruction is provided at design stage provide detailed documentary evidence (as listed for design stage) representing the dwellings as-built **OR** Where different from design stage, provide detailed documentary evidence (as listed for design stage) representing the dwellings as- built **OR** *Site Inspection Report* confirming compliance
For *communal/community composting* schemes, detailed documentary evidence stating; • distance of storage from dwelling • management arrangements • location and size of storage • details of the scheme including opening times and access restrictions • confirmation that an information leaflet will be supplied **AND** Completed Checklist IDP	
Where applicable, detailed documentary evidence stating: • Details of the Local Authority kitchen/ garden waste collection scheme • Details of the automated waste collection system	A copy of the composting information leaflet

| Where detailed documentary evidence is not available at this stage;

A letter of instruction to a contractor/ supplier, a formal letter from the developer giving the specific undertaking or the manufacturer's information, for all the above required details. | |

Definitions

Communal/community composting

Communal or community composting is where a group of people share a composting system. The raw materials are provided by all who take part in the scheme, and the compost is then used in the community, either by individuals in their own gardens, or for use on larger projects within the local environment. The distance between the site entrance and the communal/community containers must not usually exceed 30 m.

Composting

Composting is a natural process which converts organic waste into an earth-like mass by means of bacteria and micro-organisms. The composting process is also supported by larvae, wood lice, beetles, worms and other such creatures.

Facilities

All facilities must be in a dedicated position, meet the requirements of Checklist IDP and have an information leaflet that is delivered to each dwelling. External composting facilities and storage need to be located within a maximum distance of 30 m from the entrance door of the dwelling and/or the building (if a block of flats). The requirements are:

- Space for a kitchen waste container in the home and for an exterior composter accessed by an inclusive route must be provided for home composting.

- Space for a container in the home and for an exterior composter accessed by an inclusive route must be provided for community/communal composting.

- Space for a container in the home and external storage space accessed by an inclusive route, with a local green/kitchen waste collection scheme in operation must be provided for green/kitchen waste collection scheme.

The internal kitchen waste container space should be large enough to hold at least a 7-litre container.

In all cases, the composting solution/scheme must achieve full compliance with the Animal By-products Regulations (2005). If applicable, the composting solution/ scheme must be registered with the Environment Agency (EA), in England and

Wales and have either a waste management licence, an environmental permit or an exemption from the EA.

Home composting facilities

Home composting facilities must consist of an external composting container, specifically designed for composting, sited according to the manufacturer's instructions and accessed by route in accordance with the requirement of Checklist IDP. Such containers must not be sited in close proximity to windows, doors or ventilation intakes for habitable areas within the dwelling or surrounding dwellings.

Inclusive access and usability

The purpose of the Code is not to deliver purpose-designed wheelchair housing but rather inclusive general needs housing that caters for the widest possible segment of the population (including older people), and which can easily be adapted to meet the needs of wheelchair users. The principles of inclusive design are embedded within the Was 1, Was 3, Hea 3 and Hea 4 issues of the Code. They aim to prevent barriers that create undue effort and separation and enable everyone to participate equally, confidently and independently in everyday activities such as taking out rubbish and spending time outside.

Information leaflet

The leaflet must provide information on:

- How composting works and why it is important
- The materials that can be composted (e.g. raw vegetable peelings and fruit, shredded paper, teabags etc)

AND

- Where home composting facilities are provided, troubleshooting information (e.g. what to do if the compost gets too dry or too wet)

AND

- Details of the operation and management plan for communal schemes
- Where a green/kitchen waste collection scheme is in operation, the information leaflet provided by the local authority is sufficient to meet the information leaflet criteria.

Kitchen waste collection scheme

A kitchen waste collection scheme run by the local authority is an acceptable alternative to communal/community composting facilities. Many local authorities now offer kitchen waste collection schemes in addition to garden waste collection schemes.

Site Inspection Report

This is a report prepared by the Code assessor during a post construction stage assessment and provided as evidence with the assessment.

Assessment Methodology

The assessment criteria should be read with the methodology and definitions in this section. Credits are awarded where the performance requirements (set out in the assessment criteria table) have been met.

Design Stage

- Confirm the provision of a home composter and internal space for a container, communal/community composting service or Local Authority kitchen/garden collection service as appropriate.

- Confirm that the composting facilities are suitable for normal domestic green/garden, food and other compostable household waste and cover both kitchen and garden waste (see Common Cases of Non-Compliance for further information).

- Check that the facility offers inclusive access and usability by meeting the applicable requirements of Checklist IDP.

- Check that the size of the facility is compliant.

- Check that an information leaflet will be supplied.

- Check that details of communal/community composting and Local Authority collection schemes are provided (where applicable): management, opening times, access restrictions, frequency, etc.

Note: It is acceptable for the bin to be beside other recycling bins in a communal collection site providing it is clearly identifiable as being connected to a licensed community composting scheme.

Post Construction Stage

- Confirm which specifications and evidence provided at the design stage are still valid.

- Assess all the new specifications and evidence provided at the post construction stage.

Calculation Procedures

None.

Checklists and Tables

Checklist IDP must be used to assess inclusive access and usability.

Common Cases of Non-Compliance

Credits can be awarded only where the collection scheme collects from all dwellings seeking this credit.

Where a dwelling is serviced by a kitchen waste collection service, has a garden of its own and no individual composting facilities in the garden, credits cannot be awarded.

Special Cases

Existing and proposed community schemes are acceptable under this issue providing they comply with all the specifications in the technical guide.

Where Credits in the Security Issue are sought, attention should also be given to the requirements of Secured by Design when locating the external composting facility.

Category 6: Pollution

Issue ID	Description	No. of Credits Available	Mandatory Elements
Pol 1	Global Warming Potential (GWP) of Insulants	1	No

Aim

To promote the reduction of emissions of gases with high *GWP* associated with the manufacture, installation, use and disposal of foamed thermal and acoustic insulating materials.

Assessment Criteria

Criteria	Credits
Credits are awarded where all insulating materials in the elements of the dwelling listed below only use substances that have a GWP < 5 (in manufacture *AND* installation): • Roofs: including loft access • Walls: internal and external including lintels and all acoustic insulation • Floors: including ground and upper floors • Hot water cylinder: pipe insulation and other thermal stores • Cold water storage tanks: where provided • External doors	1
Default Cases None	

Information Required to Demonstrate Compliance

Schedule of Evidence Required	
Design Stage	**Post Construction Stage**
Completed Checklist Pol 1 showing the proposed insulation materials (or none) for each element and whether they are foamed using *blowing agents* or are unfoamed (from table Cat 6.1)	For post construction stage only assessments, completed Checklist Pol 1 showing the proposed insulation materials (or none) for each element and whether they are foamed using blowing agents or are unfoamed (from table Cat 6.1) **OR** Written confirmation from the developer that all insulants are as specified at design stage **OR** Where different from design stage, completed Checklist Pol 1 showing the proposed insulation materials (or none) for each element and whether they are foamed using blowing agents or are unfoamed (from table Cat 6.1)

Definitions

Blowing agents

Any material used to produce a cellular structure in either a plastic or other foam insulation used in either manufacture or installation.

Deemed to satisfy

The blowing agents listed in table Cat 6.2 are deemed to satisfy this credit since their GWP is known to be sufficiently low to justify this. All are currently believed to have a GWP of less than 5.

Global Warming Potential (GWP)

Global Warming Potential is defined as the potential for global warming that a chemical has relative to 1 unit of carbon dioxide, the primary greenhouse gas. In determining the GWP of the blowing agent, the Intergovernmental Panel on Climate Change (*IPCC*) methodology using a 100-year Integrated Time Horizon (ITH) must be applied.

Intergovernmental Panel on Climate Change (IPCC)

The Intergovernmental Panel on Climate Change (IPCC) was established by the United Nations Environment Programme (UNEP) and the World Meteorological Organization (WMO) in 1988 to assess the scientific, technical and socio-economic information relevant for the understanding of human induced climate change, its potential impacts and options for mitigation and adaptation. The IPCC has completed three full assessment reports, guidelines and methodologies, special reports and technical papers. For more information on the IPCC, its activities and publications see www.ipcc-wg2.org

Assessment Methodology

The assessment criteria should be read with the methodology and the definitions in this section. Credits are awarded where the performance requirements (set out in the assessment criteria table) have been met.

Design Stage

- Complete Checklist table: Cat 6.1 Pol 1 for all elements.

- Check drawings and specification clauses for all materials identified.

- For foamed materials, or propellants used to spray or inject insulation, provide manufacturer/installer's documentation confirming that their product uses either blowing agents *deemed to satisfy* the requirement from table Cat 6.2 in isolation or a blowing agent or blend of blowing agents which can be shown to have a GWP of less than 5.

Post Construction Stage

- Confirm which specifications and evidence provided at the design stage are still valid.

- Assess all the new specifications and evidence provided at the post construction stage.

Calculation Procedures

None.

Pol

Checklists and Tables

Table: Cat 6.1: Foamed and Non-foamed Insulating Materials	
Foamed Insulation	**Non-foamed Insulation**
Expanded polystyrene	Mineral wool or fibre
Extruded polystyrene	Glass wool or fibre
Polyurethane (PU) insulation	Cork
Cellular glass or foamed glass	Cellulose insulation
Nitrile rubber or elastomeric insulation	Wood fibre board
Phenolic insulation	Wool
Polyisocyanurate foam	Flax
Icynene foam	Recycled newspaper and jute
Tripolymer foam	Straw or strawboard
Foamed polyethylene	

Table: Cat 6.2: Blowing agents deemed to satisfy the issue requirements and/or believed to have a GWP of less than 5
Air
Carbon dioxide (CO_2)
Pentane (iso-pentane, cyclopentane, n-pentane)
Isobutene

Checklist Pol 1: GWP of Insulants

Element	Proposed Insulation Materials	Unfoamed [U]/ Foamed [F]/ Installed Using Propellants [P]	Manufacturer	Product Name	GWP (if foamed)	Name of Blowing Agent Used (where installed using a propellant)	GWP of Blowing Agent (if present)	Reference to Literature Confirming GWP (if foamed or installed using a propellant)
Roofs								
Roof Type 1								
Roof Type 2								
Loft Access								
Walls								
External Walls								
Internal Walls								
Doors								
Lintels								
Thermal and Acoustic Insulation								

continued

Pol

Checklist Pol 1: GWP of Insulants

Element	Proposed Insulation Materials	Unfoamed [U]/ Foamed [F]/ Installed Using Propellants [P]	Manufacturer	Product Name	GWP (if foamed)	Name of Blowing Agent Used (where installed using a propellant)	GWP of Blowing Agent (if present)	Reference to Literature Confirming GWP (if foamed or installed using a propellant)
Floors								
Ground Floor								
Upper Floors								
Basement								
Foundations								
Thermal Stores								
Hot Water Cylinder								
Cold Water Storage Tanks								
Pipe Insulation								
Other Thermal Stores								

Note: The manufacturing process of insulating materials changes regularly. Because of this, this document does not include a complete list of insulating materials that comply and manufacturers should be approached for up-to-date information on their products.

Pol

Common Cases of Non-Compliance

Where any insulation material contains substances which are controlled under the Montreal Protocol or where the release of such substances forms a significant part of the manufacturing process, this credit should be withheld. Such substances are prohibited within the EU and so they could only be contained in products manufactured outside the EU.

Special Cases

None.

Issue ID	Description	No. of Credits Available	Mandatory Elements
Pol 2	NO$_X$ Emissions	3	No

Aim

To promote the reduction of nitrogen oxide (NO$_X$) emissions into the atmosphere.

Assessment Criteria

Criteria		
Dry NO$_X$ Level (mg/kWh)	Boiler Class (BS EN 297: 1994)	Credits
≤ 100	4	1
≤ 70	5	2
≤ 40	–	3
Default Cases		
Where all space heating and hot water energy requirements are fully met by systems which do not produce NO$_X$ emissions.		3

Note:

1. No credits may be awarded for open flue space and/or water heating systems.

Pol

Information Required to Demonstrate Compliance

Schedule of Evidence Required	
Design Stage	**Post Construction Stage**
Detailed documentary evidence describing: • The primary and any secondary heating systems and flue type • *Dry NO$_x$* levels and/or *boiler class* of the primary and any secondary heating systems	For post construction stage only assessments, provide detailed documentary evidence (as listed for design stage) representing the dwellings as built **OR** Written confirmation from the developer that heating systems have been installed as specified in the design stage detailed documentary evidence **OR** Where only a letter of instruction is provided at design stage provide detailed documentary evidence and NO$_x$ averaging calculations (as listed for design stage but based on as built SAP outputs) representing the dwellings as built **OR** Where different from design stage, provide detailed documentary evidence (as listed for Design Stage) representing the dwellings as built **OR** *Site inspection report* confirming compliance
Where NO$_x$ averaging is required due to multiple heating systems within the dwelling: Copy of calculations as detailed in the methodology based on design stage *SAP outputs*	
Where detailed documentary evidence is not available at this stage; A letter of instruction to a contractor/ supplier or a formal letter from the developer to the Code assessor giving the specific undertaking	

Definitions

Accredited energy assessor

A person registered with an accredited energy assessment scheme provider. The scheme provider will be licensed by Communities and Local Government to accredit competent persons to assess the CO_2 emission rates of domestic buildings for the purposes of demonstrating compliance with *Building Regulations*.

(AD L1A) Approved Document L1A

The Building Regulations for England and Wales Approved Document L1A: Conservation of Fuel and Power in New Dwellings (2010 Edition).

Boiler class

An indication of a boiler's NO_X emissions. Boilers are classified on a scale of 1 to 5, with 1 indicating high NO_X emissions through to relatively low NO_X emissions for a class 5.

Boiler class (BS EN 297: 1994)

The relevant British Standard that defines and classifies boilers based on their NO_X emissions. Applies to boilers fitted with atmospheric burners of nominal heat input not exceeding 70 kW.

Building Control Body

The body responsible for ensuring that construction works are according to plan and compliant with applicable requirements through periodic inspection.

Building Regulations

Building Regulations apply in England and Wales and promote:

- Standards for most aspects of a building's construction, including structure, fire safety, sound insulation, drainage, ventilation and electrical safety
- Energy efficiency
- The needs of all people, including those with disabilities, in accessing and moving around buildings.

Dry NO_X

The NO_X emissions (mg/kWh) resulting from the combustion of a fuel at zero per cent excess oxygen levels. If electricity is sourced from the national grid, the associate Dry NO_X emissions are approximately 1200 mg/kWh.

SAP Output (design & as built stage)

This is a dated output from accredited SAP software produced by an *accredited energy assessor*. The output must summarise the data necessary to determine performance against the requirements of this issue and include the name and registration number of the accredited energy assessor, the assessment status, plot number and development address. It is not necessary to produce individual SAP outputs for identical dwellings for the purposes of a Code assessment.

The output will be based on either design stage information or on the dwelling as constructed. Design stage outputs are normally used when assessing design stage Code performance and as built outputs for post construction Code assessments.

Where SAP outputs are not produced by an accredited energy assessor they must be verified by either an accredited energy assessor or a member of the *building control body* responsible for assessing the dwelling for compliance with Part L of the Building Regulations.

For the purposes of assessing this issue the applicable SAP outputs are:

- SAP DER worksheet

(SAP) Standard Assessment Procedure for Energy Rating of Dwellings

The Government's approved methodology for assessing the energy performance of new dwellings. The current version is SAP 2009 version 9.90, dated March 2010, revision October 2010. The procedure accounts for energy used in:

- Space heating and cooling
- Hot water provision
- Fixed lighting.

The indicators of energy performance are energy consumption per unit floor area, energy cost rating (SAP rating), environmental impact rating based on CO_2 emissions (EI rating) and dwelling CO_2 emission rate (DER). They are used in the production of Energy Performance Certificates (EPCs) and to demonstrate compliance with *AD L1A* and the Code for Sustainable Homes.

To contribute to reducing CO_2 emissions as calculated by SAP, heat and power must be generated either on or in the home, on the development or through other local community arrangements (including district heat and power).

Site inspection report

This is a report prepared by the Code assessor during a post construction stage assessment and provided as evidence with the assessment.

Assessment Methodology

The assessment criteria should be read with the methodology and the definitions in this section. Credits are awarded where the performance requirements (set out in the assessment criteria table) have been met.

Design Stage

- Determine the specification and NO$_X$ emissions of all heating systems in the dwelling. If a secondary space and/or water heating system supplies less than 8% of the dwelling's combined space heating and hot water demand, it can be omitted from the assessment.

- Confirm that NO$_X$ emissions are estimated under normal operating conditions i.e. dry NO$_X$ in mg/kWh. If mains electricity meets some or all of the heating demand, assume a NO$_X$ emission rate of 1200 mg/kWh supplied.

- If the figures are not stated in dry NO_X and/or in mg/kWh as required, apply any necessary conversion/correction factors to the NO_X figure(s) stated for the heating system(s). (See Sections A & B in Calculation Procedures below for guidance.)

- Where applicable, calculate the average NO_X emissions using the methodology detailed in Section C of Calculation Procedures.

Post Construction Stage

- Confirm which specifications and evidence provided at the design stage are still valid.

- Assess all the new specifications and evidence provided at the post construction stage.

- Where the heating system has not been commissioned at the time of the post construction stage assessment, a contractual commitment must be in place to ensure that the heating system will be servicing the dwelling either before more than 60% of dwellings on the development are certified or within 18 months of the dwelling's completion.

Calculation Procedures

A: Conversion Factors

Manufacturers should supply dry NO_X emissions data in mg/kWh. Where this is not possible the assessor should use the following conversion factors to convert figures in mg/m³' ppm or wet NO_X (derived using data from BS EN 297:1994). It should be noted that these conversion factors assume worst-case efficiencies and are likely to give a high estimate. This could have the effect of lowering the number of credits achieved.

1. Figures in mg/m³ should be multiplied by 0.857 in order to show emissions in mg/kWh. A conversion may also be necessary for data not calculated at 0% excess oxygen (see B below).

2. Figures in parts per million (ppm) should be multiplied by 1.76 in order to show emissions in mg/kWh. A conversion may also be necessary for data not calculated at 0% excess oxygen (see B below).

3. Figures in mg/MJ should be multiplied by 3.6 in order to show emissions in mg/kWh (1 kWh = 3.6 MJ). A conversion may also be necessary for data not calculated at 0% excess oxygen (see B below).

The assessment criteria are based on dry NO_X values – almost all manufacturers quote emissions in dry NO_X. However if wet NO_X figures are supplied, these should be converted to dry NO_X. This can be done by multiplying wet NO_X figures by 1.75.

B: Excess Oxygen Correction

If a NO_X emission rate is quoted by the manufacturer in mg/m³ or ppm, then it should be established at what % oxygen this emission was made.

The greater the amount of excess oxygen in the flue gases at the time of measurement, the more 'diluted' the NO$_x$. It is therefore important to convert any emission rate back to 0% excess oxygen. For the purpose of this assessment, use the following conversion factors for the most frequently used rates supplied by manufacturers:

% excess O$_2$	Conversion (c)
3%	× 1.17
6%	× 1.40
15%	× 3.54

Conversion factor c = 20.9 / (20.9 – x)

Where x = % excess O$_2$ (NOT excess air) and 20.9 is the percentage of O$_2$ in the air.

C: Calculating the average NOx emissions for dwellings with more than one heating/hot water system

Where heat and hot water is provided by more than one system in a dwelling (i.e. there is more than one 'main' heating system and/or a 'secondary' system) it may be necessary to calculate the total NO$_x$ emissions for the systems combined. For the purposes of this assessment, this is only necessary when the secondary system satisfies more than 8% of the dwelling's combined total space heating and hot water demand. Where any heating system supplies less than 8% of the combined space and water heating demand it can be omitted from the assessment. However, including a low NO$_x$ heating system that supplies less than 8% of the combined demand can lower the average NO$_x$ figure. Where this is the case inclusion of the secondary system is at the discretion of the developer and assessor. The procedure to calculate average dry NO$_x$ levels is detailed in tables: Cat 6.1 and 6.2.

D: Calculation method for Combined Heat and Power (CHP) systems

Where CHP systems are specified, it is only necessary to consider the heat related NO$_x$ emissions for the assessment of this issue.

NO$_x$ emissions are allocated to heat and electricity in line with the respective power outputs. A NO$_x$ emission rate equivalent to the current rate for grid electricity should be assumed for the electrical output (i.e. 1200 mg/kWh supplied) and the remaining NO$_x$ should be allocated to heat output. Only the heat-related component is then compared to the assessment criteria. The following formula must be used to determine this:

X = (A – B)/C

Where:

X = NO$_x$ emissions per unit of heat supplied (mg/kWh)

A = NO$_x$ emissions per unit of electricity generated (mg/kWh)

Note: This is the NO_x emitted by the CHP system per unit of electricity generated and should be obtained from the supplier. Where data is provided in different units or at a level of excess oxygen above zero it must be corrected using the factors above.

B = NO_x emissions per unit of electricity supplied from the grid (mg/kWh).

Note: this should be assumed to be 1200mg/kWh supplied

C = Heat to Electricity Ratio of the CHP scheme

The above methodology determines the net NO_x emissions from CHP generated electricity compared to central generation of electricity and allocates this amount to the heat production. Where X is calculated to be negative it should be assumed to be zero.

Where the CHP system operates in conjunction with other heat sources, the calculation methodology outlined in table Cat 6.2 must be used and steps [2] and [4] repeated as appropriate.

Table Cat 6.1 Calculation of average NO_x emissions				
Systems assessed under Section A of SAP				
System and Data Source Guidance [See note 1]		Energy demand (kWh/year)	NOx emission rate (mg/kWh)	NOx Emissions (mg/yr)
		(A)	(B)	(A) × (B) = (C)
(1a)	Space heating fuel (main heating system 1) **[SAP box 211]**			
(2a)	Space heating fuel (main heating system 2) **[SAP box 213]**			
(3a)	Space heating fuel (secondary) **[SAP box 215]**			
(4a)	Energy generating technologies **[Σ SAP boxes 233 to 235]**			
(5a)	Energy saving technologies **[(Σ SAP boxes 236a to n) – (Σ SAP boxes 237a to n)]** (n = all eligible technologies) [See note [2]]			
(6a)	Water heating fuel **[Σ SAP boxes 62$_{1 \text{ to } 12}$]** OR **[SAP box 62 × 303a or b × 305a × 306 as applicable]** For DHW only community schemes			*continued*

Table Cat 6.1 Calculation of average NO$_X$ emissions Systems assessed under Section A of SAP			
System and Data Source Guidance [See note 1]	Energy demand (kWh/year) (A)	NOx emission rate (mg/kWh) (B)	NOx Emissions (mg/yr) (A) × (B) = (C)
(7a)	Solar DHW input **[Σ SAP boxes 63$_{1\ to\ 12}$]**			
Totals				
(8a)	Total Annual NO$_x$ Emissions (mg/yr) **[Σ Value at step (1a)(C) to Value at (7a)(C) = (8a)]**			
(9a)	Total Annual Energy Demand (kWh/yr) **[Σ Value at (1a)(A) to Value at (7a)(A) = (9a)]**			
(10a)	Average NO$_x$ Emissions (mg/kWh) **[Value at (8a) ÷ Value at (9a) = (10a)]**			

Note: If the value displayed in any of the required SAP boxes is negative, consider it positive when entering in to table Cat 6.1 e.g. if −250 is displayed, enter 250

Table Cat 6.2 Calculation of average NO$_X$ emissions for a dwelling Systems assessed under Section B of SAP			
System and Data Source Guidance [See note 1]	Energy demand (kWh/year) (A)	NOx emission rate (mg/kWh) (B)	NOx Emissions (mg/yr) (A) × (B) = (C)
(1b)	Space heat from CHP **[SAP box 307a]**			
(2b)	Space heat from heat source N (N = 2,3,4 or 5) **[SAP box 307b, 307d, 307d or 307e as applicable]**			
(3b)	Energy generating technologies **[Σ SAP boxes 333 to 334]**			
(4b)	Energy saving technologies **[(Σ SAP boxes 336a to n) − (Σ SAP boxes 337a to n)]** (n = all eligible technologies) [See note [2]]			
(5b)	Water heat from CHP **[SAP box 310a]**			*continued*

continued

Pol

Table Cat 6.2 Calculation of average NO$_x$ emissions for a dwelling Systems assessed under Section B of SAP				
System and Data Source Guidance [See note 1]		Energy demand (kWh/year) (A)	NOx emission rate (mg/kWh) (B)	NOx Emissions (mg/yr) (A) × (B) = (C)
(6b)	Water heat from heat source n (n = 2,3,4 or 5) **[SAP box 310b, 310c, 310d or 310e as applicable]**			
(7b)	Solar DHW input **[Σ SAP boxes 63$_{1\ to12}$]**			
Totals				
(8b)	Total Annual NO$_x$ Emissions (mg/yr) **[Σ Value at step (1b)(C) to Value at (7b)(C) = (8b)]**			
(9b)	Total Annual Energy Demand (kWh/yr) **[Σ Value at (1b)(A) to Value at (7b)(A) = (9b)]**			
(10b)	Average NO$_x$ Emissions (mg/kWh) **[Value at (8b) ÷ Value at (9b) = (10b)]**			

Note: If the value displayed in any of the required SAP boxes is negative, consider it positive when entering in to table Cat 6.2 e.g. if –250 is displayed, enter 250

Notes to tables Cat 6.1 and 6.2:

[1]   The data sources in this calculation correspond with SAP and are intended as supplementary guidance to assist in identifying each value required. It is the responsibility of the assessor to ensure that the correct value is identified and entered into the calculation, as the data source may vary dependant on the type of accredited SAP software used.

[2]   Where not accounted for on a monthly basis, energy savings from SAP Appendix Q technologies are accounted for in SAP box 236 for section A assessments and box 336 for section B assessments. These output boxes are repeated for each Appendix Q technology specified. To calculate the annual savings from Appendix Q technologies it is necessary to sum the energy savings from each system specified.

Pol

Checklists and Tables

None.

Common Cases of Non-Compliance

None.

Special Cases

None.

Category 7: Health & Well-being

Issue ID	Description	No. of Credits Available	Mandatory Elements
Hea 1	Daylighting	3	No

Aim

To promote good daylighting and thereby improve quality of life and reduce the need for energy to light the home.

Assessment Criteria

Criteria	Credits
Kitchens must achieve a minimum *Average Daylight Factor* of at least 2%	1
All living rooms, dining rooms and studies (including any room designated as a home office under Ene 9 – Home Office) must achieve a minimum Average Daylight Factor of at least 1.5%	1
80% of the *working plane* in each kitchen, living room, dining room and study (including any room designated as a home office under Ene 9 – Home Office) must receive direct light from the sky	1
Default Cases None	

Information Required to Demonstrate Compliance

Schedule of Evidence Required	
Design Stage	**Post Construction Stage**
Copy of calculations as detailed in the methodology to demonstrate: • Average daylight factor using the formula described in the definitions section (method described in Littlefair (1998) as set out in BS 8206–2) or computer simulation or scale model measurements • Position of the *no-sky line* and percentage of area of the working plane that receives direct light from the sky Confirmation from the developer that the calculations accurately reflect the dwelling as designed.	For post construction stage only assessments, calculations and additional evidence (as listed for design stage) representing the dwellings as built or on-site measurements as below **OR** A letter from the developer confirming that the dwellings have been built as detailed at design stage **OR** Where different from design stage, calculations verified by the developer for all dwellings as built **OR** On-site measurements (methodology detailed in BRE IP 23/93) in the same rooms assessed at design stage (required when scale model measurements were carried out at design stage)

Definitions

Angle of visible sky

The angle of visible sky u is the angle subtended, in the vertical plane normal to the window, by the visible sky from the centre of the window.

Where:

Hw is the height of the window

Tw is the thickness of the wall

D is the distance from the window to the obstruction

H is the height of the obstruction above the mid-height of the window

And: $u = 90 - a - b$

With:

$$\tan a = \frac{H}{D}$$

$$\tan b = \frac{T_w}{H_w}$$

Average daylight factor

The average daylight factor is the average indoor illuminance (from daylight) on the working plane within a room, expressed as a percentage of the simultaneous outdoor illuminance on a horizontal plane under an unobstructed CIE 'standard overcast sky'. The average daylight factor can be calculated using the following equation:

$$DF = \frac{MW_uT}{A(1 - R^2)}$$

Where:

W = total glazed area of windows or roof lights

A = total area of all the room surfaces (ceiling, floor, walls and windows)

R = area-weighted average reflectance of the room surfaces

M = a correction factor for dirt

T = glass transmission factor

u = *angle of visible sky*

Guide values for a typical dwelling with light-coloured walls are as follows (for more accurate values, refer to CIBSE Lighting Guide 10):

R = 0.5

M = 1.0 (vertical glazing that can be cleaned easily)

0.8 (sloping glazing)

0.7 (horizontal glazing)

T = 0.7 (double glazing)

0.6 (double glazing with low emissivity coating)

0.6 (triple glazing)

u = 65° (vertical glazing)

It is advised that this default figure for the angle of visible sky is used with caution; the methodology detailed in the angle of visible sky definition must be preferred for more accuracy.

Hea

Commission Internationale de l'Eclairage (CIE)

Commission Internationale de l'Eclairage (CIE) is the international standards body for lighting.

Daylight factor

The daylight factor is the ratio between the illuminance (from daylight) at a specific point on the working plane within a room, expressed as a percentage of the illuminance received on an outdoor unobstructed horizontal plane. This is based on an assumed overcast sky, approximated by the CIE 'standard overcast sky'.

No-sky line

The no-sky line divides those areas of the working plane which can receive direct light from the sky, from those which cannot. It is important as it indicates how good the distribution of daylight is in a room. Areas beyond the no-sky line will generally look gloomy.

As an approximation, obstructions that are parallel to the window can be considered infinite. The no sky-line will then be parallel to the window at a distance 'd' from the window wall, which can be calculated as follows:

$$d = \frac{xh}{y}$$

Where:

    h = height of the window head above the working plane

    y = height of the obstruction above the window head

    x = distance from the window to the obstruction

If d is greater than the room depth, then no part of the room lies beyond this no-sky line.

Where results using this methodology do not comply with the requirements, more accurate calculations can be carried out, as detailed in the Calculation Procedures of the issue.

Reasonableness check

A reasonableness check is carried out on daylight factor and no-sky line calculations. Checks must be performed on one room per dwelling, in 10 per cent of dwellings, up to a maximum of 10 dwellings per development. Different floors and orientations are checked, and calculation input details, such as room dimensions, window type, sizes and locations and site layout, must be consistent with the specification and the drawings.

Hea

Working plane

The working plane is a notional surface, typically at about desk or table height, at which daylight factor or the 'no-sky line' is calculated or plotted. For the calculations required under the Hea 1 issue, it is at 0.85 m above the floor.

Assessment Methodology

The assessment criteria should be read with the methodology and the definitions in this section. Credits are awarded where the performance requirements (set out in the assessment criteria table) have been met.

Design Stage

- Confirm the Average Daylight Factor and No-Sky Line.

- Carry out a reasonableness check on average daylight factor and no-sky line calculations provided by the developer/design team. Check the calculations are signed off by the developer or a member of the design team.

- Carry out an internal reasonableness check on calculations performed by the appointed assessor. Check that these have been signed off by the developer or a member of the design team.

Post Construction Stage

- Confirm which specifications and evidence provided at the design stage are still valid.

- Assess all the new specifications and evidence provided at the post construction stage.

- Check that the average daylight factor and no-sky line calculation input details, such as room dimensions, window type, sizes and locations, and site layout are correct by site inspection.

- Where any changes have occurred, seek revised calculations and check these as described above. Check the final specification and drawings.

Calculation Procedures

It is recommended that calculations are supplied by a daylighting expert:

1. Calculation procedures for *daylight factor* and typical values are detailed in Littlefair (1998):

   The DF formula can be used to model daylighting conditions in any simple rectangular room with a continuous external obstruction or none. For L-shaped rooms, it is acceptable to divide the room into two sections and calculate the DF for each section based only on the windows present in that section. The DF of both sections can then be averaged to give a final result.

Where external obstructions are of complex geometry and cannot be approximated by a continuous object, it is advisable to use the methodology in Littlefair (1998). Individual trees can be ignored.

More complex room geometries can be modelled using computer simulation software, physical scale modelling or advanced manual calculations. The Code does not specify 'compliant' computer software; the daylighting expert must select which is most appropriate.

Where there are two types of room which form part of the same large space, for example, an open-plan kitchen-dining room, calculate as one room as there is no solid partition present to block the distribution of the daylight. Credits will then be awarded on the basis of the DF of the whole space. For example, if the space is used as a kitchen, a living room and a dining room, the same DF will be used when assessing all these areas against the levels set out above.

When two or more windows in a room face different obstructions (e.g. vertical windows and roof lights) or differ in transmittance, the DF should be found separately for each window, and the results summed.

2. Plotting of the no-sky line or estimating the percentage of the working plane that receives direct light from the sky can be done using the methodology in Annex 3. It must be understood that this methodology will underestimate the actual percentage of the working plane that receives direct light from the sky because obstructions are unlikely to be infinite. Where obstructions are not horizontal, parallel to the window or considered infinite, refer to Littlefair (1998) for a more accurate methodology.

3. It is acceptable that daylighting calculations are carried out in selected dwellings (or rooms) when the reasoning behind their selection clearly demonstrates that the rooms in the dwellings for which the calculations are not provided will perform better than those backed up by the calculations.

4. Seeking expert advice is recommended to carry out daylighting calculations as mentioned above. However, assessors are not prohibited from performing calculations themselves. It is up to the assessor and design team to judge whether the assessor has sufficient expertise perform this function. Any calculations provided by the assessor should be signed off by the developer or a member of the design team before being submitted as evidence. The Technical Guide is intended only to provide the information necessary to perform a reasonableness check on calculations provided by a competent daylighting expert – further guidance on how to complete calculations can be found in BS 8206-2:2008 Lighting for buildings – Part 2: Code of practice for daylighting.

Checklists and Tables

None.

Common Cases of Non-Compliance

None.

Special Cases

Sun pipes: As a general rule, sun pipes should be treated as roof lights, i.e. if there are no obstructions use a **u** of 180°. There are a wide range of light pipes on the market with different reflective linings and some include lenses/mirrors etc. If no transmission factor is stated, use T = 0.5 for a 1 m length pipe and T = 0.25 for a 2 m length pipe.

Issue ID	Description	No. of Credits Available	Mandatory Elements
Hea 2	Sound Insulation	4	No

Aim

To promote the provision of improved sound insulation to reduce the likelihood of noise complaints from neighbours.

Assessment Criteria

Criteria	Credits
Where:	
• airborne sound insulation values are at least 3dB higher	1
• impact sound insulation values are at least 3dB lower	
OR	
• airborne sound insulation values are at least 5dB higher	3
• impact sound insulation values are at least 5dB lower	
OR	
• airborne sound insulation values are at least 8dB higher	4
• impact sound insulation values are at least 8dB lower	
than the performance standards set out in the Building Regulations approved for England and Wales, *Approved Document E* (2003 Edition, with amendments 2004).	
This can be demonstrated through EITHER	
A programme of pre-completion testing based on the Normal programme of testing described in Approved Document E, for every *group* or *sub-group* of houses or flats, demonstrating that the above standard or standards are achieved.	
OR	
Use of constructions for all relevant building elements that have been assessed and approved as *Robust Details* by Robust Details Limited (RDL) and found to achieve the performance standards stated above. All relevant dwellings must be registered with RDL.	
Default cases	
Detached dwellings	4
Attached dwellings where separating walls or floors occur only between non-habitable rooms	3

Note: these criteria apply only to walls, floors and staircases that perform a dwelling to dwelling separating function. Internal partitions are beyond the scope of this issue.

Hea

Information Required to Demonstrate Compliance

Schedule of Evidence Required	
Design Stage	**Post Construction Stage**
Where pre-completion testing will be carried out; A letter from the developer confirming the intent to: • Meet the relevant sound insulation performance levels • Use a *Compliant Test Body* to complete testing	Where pre-completion testing has been carried out: • Copies of the sound insulation field test results and/or a letter of confirmation that the required sound insulation performance standards as detailed in the assessment criteria have been achieved. • Evidence that the tests have been carried out by a Compliant Test Body
Where Robust Details will be used; • Confirmation that the Robust Details chosen will achieve the required performance standards for sound insulation (as applicable) • Confirmation that the relevant plots are registered with RDL (the Purchase Statement)	Where Robust Details have been used: • Completed Robust Details Ltd Compliance Certificate signed by the developer for all relevant constructions relating to the plots being assessed

Definitions

Approved Document E (AD E)

The Building Regulations for England and Wales Approved Document E: Resistance to the Passage of Sound, 2003 edition incorporating 2004 amendments.

Compliant test body

Those organisations or individuals having UKAS accreditation or accredited by a European equivalent of UKAS, as well as organisations or individuals registered with the Association of Noise Consultants (ANC) Registration Scheme.

Groups and sub-groups

As defined in the Building Regulations for England and Wales Approved Document E: Resistance to the Passage of Sound, Section 1 (paragraphs 1.11 – 1.17). The building control body should identify specific plots, groups and sub-groups to be tested.

Robust details

Robust details (RDs) are construction solutions that provide an alternative to pre-completion sound insulation testing as a method of complying with Requirement E1 of Approved Document E (2003 Edition) of the Building Regulations (England and Wales). Robust details must be approved by Robust Details Ltd (RDL) and all development sites must be registered with RDL and built in accordance with the RD specification. To give a reasonable level of assurance that these details will achieve the required minimum standards, RDL carries out random inspections during construction and random sound insulation tests after construction. A robust detail is deemed to be approved for Code credits only when it achieves a specified performance level when assessed by RDL according to the following criteria:

1. Mature robust detail (published for over 12 months and at least 100 test results) – regular assessment based on the 90th percentile of results from the last 100 site tests.

2. Low use robust detail (published for over 12 months but fewer than 100 test results) – initial assessment based on the first 30 tests needed to qualify for the robust details scheme and the site tests available, and reviewed regularly as new test results become available, until it becomes a mature robust detail or is rejected.

3. New robust detail (published for less than 12 months and fewer than 100 test results) – initial assessment based on the first 30 tests needed to qualify for the robust details scheme, and reviewed regularly as new test results become available, until it becomes a mature robust detail or is rejected.

It should be noted that not all RDs will necessarily achieve the performance levels required for Code credits. If in doubt, check the list of currently approved details with RDL directly (0870 240 8210; www.robustdetails.com).

Assessment Methodology

The assessment criteria should be read with the methodology and the definitions in this section. Credits are awarded where the performance requirements (set out in the assessment criteria table) have been met.

Design Stage

For compliance through sound insulation testing:

- Confirm there is a clear distinction between any groups and sub-groups on the development, and that there is a commitment made to conduct a programme of pre-completion testing, as set out in AD E. The building control body should identify specific plots, groups and sub-groups to be tested. In addition, confirm that there is a commitment to conduct remediation work should any test fail.

- Confirm that the Compliant Test Body that will carry out pre-completion testing is accredited by UKAS (or a European equivalent) or is covered by a 'deemed to satisfy' scheme. Members of the Association of Noise Consultants (ANC) that are registered by ANC to perform pre-completion testing meet this criterion (note: not all ANC members are registered to perform pre completion testing). If a Compliant Test Body has yet to be appointed, a commitment to employ one that fulfils one of the criteria will be sufficient. Lists of acoustic consultants by geographical location can be found at: www.ioa.org.uk and www.association-of-noise-consultants.co.uk.

- Confirm that evidence of the potential for the construction to meet the relevant performance standards has been provided (e.g. a design statement from an acoustic consultant with appropriate experience in building acoustics).

For compliance using robust details:

- Confirm that the robust detail(s) specified can achieve the sound insulation levels required for the number of credits sought (see table Cat 7.1: Credit Summary – Improvement on Approved Document E under Checklists and Tables below). This information is available on the Robust Details website (www.robustdetails.com).

Post Construction Stage

- Confirm which specifications and evidence provided at the design stage are still valid.

- Assess all the new specifications and evidence provided at the post-construction stage.

- Verify that specific post-construction stage evidence provided demonstrates that all the assessment criteria have been met.

Calculation Procedures

None.

Checklists and Tables

A commitment to achieve sound insulation values that are better than the performance standards for sound insulation in Approved Document E (2003 Edition with amendments 2004) by the stated amount in table: Cat 7.1.

Table: Cat 7.1: Credit Summary – Improvement on Approved Document E		
Credits	Improvement on Approved Document E (dB)	
	Airborne Sound $DnT,w + Ctr$	Impact Sound $L'nT,w$
1	+3	−3
3	+5	−5
4	+8	−8

The number of credits awarded to a dwelling is determined by the lowest performing separating wall or floor, regardless of whether the assessment is based on pre-completion testing, the use of robust details, or a mixture of both.

The dwellings in a group or sub-group that have been tested are awarded credits appropriate to their measured performance. Other dwellings in the group or sub-group that were not tested are awarded the same number of credits as the lowest performing separating walls or floors in the same group or sub-group that was tested.

For the purposes of the two paragraphs above, the performance of the lowest performing separating wall or floor must be clearly identified by the Compliant Test Body.

Common Cases of Non-Compliance

None.

Special Cases

It is considered good acoustic design not to have habitable rooms on one side of a separating wall or floor and non-habitable rooms on the other side.

If there are no habitable rooms with separating walls or floors no testing is needed and 3 credits can be awarded by default, to allow for the small amount of sound nuisance that can occur in such cases.

Where there are insufficient suitable separating walls or floors in a development to carry out the number of tests specified in AD E, all of the available suitable separating walls or floors must be tested according to the requirements of the Building Control body. Credits will then be awarded as appropriate.

The performance requirements set out in table 1a of AD E are appropriate for the walls, floors and stairs that separate spaces used for normal domestic purposes. A higher standard of sound insulation may be required between spaces used for normal domestic purposes and communal or non-domestic purposes. In these situations, the appropriate level of sound insulation will be set by the building control body or other appropriate party; Hea 2 credits can then be achieved by exceeding these requirements, as detailed in the assessment criteria table.

Issue ID	Description	No. of Credits Available	Mandatory Elements
Hea 3	Private Space	1	No

Aim

To improve quality of life by promoting the provision of an inclusive outdoor space which is at least partially private.

Assessment Criteria

Criteria	Credits
Where *outdoor space* (private or semi-private) has been provided that is: • Of a *minimum size* that allows all occupants to use the space. • Provided with *inclusive access and usability* (Checklist IDP). • *Accessible only to occupants of designated dwellings.*	1
Default Cases None	

Information Required to Demonstrate Compliance

Schedule of Evidence Required	
Design Stage	Post Construction Stage
Detailed documentary evidence confirming: • The number of bedrooms served by the outdoor space • That the outdoor space meets the minimum size requirements **AND** Completed Checklist IDP	For post construction stage only assessments, provide detailed documentary evidence (as listed for design stage) representing the dwellings as built **OR** Written confirmation from the developer that the dwellings have been constructed as specified in the design stage detailed documentary evidence **OR** Where only a letter of instruction is provided at design stage provide detailed documentary evidence (as listed for design stage) representing the dwellings as built **OR** Where different from design stage, provide detailed documentary evidence (as listed for design stage) representing the dwellings as built **OR** *Site Inspection Report* confirming compliance
Where a shared outdoor space is provided, detailed documentary evidence demonstrating: • The private space is accessible only to occupants of designated dwellings	
Where detailed documentary evidence is not available at this stage; A letter of instruction to a contractor/supplier or a formal letter from the developer to the assessor giving a specific undertaking	

Definitions

Accessible only to occupants of designated dwellings

The space must be designed in a way that makes it clear that the space is to be used only by occupants of designated dwelling(s). This could be achieved by using the buildings themselves, or fencing, planting or other barrier to seal off the space.

Inclusive access and usability

The purpose of the Code is not to deliver purpose-designed wheelchair housing but rather inclusive general needs housing that caters for the widest possible segment of the population (including older people), and which can easily be adapted to meet the needs of wheelchair users. The principles of inclusive design are embedded within the Was 1, Was 3, Hea 3 and Hea 4 issues of the Code. They aim to prevent barriers that create undue effort and separation and enable everyone to participate equally, confidently and independently in everyday activities such as taking out rubbish and spending time outside.

Minimum size for outdoor space

Minimum space requirements:

- Private space: 1.5 m^2 per bedroom
- Shared space: minimum 1 m^2 per bedroom.

Outdoor space

An outdoor space could be:

- A private garden
- A communal garden or courtyard
- Balconies
- Roof terraces
- Patios

Site Inspection Report

This is a report prepared by the Code assessor during a post construction stage assessment and provided as evidence with the assessment.

Assessment Methodology

The assessment criteria should be read with the methodology and the definitions in this section. Credits are awarded where the performance requirements (set out in the assessment criteria table) have been met.

Design Stage

- Measure the area of the outdoor space and check it is of a sufficient size for the number of bedrooms.
- Check that the facility offers inclusive access and usability by meeting the applicable requirements of Checklist IDP.
- Where a shared space is provided, check the features make clear that the space is private and only to be used by occupants of designated dwelling(s).

Post Construction Stage

- Confirm which specifications and evidence provided at the design stage are still valid.
- Assess all the new specifications and evidence provided at the post construction stage.

Calculation Procedures

None.

Checklists and Tables

Use Checklist IDP to assess inclusive access and usability.

Common Cases of Non-Compliance

'Juliet' balconies generally do not comply with the criteria, as they are normally too small.

Conservatories and other enclosed areas do not comply with the criteria.

Winter gardens will comply with the criteria only if at least one side can be fully opened to the exterior (using e.g. shutters, sliding walls, or wing or terrace doors). Without this feature, winter gardens are regarded as a conservatory and do not comply with the criteria.

Special Cases

Balconies must meet criterion 6 of Checklist IDP only. Roof terraces or balconies over habitable rooms, which require a step up to increase slab thickness (e.g. for thermal insulation to the accommodation below), are exempt from requirement 6a.

Issue ID	Description	No. of Credits Available	Mandatory Elements
Hea 4	Lifetime Homes	4	Yes (For level 6)

Aim

To promote the construction of homes that are accessible and easily adaptable to meet the changing needs of current and future occupants.

Assessment Criteria

Criteria	Credits	Mandatory Levels
Where all principles of *Lifetime Homes*, applicable to the dwelling being assessed, have been complied with. **OR**	4	Level 6
Where an exemption from Lifetime Homes criteria 2 and/or 3 is applied to selected pathways subject to a steeply sloping plot gradient, but all other principles of Lifetime Homes, applicable to the dwelling being assessed, have been complied with.	3	
Default Cases None		

Information Required to Demonstrate Compliance

Schedule of Evidence Required	
Design Stage	**Post Construction Stage**
Confirmation from the developer that all 16 of the Lifetime Homes design criteria are met **OR** Where an exemption from Lifetime Homes criteria 2 and/or 3 is sought: • Confirmation from the developer that all other design criteria are met **AND** Detailed documentary evidence demonstrating access routes subject to steeply sloping gradients at pre development and completion	For Post Construction Stage only assessments, evidence as listed for Design Stage but based on the dwelling as built. **OR** Where different from design stage written confirmation that the dwellings as built meet all 16 of the Lifetime Homes design criteria (aside from criteria 2 and/or 3 where an exemption is applied) Where an exemption from criteria 2 and/or 3 is sought Detailed documentary evidence describing the alternative access route as built **OR** *Site Inspection Report* confirming that an alternative access route meeting the requirements of the exemption framework has been provided

Definitions

Inclusive access and usability

The purpose of the Code is not to deliver purpose-designed wheelchair housing but rather inclusive general needs housing that caters for the widest possible segment of the population (including older people), and which can easily be adapted to meet the needs of wheelchair users. The principles of inclusive design are embedded within the Was 1, Was 3, Hea 3 and Hea 4 issues of the Code. They aim to prevent barriers that create undue effort and separation and enable everyone to participate equally, confidently and independently in everyday activities such as taking out rubbish and spending time outside.

Lifetime Homes

Lifetime Homes was developed by the Habinteg Housing Association, the Helen Hamlyn Foundation and the Joseph Rowntree Foundation in the early 1990s. The scheme involves the incorporation of 16 design features that together create a flexible blueprint for accessible and adaptable housing in any setting.

Site Inspection Report

This is a report prepared by the Code assessor during a post construction stage assessment and provided as evidence with the assessment.

Assessment Methodology

The assessment criteria should be read with the methodology and the definitions in this section. Mandatory requirements are met and credits are awarded where the performance requirements (set out in the assessment criteria table) have been met.

Design Stage

- Confirm that the developer/designer has completed the Lifetime Homes checklist. Four credits are awarded where the developer/designer confirms that all 16 criteria have been met by the dwelling as designed.

- Obtain comparative plans from the developer/designer to demonstrate that an exemption from meeting Lifetime Homes criteria 2 and/or 3 (as set out in Special Cases) can be applied at steeply sloping plots. Three credits are awarded where the developer/designer confirms that all other criteria have been met by the dwelling as designed.

- Where issues arise regarding the applicability of criteria (other than 2 and 3) to specific developments, guidance must be sought from Habinteg Housing Association which owns and manages the Lifetime Homes standard as well as the checklist published in the Code Technical Guidance. For more information visit: www.lifetimehomes.org.uk.

Post Construction Stage

- Confirm that the developer/designer has completed a Lifetime Homes checklist for the dwelling as built.

- Verify that the Lifetimes Homes criteria are achieved by the dwelling as built, either by a site inspection or as built drawings.

- If not provided at the design stage, obtain comparative plans from the developer/designer to demonstrate that an exemption from meeting Lifetime Homes criteria 2 and/or 3 (as set out in Special Cases) can be applied to steeply sloping plots. Verify through site inspection or as built drawings that an alternative access route meeting the requirements of the exemption framework has been provided.

Calculation Procedures

None.

Checklists and Tables

The Lifetime Homes checklist must be used by the developer/designer to demonstrate whether the assessment criteria have been met. Additional useful guidance can be found at: www.lifetimehomes.org.uk/codeassessors

Common Cases of Non-Compliance

None.

Special Cases

For dwellings on plots with topography exceeding 1:15, an exemption from meeting criteria 2 and/or criteria 3 of Lifetime Homes can be applied, where requested by the developer. Subject to all other Lifetimes Homes criteria applicable to the dwelling being achieved, this exemption will allow for three credits and the mandatory element of Hea 4 to be awarded. [Where an exemption is applied to either criterion, under no circumstances shall the dwelling be marketed or classified as meeting the Lifetime Homes standard and neither must the Lifetime Homes logo be used in any advertising/promotional material.]

Plot gradients must be measured between two points according to the table below:

LTH criterion	Start	Finish
2	Car parking spaces or drop-off points (subject to criterion 1 of Lifetime Homes)	The finished floor level at: a. The principal or secondary entrance doors to an individual dwelling (where a footpath link exists) b. The main communal entrance door to a block of dwellings c. In the case of basement parking, the entrance door to the lift core
3	The start of all footpath approach routes leading to the dwelling, taken from the plot boundary	All individual or communal entrances where a footpath link to the plot boundary exists.

Any pathways identified in the table above, that are subject to a pre-development or finished plot gradient of less than 1:15, will need to meet the full requirements of the relevant Lifetime Homes criterion for credits to be awarded. An exemption would not apply in these cases.

Where only certain sections of the route have gradients exceeding 1:15 but the whole plot gradient is less than 1:15, an exemption cannot be applied. Designers must manage the existing gradient so that a level or gently sloping route is achieved (i.e. the gradients must comply with criterion 3).

For this exemption to apply, gradients must exceed 1:15 owing to pre-development topography and not due to re-grading carried out at any stage in the project. Exemptions can not be granted where; as a result of earth movement undertaken throughout the project, pre-development gradients are reduced so that finished levels give gradients shallower than 1:15.

Exemptions are considered on a dwelling-by-dwelling basis.

Evidence required to demonstrate compliance with this exemption includes the following:

- Comparative plans that adequately demonstrate gradients for the site at pre-development and completion.
  - Plans must be drawn to an identified scale and give levels (at both project stages)
  - Plans must highlight all routes subject to Lifetime Homes criteria 2 and 3 with plot gradients exceeding 1:15 (at both project stages)

Where an exemption is approved, a stepped route according to Section 6 of Approved Document Part M may be provided in place of a gently sloping pathway.

Approved Document Part M sets out the following requirements for a staircase (section 6.17):

1. Has flights whose unobstructed widths are at least 900 mm;
2. The rise of a flight between landings is not more than 1.8 m;
3. Has a top and bottom and, if necessary to comply with the AD, intermediate landings, each of whose lengths is not less than 900 mm;
4. Has steps with suitable tread nosing profiles (see Diagram 27 of the AD) and the rise of each step is uniform and between 75 mm and 150 mm;
5. The going of each step is not less than 280 mm, which for tapered treads, must be measured at a point 270 mm from the 'inside' or the tread; and
6. Where the flight comprises three or more risers, there is a suitable continuous handrail on at least one side of the flight. A suitable handrail should have a grippable profile; be between 850 mm and 1000 mm above the pitch line of the flight; and extend 300 mm beyond the top and bottom nosings.

Category 8: Management

Issue ID	Description	No. of Credits Available	Mandatory Elements
Man 1	Home User Guide	3	No

Aim

To promote the provision of guidance enabling occupants to understand and operate their home efficiently and make the best use of local facilities.

Assessment Criteria

Criteria	Credits
Provision of a *Home User Guide*, compiled in accordance with Checklist Man 1, Part 1, together with confirmation that the guide is available in *alternative formats*.	2
Where the guide includes additional information relating to the site and its surroundings and is compiled in accordance with Checklist Man 1, Part 2.	1
Default Cases None	

Information Required to Demonstrate Compliance

Schedule of Evidence Required	
Design Stage	**Post Construction Stage**
Where a home user guide will be supplied covering operational issues only: Confirmation in the form of a letter from the developer or in the specification that the guide will be: • Supplied to all dwellings within the development • Be developed to the required standards (as a minimum including a list of contents showing that the guide will cover all of the issues required in Checklist Man 1 Part 1)	The provision of: • A sample copy of the home user guide covering all the issues required in Checklist Man 1 Part 1 or Parts 1 and 2 **AND** • Confirmation that the home user guide has been supplied to all home(s) NOTE: Where home user guides are to be provided on the internet or CD occupants must be given a letter regarding the home user guide and a hard copy of the home user guide contents page
Where a home user guide covering operational issues and issues relating to the site and surroundings will be supplied: As above and including information covered in Checklist Man 1 Part 2	

Definitions

Alternative formats for a home user guide

The home user guide must be provided in an appropriate format for users. This might include translation into foreign languages, Braille, large print or audio cassette/CD.

Home user guide

A guide to occupants of the dwelling that contains necessary details about the everyday use of the home in a form that is easy for users to understand.

Volatile organic compound (VOC)

VOC's are emissions from furnishings and some structural materials which may have a deleterious effect on occupants. VOCs are commonly found in the solvents of glues and non-water-based paints and varnishes, and in some preservative treatments.

Man

Assessment Methodology

The assessment criteria should be read with the methodology and the definitions in this section. Credits are awarded where the performance requirements (set out in the assessment criteria table) have been met.

Design Stage

- Confirm whether the home user guide has been compiled in accordance with Checklist Man 1, Part 1.
- Confirm whether the home user guide includes additional information regarding the site and surroundings in accordance with Checklist Man 1, Part 2.
- Confirm whether the home user guide will be provided to all dwellings and that there is a process in place to make the guide available in alternative formats.

Post Construction Stage

- Confirm that a home user guide has been provided and the contents have been compiled in accordance with Checklist Man 1, Parts 1 and/or 2.
- Confirm that the home user guide will be provided to all dwellings or that a hard copy of the contents page will be provided to all dwellings where the guide is being provided in an alternative medium, e.g. via the internet or on CD.

Calculation Procedures

None.

Checklists and Tables

Checklist Man 1 – Home User Guide		YES/NO
Part 1 – Operational Issues		
The list below indicates the type of information that should be included		
a. Environmental strategy/design and features	• Details of any specific environmental/energy design strategy/features including an overview of the reasons for their use (e.g. environmental and economic savings and restrictions on making alterations) and how they should best be operated (where they are not passive features such as insulation and SUDS). Strategies/features could include passive solar design, super insulation, energy efficient timber windows, heat recovery systems, solar hot water systems, photovoltaics, passive vents or the use of certified timber or SUDS within the boundary of individual properties. (Each dwelling will in any case be issued with a copy of the Code Certificate.)	
b. Energy	• Information as described in the Building Regulations ADL1A (Schedule 1 requirement c) i.e. Sufficient information about the building, the fixed building services (this should include things like the implication of covering	*continued*

Man

Checklist Man 1 – Home User Guide		YES/NO
Part 1 – Operational Issues **The list below indicates the type of information that should be included**		
	heating outlets with bags etc and other hazards) and their maintenance requirements so that the building can be operated in such a manner as to use no more fuel and power than is reasonable in the circumstances	
	• A way of complying would be to a provide suitable set of operating and maintenance instructions aimed at achieving economy in the use of fuel and power in a way that householders can understand. The instructions should be directly related to the particular system/s installed in the dwelling	
	• The instructions should explain to the occupier how to operate the system(s) efficiently. These should include: the making of seasonal adjustments to control settings and what routine maintenance is needed to enable operating efficiency to be maintained at a reasonable level through the service live/s of the system/s	
	• Details of any renewable system/s and how it/they operate/s	
	• Details of low-energy light fittings, their use and their benefits, e.g. how much energy they save compared to traditional light fittings and what this can mean in terms of reduced energy bills	
	• Information should also be provided explaining lamp efficacy and the benefits of purchasing high efficacy lamps.	
	• Details of the EU labelling scheme for white goods	
	• General information on energy efficiency	
c. Water Use	• Details of water-saving measures and tips	
	• External water use and efficiency, e.g. the use of water butts or other type of rainwater recycling systems	
d. Recycling & Waste	• Information about the Local Authority collection scheme (if applicable)	
	• If the home is not covered by a Local Authority collection scheme, details and location of communal recycling bins/skips/facilities	
	• Information on the location and use of any recycling bins	
	• Information on the location and use of any compost bins	
	• Information on WRAP which can offer guidance on recycling and sustainable waste disposal	
e. Sustainable DIY	• Environmental recommendations for consideration in any home improvement works, such as the use of low VOC products or the purchase of certified timber	
f. Emergency Information	• Information on smoke detector/s	
g. Links, References & Further Information	• Include references/links to other information including websites, publications and organisations providing information on how to run the home efficiently and in the best environmentally sound way. As a minimum, this should include links to: – The Energy Saving Trust good practice guidance (*www. energysavingtrust.org.uk*) – The Local Authority – The company responsible for the construction of the property	*continued*

Checklist Man 1 – Home User Guide		YES/NO
Part 1 – Operational Issues		
The list below indicates the type of information that should be included		
	– The company responsible for the management of the home (where applicable) • In all instances both an address/telephone contact number and a web link will need to be provided	
h. Provision of Information in Alternative Formats	• Include details of the procedure for obtaining a copy of the guide in alternative formats, including foreign languages, Braille, large print or audio cassette / CD. It should include the contact details of the person/ organisation responsible for producing the guide	
Part 2 – Site and Surroundings		
The list below indicates the type of information that should be included		
a. Recycling & Waste	• Information on what to do with waste not covered by the standard weekly Local Authority collection scheme for example fridges/freezers, computer equipment, batteries and other potentially hazardous equipment. In some areas the Local Authority will collect these items. If this is the case details and information of such a collection should be provided • Information and location of local recycling facilities and waste tips	
b. Sustainable (Urban) Drainage Systems (SUDS)	• Details of SUDS within the site boundary including an overview of the reasons and benefits behind their use (e.g. prevention of localised flooding) and advice on maintenance and operation	
c. Public Transport	• Details of local public transport facilities including maps and timetables and the location of nearby bus stops and/or train/tube stations • Details of cycle storage and cycle paths in the area including, if available, cycle path network maps for the whole town/local area • Details of car parking and information on available park and ride, car sharing schemes and/or car pools/car hire in the area • Details on how to get to local amenities in the area by public transport or cycling	
d. Local amenities	• The location of food shops, post boxes, postal facilities, bank/cash points, pharmacies, schools, medical centres, leisure centres, community centres, places of worship, public houses, children's play areas, outdoor open access public areas • Other local amenities such as places of interest/cultural value, areas of beauty / wildlife / conservation / allotments etc.	
e. Responsible Purchasing	• Include information about the purchasing of: – Low energy/low water white goods – Electrical equipment, including light fittings and bulbs – Timber products from sustainable sources – Organic food procurement/food growing/local produce/local food provision, e.g. farmers markets, organic box schemes etc	
f. Emergency Information	• Contact details for emergency services including: • Location of local minor injuries clinics and A&E departments • Location of nearest police/fire station	*continued*

Man

Checklist Man 1 – Home User Guide	YES/NO
Part 1 – Operational Issues	
The list below indicates the type of information that should be included	
g. Links, References & Further Information. • This should include references/links to other information including websites, publications and organisations providing information on how to reduce the environmental impact in terms of transport, the use of local amenities, responsible purchasing etc. Such links/references may include links to: – Sustrans (for cycle networks, www.sustrans.org.uk) – The local authority (including information about recycling and waste tips) – Local transport providers (e.g. bus or train companies) – Local amenities • In all instances both an address/telephone contact number and a web link will need to be provided	
Developer Confirmation	
By entering a 'YES' against the criteria above, I confirm that all dwellings of this specification type on the **ENTER SITE NAME** site meet the stated criteria.	
Signature: Date: Print Name:	

Common Cases of Non-compliance

None.

Special Cases

It is acceptable for a home user guide to be provided on the internet or CD. Where this is the case, all occupants:

- Must be given a hard copy of the home user guide contents page and a letter explaining the benefits of using the guide.

AND

- Must be given a contact number and the address of where they can obtain a hard copy of the home user guide, if they request this. These contact details must remain current for at least 12 months from handover.

A system must be in place to provide a hard copy of the home user guide to occupants on request.

Issue ID	Description	No. of Credits Available	Mandatory Elements
Man 2	Considerate Constructors Scheme	2	No

Aim

To promote the environmentally and socially considerate, and accountable management of construction sites.

Assessment Criteria

Criteria	Credits
Where there is a commitment to meet *best practice* under a nationally or locally recognised certification scheme such as the *Considerate Constructors Scheme*	1
Where there is a commitment to go *significantly beyond best practice* under a nationally or locally recognised certification scheme such as the Considerate Constructors Scheme	2
Default Cases None	

Man

Information Required to Demonstrate Compliance

Schedule of Evidence Required	
Design Stage	**Post Construction Stage**
For Considerate Constructors Scheme: Specification clause or other confirmation of commitment from the contractor or developer to comply with the Considerate Constructors Scheme and achieve formal certification under the scheme with either a pass score or a score of 32 points and above **AND** Confirmation that registration with the Considerate Constructor Scheme has taken place no later than the commencement of the construction phase	For Considerate Constructors Scheme: • A copy of the Considerate Constructors Certificate **AND** • The final Considerate Constructors Monitor's report highlighting the total score and the sub-scores in each section NOTE: Where developments are phased and the Considerate Constructor Certificate is not yet available the intermediate report covering the developed site completed by the Considerate Constructors Monitor will be accepted. Where no inspection has yet taken place details of registration and a commitment from the contractor or developer to achieve either a pass score or a score of 32 points and above will be accepted until such time as the first inspection takes place.
For an *alternative locally or nationally recognised scheme*: The independent scheme assessor must complete Checklist Man 2 (October 2010) and provide the assessor with a copy as evidence NOTE: The Assessor must seek confirmation from the Code Service Provider that an alternative scheme is acceptable prior to formal submission of an assessment	For an alternative scheme: A copy of the alternative scheme's Certificate of Compliance or equivalent documentary evidence (from an independent third party assessor) confirming that all the mandatory elements items plus 50% or 80% (as applicable) of the optional items have been achieved

Definitions

Alternative locally or nationally recognised schemes

An alternative scheme may demonstrate compliance by fulfilling the criteria stated in Checklist Man 2 (Oct 2010) for other locally and nationally recognised schemes. Any such scheme must be approved by the Code service provider prior to assessment. This can be achieved by submitting a completed Checklist Man 2 (Oct 2010) – Compliance with an Alternative Scheme.

Best practice

Achieving a score of at least 3 in every section, and a total score between 24 and 31.5, of the Considerate Constructors Scheme's Code of Considerate Practice indicates that a site is being managed in accordance with best practice.

Alternative schemes demonstrate this where, in addition to meeting all the mandatory requirements, 50 per cent of the optional items in Checklist Man 2 (Oct 10) – Compliance with an Alternative Scheme, are addressed.

Considerate Constructors Scheme (CCS)

The Considerate Constructors Scheme is a UK certification scheme that encourages the considerate management of construction sites. The scheme is operated by the Construction Confederation and points are awarded in increments of 0.5 over the following eight sections:

- Considerate
- Environmentally Aware
- Site Cleanliness
- Good Neighbour
- Respectful
- Safe
- Responsible
- Accountable.

To achieve certification under this scheme, a score of at least 24 is required.

Alternative locally or nationally recognised schemes

An alternative scheme may demonstrate compliance by fulfilling the criteria stated in Checklist Man 2 (Oct 2010) for other locally and nationally recognised schemes. Any such scheme must be approved by the Code service provider prior to assessment. This can be achieved by submitting a completed Checklist Man 2 (Oct 2010) – Compliance with an Alternative Scheme.

Significantly beyond best practice

Achieving a score of at least 4 in every section, and a total score of between 32 and 40 of the Considerate Constructors Scheme's Code of Considerate Practice indicates that a site is being managed significantly beyond best practice.

Alternative schemes demonstrate this where, in addition to meeting all the mandatory requirements, 80 per cent of the optional items in Checklist Man 2 (Oct 10) – Compliance with an Alternative Scheme, are addressed.

Assessment Methodology

The assessment criteria should be read with the methodology and the definitions in this section. Credits are awarded where the performance requirements (set out in the assessment criteria table) have been met.

Design Stage

- Where the site is being assessed using the Considerate Constructors Scheme, confirm the contractor's commitment as set out in the assessment criteria.

- Where the site is being assessed using an alternative scheme, the details of that scheme should be checked to confirm that it covers equivalent items. This is done by completing Checklist Man 2 – Compliance with an Alternative Scheme (available from the Code Service Provider). The checklist sets out a number of mandatory items and a wider range of issues equivalent to those in the Considerate Contractors Scheme. In addition to the mandatory issues:

- For one credit, 50% of these issues must be achieved to demonstrate compliance with best practice standards.

- For two credits, 80% of these issues must be achieved to demonstrate going significantly beyond best practice standards.

Post Construction Stage

- Where the site has been assessed using the Considerate Constructors Scheme, confirm that certification has taken place and the final score on the monitor's report.

- Where the site has been assessed using an alternative scheme, confirm that all the mandatory items and 50% (or 80%) of the optional items (as applicable) have been achieved. Confirm compliance with Checklist Man 2 – Compliance with an Alternative Scheme using information provided by the third-party certifier of the alternative scheme.

Calculation Procedures

None.

Checklists and Tables

Checklist Man 2 – Compliance with an Alternative Scheme is available from the Code service provider on request.

Common Cases of Non-Compliance

None.

Special Cases

None.

Issue ID	Description	No. of Credits Available	Mandatory Elements
Man 3	Construction Site Impacts	2	No

Aim

To promote construction sites managed in a manner that mitigates environmental impacts.

Assessment Criteria

Criteria	Credits
Where there are procedures that cover two or more of the following items: Monitor, report and set targets for CO_2 production or energy use arising from site activities Monitor and report CO_2 or energy use arising from commercial transport to and from site Monitor, report and set targets for water consumption from site activities Adopt best practice policies in respect of air (dust) pollution arising from site activities Adopt best practice policies in respect of water (ground and surface) pollution occurring on the site 80% of site timber is reclaimed, re-used or responsibly sourced **OR**	1
Where there are procedures that cover four or more of the items listed above.	2
Default Cases None	

Information Required to Demonstrate Compliance

Schedule of Evidence Required	
Design Stage	**Post Construction Stage**
Completed copy of Checklist Man 3 (signed and dated) detailing the procedures that will be employed to minimise construction site impacts.	Documentary evidence demonstrating that the procedures detailed in Checklist Man 3* have been achieved. This can take the form of: • Measurement/consumption records • Target records • Graphs comparing consumption with targets • Delivery records • Site procedures for minimising air/dust and water pollution • CoC certificates for timber/purchase orders confirming re-used/reclaimed timber/letter from the developer confirming the materials on site that were re-used * Checklist Man 3 can be completed on a site wide basis with monthly reviews.

Definitions

Key performance indicators (KPI)

Key performance indicators generated by Constructing Excellence for the construction industry. See www.kpizone.com

Assessment Methodology

The assessment criteria should be read with the methodology and the definitions in this section. Credits are awarded where the performance requirements (set out in the assessment criteria table) have been met.

Design Stage

- Confirm whether the developer is committed to achieving any of the requirements set out in Checklist Man 3 – Construction Site Impacts under Checklists and Tables.

Post Construction Stage

- Confirm which commitments and evidence provided at the design stage are still valid.

- Assess all the new evidence provided at the post construction stage.

Man

Calculation Procedures

None.

Checklists and Tables

Checklist Man 3: Construction Site Impacts			
Criteria	Evidence Demonstrating how Criteria will be Met	Reference	Tick
a. Commitment to monitor, report and set targets for CO_2 production or energy use arising from site activities			
1) Confirm that monthly measurements of energy use will be recorded and displayed on site.			
2) Set and display appropriate target* levels of energy consumption (targets could be annual, monthly or project targets).			
3) As a minimum, monitoring must include checking the meters and displaying some form of graphical analysis in the site office to show consumption over the project duration and how actual consumption compares to the targets set.			
4) The design/site management team is to nominate an individual who will be responsible for the monitoring and collection of data.			
* Targets for energy consumption during the construction process should be set using UK Construction Industry *KPIs*. These documents do not specify targets but facilitate projects in setting appropriate targets (see References section of main credit for further details). Note: The Code does not require targets to be met but is encouraging the process of setting, monitoring and reporting against targets.			
b. Commitment to monitor and report CO_2 or energy use arising from commercial transport to and from the site			
1) Confirm that a site monitoring system will be in place to monitor and record deliveries *. The system will need to record: • The number of deliveries. • The mode of transport. • The kilometres/miles travelled for all deliveries. • Where the delivery is specifically for the site, a figure of total distance travelled should be used, i.e. a round trip (from the point of origin, to the site and back to the point of origin). • Where the delivery to the site is part of a multiple delivery route, the recorded figure should be the distance travelled to the site (from the previous delivery) plus the distance to the next delivery or return.			

continued

Man

Checklist Man 3: Construction Site Impacts			
Criteria	Evidence Demonstrating how Criteria will be Met	Reference	Tick
This information can then be used to estimate a total figure for kg of CO_2 for the project. The Code does not require this information to be converted to CO_2 but the information must be made available to the senior project and site management staff/suppliers to establish benchmarks and aid future decision-making towards improving site and transport efficiency. If the project team wishes to convert this information into CO_2 emissions, there are tables provided at the end of this checklist, which can be used.			
2) If the design team or contractor confirms that the project is aiming to achieve the measures in *Construction Site Transport – measures for traffic movements and distances* (published April 2003, see references) then this aspect has been achieved automatically. The information obtained for this item can also be used to satisfy the UK Construction Industry KPIs on transport.			
3) The design/site management team is to nominate an individual who will be responsible for the monitoring and collection of data.			
* Please see *Tables 8.1–8.4* below on monitoring site transport CO_2			
c. Commitment to monitor, report and set targets for water consumption arising from site activities			
1) Demonstrate compliance by the design/site management team confirming, in writing, that monthly measurements of water consumption will be recorded and displayed on site.			
2) Set and display appropriate target* levels of water consumption (targets could be annual, monthly or project targets).			
3) As a minimum, monitoring must include checking the meters and displaying some form of graphical analysis in the site office to show consumption over the project duration and how actual consumption compares to targets set.			
4) The design/site management team is to nominate an individual who will be responsible for the monitoring and collection of data.			

* Targets for water consumption during the construction process should be set using UK Construction Industry KPIs . These documents do not specify targets but facilitate projects in setting appropriate targets (see *References and Further Information* for details).

Note: The Code does not require targets to be met but is encouraging the process of setting, monitoring and reporting against targets.

continued

Checklist Man 3: Construction Site Impacts			
Criteria	Evidence Demonstrating how Criteria will be Met	Reference	Tick
d. Commitment to adopt best practice policies in respect of air (dust) pollution arising from site activities			
1) Confirm the site's procedures to minimise air (dust) pollution. These can include: • 'Dust sheets' • Proposals to regularly damp down the site in dry weather • Covers to skips etc.			
2) The site team must indicate how this information is disseminated to site operatives.			
Note: Further information can be obtained from DTI/BRE publications *Control of Dust from Construction and Demolition Activities* and *Pollution Control Guide* Parts 1–5 which provide good practice guidelines on construction-related pollution (see *References and Further Information* for details).			
e. Commitment to adopt best practice policies in respect of water (ground and surface) pollution occurring on the site			
1) Confirm the site's procedures to minimise water pollution following best practice guidelines outlined in the following Environment Agency documents: • PPG 1 – General guide to the prevention of pollution. • PPG 5 – Works in, near or liable to affect watercourses. • PPG 6 – Working at demolition and construction sites. 2) The site team must indicate how this information is disseminated to site operatives.			
f. 80% of site timber is reclaimed, re-used or responsibly sourced			
1) 80% of timber used during construction, including formwork, site hoardings and other temporary site timber used for the purpose of facilitating construction, is to be procured from sustainably managed sources, independently certified by one of the top two levels as set out in the Responsible Sourcing of Materials Issues (Mat 2 and Mat 3) in the Materials section of this document. All timber used during construction must be legally sourced. Re-used timber from off site can be counted as equivalent, but re-usable formwork complies only if it meets the above criterion. This credit can be awarded where all the timber used is reclaimed timber.			
Signed:		Date:	

Table: Cat 8.1: Standard Road Transport Fuel Conversion Factors					
Fuel Used	Units	Total Units Used	x	kg CO$_2$ per Unit	Total kg CO$_2$
Petrol	Litres		x	2.315	
Diesel	Litres		x	2.630	
Compressed natural gas (CNG)	kg		x	2.728	
Liquid petroleum gas (LPG)	Litres		x	1.495	

Source: UK Greenhouse Gas Inventory for 2006 (produced for Defra by AEA Energy & Environment), Digest of UK Energy Statistics (DTI) and Carbon factors for fuels (UKPIA, 2004)

Table: Cat 8.2: Standard Road Transport Fuel Conversion Factors					
Size of Car	Units	Total Units Travelled	x	kg CO$_2$ per Unit	Total kg CO$_2$
Small petrol car, up to 1.4 litre engine	Miles		x	0.291	
	km		x	0.181	
Medium petrol car, from 1.4 to 2.0 litres	Miles		x	0.344	
	km		x	0.214	
Large petrol car above 2.0 litres	Miles		x	0.476	
	km		x	0.296	
Average petrol car	Miles		x	0.333	
	km		x	0.207	

Source: Revised factors developed by AEA Energy & Environment and agreed with the Department for Transport (2008)

Table: Cat 8.3: Standard Road Transport Fuel Conversion Factors					
Size of Car	Units	Total Units Travelled	x	kg CO$_2$ per Unit	Total kg CO$_2$
Small diesel car, up to 1.7 litre engine	Miles		x	0.244	
	km		x	0.151	
Medium diesel car, from 1.7 to 2.0 litres	Miles		x	0.303	
	km		x	0.188	
Large diesel car above 2.0 litres	Miles		x	0.415	
	km		x	0.258	
Average diesel car	Miles		x	0.319	
	km		x	0.198	

Source: Revised factors developed by AEA Energy & Environment and agreed with the Department for Transport (2008)

Table: Cat 8.4: Van/Light Commercial Vehicle Road Freight Mileage Conversion Factors						
Type of Van	Gross Vehicle Weight (tonnes)	Units	Total Units Travelled	x	kg CO_2 per Unit	Total kg CO_2
Petrol	up to 1.25t	Miles		x	0.360	
		km		x	0.224	
Diesel	up to 3.5t	Miles		x	0.438	
		km		x	0.272	
LPG or CNG	up to 3.5t	Miles		x	0.438	
		km		x	0.272	

Source: Factors developed by AEA Energy & Environment and agreed with the Department for Transport (2008)

Table: Cat 8.5: Diesel HGV Road Freight Mileage Conversion Factors (based on UK average load)						
Type of Lorry	Gross Vehicle Weight (tonnes)	Units	Total Units Travelled	x	kg CO_2 per Unit	Total kg CO_2
Rigid	>3.5–7.5t	Miles		x	0.906	
		km		x	0.563	
Rigid	>7.5–17t	Miles		x	1.202	
		km		x	0.747	
Rigid	>17t	Miles		x	1.559	
		km		x	0.969	
Articulated	>3.5–33t	Miles		x	1.315	
		km		x	0.817	
Articulated	>33t	Miles		x	1.495	
		km		x	0.929	

Source: Revised factors developed by AEA Energy & Environment and agreed with the Department for Transport (2008)

Common Cases of Non-Compliance

None.

Special Cases

None.

Issue ID	Description	No. of Credits Available	Mandatory Elements
Man 4	Security	2	No

Aim

To promote the design of developments where people feel safe and secure- where crime and disorder, or the fear of crime, does not undermine quality of life or community cohesion.

Assessment Criteria

Criteria	Credits
An Architectural Liaison Officer (ALO) or Crime Prevention Design Advisor (CPDA) from the local police force is consulted at the design stage and their recommendations are incorporated into the design of the dwelling. **AND** *Section 2 – Physical Security from 'Secured by Design – New Homes'* is complied with (*Secured by Design* certification is not required).	2
Default Cases None	

Information Required to Demonstrate Compliance

Schedule of Evidence Required	
Design Stage	**Post Construction Stage**
Detailed documentary evidence showing: • That an ALO/CPDA has been consulted with to ensure that the requirements of Section 2 – Physical Security from 'Secured by Design – New Homes' are met • A commitment to follow the advice provided by the ALO/CPDA	Detailed documentary evidence showing: Confirmation from the developer that all of the recommendations provided by the ALO/CPDA have been incorporated in the design and that the site meets the standards required in Section 2 – Physical Security from 'Secured by Design – New Homes'
	Assessor Site Inspection Report **OR** As-Built drawings showing security features
	Where a 'Secured by Design' certificate can be provided, this will be deemed to satisfy the requirements and no other evidence will be required

Definitions

(ALO) Architectural Liaison Officer

"This is the same as the Crime Prevention Design Advisor (see definition below) and is the title given to the same role in some police forces." Taken from www.securedbydesign.com

(CPDA) Crime Prevention Design Advisor

"The Crime Prevention Design Advisor (CPDA) is a specialist crime prevention officer, trained at the Home Office Crime Reduction College, who deals with crime risk and designing out crime advice for the built environment. In addition to physical security measures the officer will consider defensible space, access, crime and movement generators all of which can contribute to a reduction in crime and disorder." Taken from www.securedbydesign.com

(SBD) Secured by Design

This is a police initiative to encourage the building industry to adopt crime prevention measures in the design of developments to assist in reducing the opportunity for, and fear of, crime, creating a safer and more secure environment. Secured by Design is owned by the Association of Chief Police Officers (ACPO), and has the support of the Home Office Crime Reduction & Community Safety Group and the Planning Section of the Department for Communities and Local Government.

Section 2 – Physical Security from 'Secured by Design – New Homes'

To be awarded, a Secured by Design award, the ALO/CPDA must be satisfied that the criteria of both Section 1 – The Development – Layout & Design, and Section 2 – Physical Security are met. The requirements of Section 1 are beyond the remit of the Code and for this issue, only the requirements of Section 2 must be met.

Site Inspection Report

A report prepared by the Code assessor during a post construction stage assessment and provided as evidence with the assessment.

Assessment Methodology

The assessment criteria should be read with the methodology and the definitions in this section. Credits are awarded where the performance requirements (set out in the assessment criteria table) have been met.

Design Stage

- Check that an *ALO/CPDA* has been appointed and that the developer confirms their advice will be followed.

Post Construction Stage

- Check that there is confirmation from the ALO/CPDA that all dwellings comply with Section 2 of 'Secured by Design' (i.e. the development is SBD-part compliant), or the development has been awarded an SBD certificate which indicates compliance with both Sections 1 and 2 of 'Secured by Design'.

Calculation Procedures

None.

Checklists and Tables

None.

Common Cases of Non-Compliance

None.

Special Cases

None.

Category 9: Ecology

Issue ID	Description	No. of Credits Available	Mandatory Elements
Eco 1	Ecological Value of Site	1	No

Aim

To promote development on land that already has a limited value to wildlife, and discourage the development of ecologically valuable sites.

Assessment Criteria

Criteria	Credits
Where the *development site* is confirmed as land of inherently *low ecological value* **EITHER** By meeting the criteria for low ecological value (using Checklist Eco 1 – Land of Low Ecological Value under Checklists and Tables below) **OR** By being confirmed by a *suitably qualified ecologist* **OR** Where an independent ecological report of the site, prepared by a suitably qualified ecologist, confirms that the *construction zone* is of low or insignificant ecological value **AND** Any land of ecological value outside the construction zone but within the development site will remain undisturbed by the construction works.	1
Default Cases None	

Information Required to Demonstrate Compliance

Schedule of Evidence Required	
Design Stage	**Post Construction Stage**
Where using Checklist Eco 1, provision of: • Site visit report from the design team/assessor confirming details adequate to meet Checklist Eco 1 based on plans of the site and surrounding area prior to the commencement of construction works/site clearance	Where using Checklist Eco 1 evidence to be provided as at design stage
Where a suitably qualified ecologist is appointed; A copy of a report or letter from the ecologist highlighting the information required as set out in the 'Code for Sustainable Homes Ecology Report Template' **AND** Detailed documentary evidence identifying the construction zone and how any areas of ecological value outside the construction zone will remain undisturbed in accordance with the ecologist's recommendations.	Where a suitably qualified ecologist is appointed; Evidence to be provided as at design stage **AND** Detailed documentary evidence confirming that any land of ecological value outside the construction zone has been and will continue to be adequately protected during construction works

Definitions

Construction zone

The construction zone includes any land used for buildings, hard-standing, landscaping, site access or where construction work is carried out (or land is being disturbed in any other way), plus a 3m boundary in either direction around these areas. It also includes any areas used for temporary site storage and buildings. If it is not known exactly where buildings, hard-standing, site access and temporary storage and buildings will be located, it must be assumed that the construction zone is the development site.

Contaminated land

A site can be defined as contaminated land where the level of site contamination prevents development unless decontamination is carried out.

Contamination includes any solid, liquid or gaseous material in or on the ground to be covered by the building, and which is a pollutant or could become toxic, corrosive, explosive, flammable or radioactive and therefore likely to be a danger to health and safety or the environment. This also includes non-native invasive plant species as defined below.

Where the only decontamination required is for the removal of asbestos within an existing building fabric to be demolished, this cannot be classified as contaminated land. Where asbestos is found to be present in the ground, this will be classed as contamination for the purposes of this issue.

Development site

The development site is the whole site up to and including the boundary.

Ecological features

Ecological features are defined in Checklist Eco 1 – Land of Low Ecological Value, and include trees, hedges, ponds, streams, rivers, marshes, wetlands, meadows, species-rich grassland, heathland and heather.

Low ecological value

Land defined as having low ecological value using Checklist Eco 1 or defined by a suitably qualified ecologist as having low or insignificant ecological value.

Non-native invasive species

These are non-indigenous species (e.g. plants or animals) that adversely affect the habitats they invade economically, environmentally or ecologically. For the purposes of the Code, this currently includes only Japanese Knotweed and Giant Hogweed. Further information on their control and disposal and how this fits into the legislative framework relating to such species can be obtained from DEFRA.

Suitably qualified ecologist

A suitably qualified ecologist is defined as an individual who:

- Holds a degree or equivalent qualification (e.g. N/SVQ Level 5) in ecology or a related subject

- Is a practising ecologist, with a minimum of three years' relevant experience (within the last five years). Such experience must clearly demonstrate a practical understanding of factors affecting ecology in relation to construction and the built environment, including acting in an advisory capacity to provide recommendations for ecological protection, enhancement and mitigation measures. Examples of relevant experience are ecological impact assessments, Phase 1 and 2 habitat surveys, and habitat restoration

- Is covered by a professional code of conduct and subject to peer review.

Peer review is defined as the process employed by a professional body to demonstrate that potential or current full members maintain the standard of knowledge and experience required to ensure compliance with a code of conduct and professional ethics.

Full members of the following organisations who meet the above requirements are deemed to be suitably qualified ecologists:

- Association of Wildlife Trust Consultancies (AWTC)
- Chartered Institution of Water and Environmental Management (CIWEM)
- Institute of Ecology and Environmental Management (IEEM)
- Institute of Environmental Management and Assessment (IEMA)
- Landscape Institute (LI).

Verified ecological report

A verified ecological report is a report carried out by an ecologist who does not fully meet the requirements of a suitably qualified ecologist. For the report to comply, as a minimum a suitably qualified ecologist must have read and reviewed the report and confirmed in writing that it:

- Represents sound industry practice
- Reports and recommends correctly, truthfully and objectively
- Is appropriate given the local site conditions and scope of works proposed
- Avoids invalid, biased and exaggerated statements
- Additionally, written confirmation from the third-party verifier that they comply with the definition of a suitably qualified ecologist.

Assessment Methodology

The assessment criteria should be read with the methodology and the definitions in this section. Credits are awarded where the performance requirements (set out in the assessment criteria table) have been met.

Design Stage

- For Checklist Eco 1 – Land of Low Ecological Value, verify that the answer to all questions in Section 1 is 'No' and that 'Yes' has been answered to at least one question in Section 2.
- Where a suitably qualified ecologist has been appointed, confirm that the ecologist's report verifies that the construction zone is of low or insignificant value and that any land of ecological value outside the construction zone will remain undisturbed by the construction works.
- Confirm that the ecologist meets the definition of a suitably qualified ecologist, as defined above. If the ecologist does not meet the requirements, confirm that the report is a *verified ecological report*.

Eco

Post Construction Stage

- Where the construction zone was of low ecological value, ensure that the area designated as the construction zone has not changed from the design stage.

- Where any land of ecological value was present outside the construction zone but within the development site, ensure that this has remained undisturbed by the construction works.

Calculation Procedures

None

Checklists and Tables

Checklist Eco 1: Land of Low Ecological Value		
General information: For the development to be defined as 'land of low ecological value', the assessor must answer NO to all of the questions in Section 1 and YES to any of the questions in Section 2.		
Section 1: *Ecological features* of the site		
Instruction: Criteria 1.1–1.5 can be used to determine the presence of existing ecological features across the site. If YES is recorded against any question in Section 1 then the site cannot be defined as having land of low ecological value and the credit cannot be awarded. If NO is recorded against all the questions in Section 1 then proceed to Section 2.		
1.1	Does the site contain any trees or hedges above 1 m high or with a trunk diameter greater than 100 mm?	YES ☐ NO ☐
1.2	Are there any ponds, streams or rivers on, or running through, the site?	YES ☐ NO ☐
1.3	Is there any marsh or other wetland present on the site?	YES ☐ NO ☐
1.4	Are there any meadows or species-rich grassland present on the site?	YES ☐ NO ☐
1.5	Is there any heath land, consisting of heather and/or scrub present on the site?	YES ☐ NO ☐

continued

Checklist Eco 1: Land of Low Ecological Value		
Section 2: Type of land		
Instruction: In addition to answering NO to all the questions in Section 1, if YES is recorded against one or more of the questions in Section 2, the development site can be defined as having land of low ecological value and the credit can be awarded. (The assessor MUST check that these agree with the site drawings.)		
2.1	Does the development site consist of land which is entirely within the floor plan(s) of existing building(s) or building(s) demolished within the past two years?	YES ☐ NO ☐
2.2	Does the development site consist of land which is entirely covered by other constructions such as sporting hard surfaces, car parking or such constructions which have been demolished within the past two years?	YES ☐ NO ☐
2.3	Does the development site consist of land which is contaminated by industrial or other waste to the extent that it would need decontamination before building commences?	YES ☐ NO ☐
2.4	Does the development site consist of land which is a mixture of existing buildings, hard surfaces and/or *contaminated land*?	YES ☐ NO ☐
2.5	Does 80% of the land within the development site comply with statements 2.1, 2.2 or 2.3 and the remaining 20% of the building's ground area extend into land which has been either used for single-crop arable farming for at least five years, OR consists of regularly cut lawns and sports fields.	YES ☐ NO ☐

Common Cases of Non-Compliance

A site that consists of buildings, hard surfaces, car parking or other such construction which has been derelict for more than two years cannot achieve the credit unless it can be verified by a *suitably qualified ecologist* that the site is of low or insignificant ecological value.

Special Cases

Areas of high ecological importance can be omitted from the construction zone if the *suitably qualified ecologist* is satisfied that they will not be disturbed by actions on site. Confirmation from the *ecologist* is required in writing, including details of the features and their locations. At the post construction stage, the ecologist must confirm that these areas were not affected by site activities.

Eco

Issue ID	Description	No. of Credits Available	Mandatory Elements
Eco 2	Ecological Enhancement	1	No

Aim

To enhance the ecological value of a site.

Assessment Criteria

Criteria	Credits
Where a *suitably qualified ecologist* has been appointed to recommend appropriate ecological features that will positively enhance the ecology of the site. **AND** Where the developer adopts all key *recommendations* and 30% of additional recommendations.	1
Default Cases None	

Information required to Demonstrate Compliance

Schedule of Evidence Required	
Design Stage	**Post Construction Stage**
A copy of the ecologist's report highlighting the information required as set out in 'Code for Sustainable Homes Ecology Report Template' **AND** Detailed documentary evidence stating: • How the key recommendations and 30% of additional recommendations will be incorporated into the design • The planting schedule of any species to be incorporated from suitably qualified ecologists recommendations	For post construction stage only assessments, provide evidence (as listed for design stage) representing the dwellings as built and confirmation that the ecologists recommendations were implemented, by providing plans or other detailed documentary evidence **OR** Confirmation from the ecologist that what was agreed at design stage was implemented, by providing plans or other detailed documentary evidence **OR** Where different from design stage, provide ecologists report and detailed documentary evidence (as listed for design stage) representing the dwellings as built

Definitions

Development site

The development site is the whole site up to and including the boundary.

Recommendations

Recommendations are defined as measures adopted to enhance the ecology of the site, which may include:

- The planting of native species

- The adoption of horticultural good practice (e.g. no or low use of residual pesticides)

- The installation of bird, bat and/or insect boxes at appropriate locations on the site

- Development of a full biodiversity management plan including avoiding clearance/works at key times of the year (e.g. breeding season)

- The proper integration, design and maintenance of SUDS and green roofs, community orchards etc.

Only native floral species or those with a known attraction or benefit to local wildlife can be considered for the purpose of enhancing the ecological value of the site.

RIBA Outline Plan of Work

The Royal Institute of British Architects publishes an Outline Plan of Work (Royal Institute of British Architects, 1991) which describes the UK traditional approach to the project delivery process in 12 well-defined steps, labelled A to M. The RIBA process begins at the project inception (A), where a general outline of requirements and a plan of action are produced by an architect and the commissioning client, and it ends at feedback (M) following the completion and handover of the building to the client.

Suitably qualified ecologist

A suitably qualified ecologist is defined as an individual who:

- Holds a degree or equivalent qualification (e.g. N/SVQ Level 5) in ecology or a related subject
- Is a practising ecologist, with a minimum of three years' relevant experience (within the last five years). Such experience must clearly demonstrate a practical understanding of factors affecting ecology in relation to construction and the built environment, including acting in an advisory capacity to provide recommendations for ecological protection, enhancement and mitigation measures. Examples of relevant experience are ecological impact assessments, Phase 1 and 2 habitat surveys, and habitat restoration
- Is covered by a professional code of conduct and subject to peer review.

Peer review is defined as the process employed by a professional body to demonstrate that potential or current full members maintain the standard of knowledge and experience required to ensure compliance with a code of conduct and professional ethics.

Full members of the following organisations who meet the above requirements are deemed to be suitably qualified ecologists:

- Association of Wildlife Trust Consultancies (AWTC)
- Chartered Institution of Water and Environmental Management (CIWEM)
- Institute of Ecology and Environmental Management (IEEM)
- Institute of Environmental Management and Assessment (IEMA)
- Landscape Institute (LI).

Eco

Assessment Methodology

The assessment criteria should be read with the methodology and the definitions in this section. Credits are awarded where the performance requirements (set out in the assessment criteria table) have been met.

Design Stage

- The assessor must confirm that a suitably qualified ecologist has been appointed to provide a report detailing key and additional recommendations for enhancing the site's ecology and that:

    a) The report has been prepared using the 'Code for Sustainable Homes Ecology Report Template', and it is recommended that this is carried out at Stage B according to the *RIBA Outline Plan of Work*

    b) The ecologist meets all the requirements stated in the definition of a suitably qualified ecologist.

    c) The suitably qualified ecologist has confirmed that all UK and EU laws in respect of protected species have been complied with and that any key and additional recommendations are beyond the requirements of such laws.

    d) The ecologist made a site visit prior to the commencement of initial site preparation works.

    e) The ecologist's recommendations are based on the existing site ecology, determined from the site visit.

    f) The site visit was made at appropriate times of year when plant and animal species were evident.

- If there has been no site visit prior to initial site preparation, this is only acceptable where the credit for Eco 1 – Ecological Value of Site has been achieved, and evidence provided to achieve Eco 1 has been passed on to the ecologist as the basis for the ecological report. This evidence must be in accordance with the Information Required to Demonstrate Compliance as detailed in Eco 1.

Post Construction Stage

- Confirm which specifications and evidence provided at the design stage are still valid.

- Assess all the new specifications and evidence provided at the post construction stage.

- Verify that the post construction stage evidence provided demonstrates that all the assessment criteria have been met.

- Where the whole site has not yet been built out, the assessor must confirm that there is either a contract in place or a letter confirming when final site wide issues such as planting will be complete.

Calculation Procedures

None.

Checklists and Tables

None.

Common Cases of Non-Compliance

The credit cannot be achieved where the developer/client has confirmed a commitment to comply with all current EU and UK legislation relating to protected species and habitats applicable to the *development site* but no ecological enhancement is proposed.

Where enhancement has been made to an unconnected area(s) outside the site boundary and no enhancement has been made within the boundary, the credit cannot be awarded.

To achieve the credit, features designed to enhance the ecology of the site must be recommended by a suitably qualified ecologist.

Special Cases

None.

Issue ID	Description	No. of Credits Available	Mandatory Elements
Eco 3	Protection of Ecological Features	1	No

Aim

To promote the protection of existing ecological features from substantial damage during the clearing of the site and the completion of construction works.

Assessment Criteria

Criteria	Credits
Where all existing features of ecological value on the *development site* potentially affected by the works are maintained and adequately protected during site clearance, preparation and construction works.	1
Default Cases The credit can be awarded by default where the site has been classified as having *low ecological value* in accordance with Section 1 of Checklist Eco 1, *Ecological features* of the site, AND no features of ecological value have been identified. If a *suitably qualified ecologist* has confirmed a feature can be removed because of its insignificant ecological value or where an arboriculturalist has confirmed a feature can be removed owing to poor health/condition (e.g. diseased trees which require felling for health and safety and/or conservation reasons), the credit can be achieved provided all other features are adequately protected in accordance with the ecologist's recommendations.	

Information Required to Demonstrate Compliance

Schedule of Evidence Required	
Design Stage	**Post Construction Stage**
Detailed documentary evidence* confirming ecological features present and how they will be protected *Where compliance with the criteria is demonstrated by the relevant documents submitted to the Planning Authority which gained planning approval, these can be used as evidence	Detailed documentary evidence confirming that any ecological features within the development site have been and will continue to be adequately protected during construction works
Where ecological features are being removed for health and safety and/or conservation reasons; Written evidence from an appropriate statutory body / arboriculturalist confirming the requirement to remove any features	Where ecological features are being removed for health and safety and/or conservation reasons; Detailed documentary evidence to demonstrate that only those features agreed by appropriate statutory body / arboriculturalist were removed.
Where ecological features are being removed and are of low ecological value; A copy of the ecologist's report highlighting the information required as set out in the Code for Sustainable Homes Ecology Report Template	Where ecological features have been removed; Confirmation from the ecologist that all features removed were identified at design stage as being of low ecological value.
Where using Checklist Eco 1, to demonstrate that there are no features to protect provision of: • Site visit report from the design team/assessor confirming details adequate to meet Checklist Eco 1 based on plans of the site and surrounding area prior to the commencement of construction works/site clearance	Where using Checklist Eco 1 evidence to be provided as at design stage

Definitions

Development site

The development site is the whole site up to and including the boundary.

Ecological features

Ecological features are defined in Checklist Eco 1 – Land of Low Ecological Value, and include trees, hedges, ponds, streams, rivers, marshes, wetlands, meadows, species-rich grassland, heathland and heather.

Low ecological value

Land defined as having low ecological value using Checklist Eco 1 or defined by a suitably qualified ecologist as having low or insignificant ecological value.

Protection of natural areas

The provision of physical barriers to prevent damage to existing natural areas. Natural areas include meadows, species-rich grassland, heathland consisting of heather and/or scrub, marshes and wetlands, ponds, streams and rivers. If such areas are remote from site works or storage, construction activity should be prevented in their vicinity.

Protection of trees and hedges

Where trees and hedges have been protected in accordance with BS 5837, *Trees in relation to construction*. This standard requires a tree protection plan to be developed which involves erecting physical barriers to prevent damage to existing trees, with an exclusion area around the trees. It also looks at defining a root protection area and requires consideration when compulsory work is carried out within the root protection area.

Protection of watercourses and wetland areas

The provision of physical barriers (e.g. bunds and cut-off ditches) and site drainage to ensure no site run-off damages the local watercourses. Specialist advice should be obtained from a suitably qualified ecologist, Natural England or the Environment Agency with reference to Pollution Prevention Guidelines 05.

Suitably qualified ecologist

A suitably qualified ecologist is defined as an individual who:

- Holds a degree or equivalent qualification (e.g. N/SVQ Level 5) in ecology or a related subject

- Is a practising ecologist, with a minimum of three years' relevant experience (within the last five years). Such experience must clearly demonstrate a practical understanding of factors affecting ecology in relation to construction and the built environment, including acting in an advisory capacity to provide recommendations for ecological protection, enhancement and mitigation measures. Examples of relevant experience are ecological impact assessments, Phase 1 and 2 habitat surveys, and habitat restoration

- Is covered by a professional code of conduct and subject to peer review.

Peer review is defined as the process employed by a professional body to demonstrate that potential or current full members maintain the standard of knowledge and experience required to ensure compliance with a code of conduct and professional ethics.

Full members of the following organisations who meet the above requirements are deemed to be suitably qualified ecologists:

- Association of Wildlife Trust Consultancies (AWTC)
- Chartered Institution of Water and Environmental Management (CIWEM)
- Institute of Ecology and Environmental Management (IEEM)
- Institute of Environmental Management and Assessment (IEMA)
- Landscape Institute (LI).

Verified ecological report

A verified ecological report is a report carried out by an ecologist who does not fully meet the requirements of a suitably qualified ecologist. For the report to comply, as a minimum a suitably qualified ecologist must have read and reviewed the report and confirmed in writing that it:

- Represents sound industry practice
- Reports and recommends correctly, truthfully and objectively
- Is appropriate given the local site conditions and scope of works proposed
- Avoids invalid, biased and exaggerated statements
- Additionally, written confirmation from the third-party verifier that they comply with the definition of a suitably qualified ecologist.

Assessment Methodology

The assessment criteria should be read with the methodology and the definitions in this section. Credits are awarded where the performance requirements (set out in the assessment criteria table) have been met.

Design Stage

- Confirm that a report has been prepared on ecological features in accordance with the Information Required to Demonstrate Compliance, together with details of ecological protection to be carried out prior to the start of any preliminary construction or preparation works (e.g. site clearance or the erection of temporary site facilities).
- Where there are no ecological features to protect and the credit is being awarded by default, the evidence provided must demonstrate this and that the requirements of Section 1 of Checklist Eco 1, Ecological features of the site, have been met.
- The assessor must check that the developer/client has confirmed compliance with all current EU and UK legislation relating to protected species and habitats

Eco

applicable to the development site. This is in addition to the protection of ecological features as set out above.

Post Construction Stage

- Confirm that any features identified at the design stage have been successfully protected.

Calculation Procedures

None.

Checklists and Tables

None.

Common Cases of Non-Compliance

Credits cannot be awarded for the relocation of ecological features.

Where ecological features (as defined above) have not been protected, credits cannot be awarded. This applies even where the developer/client has confirmed a commitment to comply with all current EU and UK legislation relating to protected species and habitats applicable to the development site.

Special Cases

None.

Issue ID	Description	No. of Credits Available	Mandatory Elements
Eco 4	Change in Ecological Value of Site	4	No

Aim

To minimise reductions and promote an improvement in ecological value.

Assessment Criteria

Criteria	Credits
The ecological value before and after development is measured, and the overall change in species per hectare is:	
• Minor negative change: between –9 and less than or equal to –3	1
• Neutral: greater than –3 and less than or equal to +3	2
• Minor enhancement: greater than 3 and less than or equal to 9	3
• Major enhancement: greater than +9	4
Default Cases	
None	

Information Required to Demonstrate Compliance

Schedule of Evidence Required	
Design Stage	Post Construction Stage
Copy of the calculations completed by the assessor and supported by the following detailed documentary evidence: • Proposed site layout • The pre-development site survey, clearly indicating natural and built features on both the site and land surrounding the site before the proposed development • Landscape and plot categories (in accordance with the Assessment Methodology) with a list of site areas provided for both before and after development	For post construction stage only assessments, provide detailed documentary evidence and calculations as design stage **OR** Written confirmation from the developer that the proposed site layout detailed at design stage has been implemented **OR** Where different from design stage, provide detailed documentary evidence and calculations as design stage
Where the advice of an ecologist is sought, the following detailed documentary evidence must be provided: Code for Sustainable Homes Ecology Report Template completed by the ecologist **AND** Written confirmation from the developer confirming how the ecologist's recommendations will be implemented including a planting schedule.	Where post construction stage assessment only, provide detailed documentary evidence as design stage **AND** Written confirmation from the developer that the ecologist's recommendations have been implemented **OR** Where the advice of an ecologist was sought at the design stage, the following detailed documentary evidence must also be provided: Written confirmation from the developer that the ecologist's recommendations have been implemented **OR** Where different from design stage, provide detailed documentary evidence as design stage

Eco

Definitions

Arable

Land dominated by cereals and other arable crops, as well as intensively managed grasslands.

Crops/weeds

Mostly highly disturbed vegetation of arable fields and their boundaries; includes cereal and vegetable crops.

Derelict land

The ecological value of derelict sites (table: Cat 9.3, Checklists and Tables) is time dependent; a linear scale has been used to determine intermediate values between zero ecological value at 1 year from dereliction/demolition to a value at 30 years based on marginal upland figures. This presents a worst case figure which can be amended on the advice of a suitably qualified ecologist.

Development site

The development site is the whole site up to and including the boundary.

Fertile grass

The bulk of agriculturally improved grasslands, intensive pasture and silage crops, but also includes mown areas of improved grasslands for recreational and amenity purposes, as well as re-sown roadside verges.

Heath/bog

Mostly heather moorland, blanket bog and upland heath, but also lowland heath and raised bog.

Infertile grass

A diverse group of semi-improved and semi-natural grasslands which includes acidic to basic, wet to dry grasslands, and tall herb vegetation mainly present in the lowlands; often found on stream sides and roadside verges.

Lowland wooded

Includes wooded vegetation of hedges and broadleaved woods in the lowlands.

Marginal upland

Areas that are on the periphery of upland and are dominated by mixtures of low-intensity agriculture, forestry and semi-natural vegetation.

Moorland grass/mosaic

Typically grazed moorland vegetation, including extensive upland acidic and peaty grassland that is species-rich with very localised flushes.

Pastoral

Grasslands used for grazing purposes.

Suitably qualified ecologist

A suitably qualified ecologist is defined as an individual who:

- Holds a degree or equivalent qualification (e.g. N/SVQ Level 5) in ecology or a related subject

- Is a practising ecologist, with a minimum of three years' relevant experience (within the last five years). Such experience must clearly demonstrate a practical understanding of factors affecting ecology in relation to construction and the built environment, including acting in an advisory capacity to provide recommendations for ecological protection, enhancement and mitigation measures. Examples of relevant experience are ecological impact assessments, Phase 1 and 2 habitat surveys, and habitat restoration

- Is covered by a professional code of conduct and subject to peer review.

Peer review is defined as the process employed by a professional body to demonstrate that potential or current full members maintain the standard of knowledge and experience required to ensure compliance with a code of conduct and professional ethics.

Full members of the following organisations who meet the above requirements are deemed to be suitably qualified ecologists:

- Association of Wildlife Trust Consultancies (AWTC)

- Chartered Institution of Water and Environmental Management (CIWEM)

- Institute of Ecology and Environmental Management (IEEM)

- Institute of Environmental Management and Assessment (IEMA)

- Landscape Institute (LI).

Tall grassland/herb

Typical vegetation of overgrown lowland field boundaries, stream sides, ditches and roadside verges.

Upland

Land generally above a height suitable for mechanised farming and frequently dominated by semi-natural vegetation.

Eco

Upland wooded

A varied group of acidic vegetation types usually associated with upland woods, including semi-natural woodland, conifer plantations, bracken, and wooded stream sides.

Urban mosaic

A complex mix of habitats located within cities, towns or villages, which include buildings, hard-standing, pockets of disused land and scrub, and areas of managed green spaces, such as gardens, allotments and parkland.

Verified ecological report

A verified ecological report is a report carried out by an ecologist who does not fully meet the requirements of a suitably qualified ecologist. For the report to comply, as a minimum a suitably qualified ecologist must have read and reviewed the report and confirmed in writing that it:

- Represents sound industry practice

- Reports and recommends correctly, truthfully and objectively

- Is appropriate given the local site conditions and scope of works proposed

- Avoids invalid, biased and exaggerated statements

- Additionally, written confirmation from the third-party verifier that they comply with the definition of a suitably qualified ecologist.

'Wildlife' garden planting

Garden planting that uses native species and those that have a known attraction or benefit to local fauna, based on the advice of a suitably qualified ecologist.

Assessment Methodology

The assessment criteria should be read with the methodology and the definitions in this section. Credits are awarded where the performance requirements (set out in the assessment criteria table) have been met.

Design Stage

- Calculate the change in ecological value of the *development site* by comparing the estimated diversity of plant species before and after construction using the method described in Calculation Procedures below.

Post Construction Stage

- Confirm which specifications and evidence provided at the design stage are still valid.

- Assess all the new specifications and evidence provided at the post construction stage.

Calculation Procedures

Before Development

1. Select the most appropriate landscape type from table: Cat 9.3 (Checklists and Tables) using the descriptions provided in Definitions. This will be based on the typology of the land surrounding the site and is likely to be the same throughout the development. However, in some cases it may differ, such as when a disused site is developed as part of a master plan for a mixed-use development. Typical of this would be a new town development (e.g. Milton Keynes), or the development of an inner-city *derelict* site.

2. Select all of the plot types from table Cat 9.3 which are applicable to the development site and calculate the area of each of them. It is important to ensure that the appropriate vegetation plot types for the site and their areas are correctly defined.

   Where areas of 'garden planting (typical)' and 'wildlife garden planting' are present, these will always record a score of zero, unless a *suitably qualified ecologist* has been appointed who will make the distinction between 'typical' and 'wildlife' garden planting species and record 'actual' species numbers.

   Enter the name of each plot type, its area and the number of species per plot type into table Cat 9.2a Follow the prompts to calculate the total average number of species before development.

   Alternatively, where a suitably qualified ecologist has conducted an ecological site survey, the habitat types, their areas and number of species per habitat type can be entered directly into table Cat 9.2a.

   The ecological report does not have to be produced by a *suitably qualified ecologist. Where this is the case a verified ecological report can be provided.*

Table: Cat 9.2a : Calculation of the Ecological Value of the Site Before Development				
Plot Type	Area of Plot Type (m²)		Species No. (from Table 2 or an SQE)	Species 3 Area of Plot Type
		X		
		X		
		X		
		X		
		X		
		X		
		X		
		X		
		X		
		X		
(1) Total Site Area =		(2) Total Σ Species × Area =		
Species per Plot Type Before Development: Total Σ Species × Area of Plot Type/Total Site Area = (2)/(1) =				

After Development

1. Repeat steps 1–2 above.

2. Enter the name of each plot type, its area and number of species per plot type (from table Cat9.3) into table Cat 9.2b. Follow the prompts to calculate the total average number of species after development.

3. Where a suitably qualified ecologist has conducted an ecological site survey and recommended new habitat types/planting schemes, their areas and number of species per habitat type can be entered directly into table Cat 9.2b.

   Where new habitats are to be created or floral species are to be planted as part of a landscape design, only those species which are native or have a known attraction to local wildlife can be included in the calculations based on the advice and recommendations of a suitably qualified ecologist.

Where 'extensive green roofs' are designed by a suitably qualified ecologist, add this area to 'wildlife garden' plot type and subtract the area from 'building' plot type.

The species value figures in table Cat 9.3 are for an existing, well-established site. It takes many years before the ecological value of a specific landscape type is established naturally. It is therefore not possible to assume that, for example, newly developed urban parkland has between 13.8 and 17.6 species just after construction without the expert knowledge of a suitably qualified ecologist. However, if the homes are to be built on existing urban parkland with part of the site left undisturbed, the ecological value of that part of the site can be assumed to be unchanged. If an urban parkland is being created on part of the site, the number of species on this part will need to be confirmed by a suitably qualified ecologist (taken from the actual number of indigenous species being planted), rather than assuming that the new parkland will immediately have a species value of 11.6 (assuming fertilisers are going to be used).

Table: Cat 9.2b : Calculation of the Ecological Value of the Site After Development				
Plot Type	Area of Plot Type (m²)		Species No. (from Table 2 or a SQE)	Species 3 Area of Plot Type
		X		
		X		
		X		
		X		
		X		
		X		
		X		
		X		
		X		
		X		
(1) Total Site Area =		(2) Total Σ Species × Area =		
Species per Plot Type Before Development: Total Σ Species × Area of Plot Type/Total Site Area = (2)/(1) =				

4. Calculation of the Change in Ecological Value

The average number of species for the site before development is calculated by multiplying the area of the different plot types and the equivalent number of 'species' for those plot types (values taken from table Cat 9.3 or given by a suitably qualified ecologist), adding these values and then dividing by the area of the whole site. The same procedure is carried out after the development, and the two values are compared to establish the change.

$$\text{Species Before Development} = \frac{\sum_{1}^{n}(\text{Area Plot Type N} \times \text{Species Plot Type N})}{\text{Total Site Area}}$$

$$\text{Species After Development} = \sum_{1}^{n}\frac{(\text{Area Plot Type N} \times \text{Species Plot Type N})}{\text{Total Site Area}}$$

$$\text{Species Change} = \text{Species After Development} - \text{Species Before Development}$$

Checklists and Tables

Ecological Value

Table Cat 9.3 below provides default values for calculating the change of ecological value of the site. This information is based on national figures from the Countryside Survey prepared for the Digest of Environmental Statistics No 20, 1998 (DEFRA).

The actual number of species may be used to replace any of the figures in table Cat 9.3 below, provided that a suitably qualified ecologist has been appointed and has reported actual species values in accordance with the calculation procedures above.

Eco

Table Cat 9.3 : Average Number of Species per Landscape and Vegetation Plot Type for Existing Habitats

Plot Type	Landscape Type									
	Arable	Pastoral	Marginal Upland	Upland	Existing Building/Hard Landscaped Areas	Urban Mosaic	Industrial Derelict Land <1 year	Industrial Derelict Land <10 years	Industrial Derelict Land <20 years	Industrial Derelict Land ≥30 years
Crop Weeds	5.4	8.3	–	–	0	–	–	–	–	–
Tall grassland/herb	12.7	15.0	–	–	0	17.6	0	6.3	15.8	21.1
Fertile grassland	11.6	12.7	15.3	–	0	11.6	0	4.6	11.5	15.3
Infertile grassland	17.1	17.6	21.1	–	0	17.6	0	6.3	15.8	21.1
Lowland wooded	12.9	12.5	–	–	0	13.8	–	–	–	–
Upland wooded	–	12.7	13.8	20.4	0	13.8	–	–	–	–
Moorland grass/mosaic	–	2.0	20.4	21.0	0	–	–	–	–	–
Heath/Bog	–	–	14.3	20.0	0	–	–	–	–	–
Hard Landscaping	0	0	0	0	0	0	0	0	0	0
Buildings	0	0	0	0	0	0	0	0	0	0
Garden Planting (Typical)	tbe	tbe	tbe	tbe	tbe	tbe	–	–	–	–
Wildlife Garden Planting	tbe	tbe	tbe	tbe	tbe	tbe	–	–	–	–

'–' insufficient data to produce national averages, as not all vegetation plot types are found in all landscape types. Values are data from: DEFRA "Digest of Environmental Statistics" No. 20. HMSO, 1998

tbe: To be evaluated by a suitably qualified ecologist – otherwise assume 0

Common Cases of Non-Compliance

Where the creation of a habitat such as garden planting or wildlife garden planting increases the site's ecological value, a suitably qualified ecologist must advise in terms of the species required and species per hectare to achieve the credit.

Special Cases

None.

Issue ID	Description	No. of Credits Available	Mandatory Elements
Eco 5	Building Footprint	2	No

Aim

To promote the most efficient use of a building's footprint by ensuring that land and material use is optimised across the development.

Assessment Criteria

Criteria	Credits
For houses, where the *net internal floor area*: *net internal ground floor area* ratio is greater than or equal to 2.5:1 **OR** For blocks of flats, where the net internal floor area: net internal ground floor area ratio is greater than or equal to 3:1 **OR** For a combination of houses and flats, the ratio of total net internal floor area: total net internal ground floor area of all houses and flats (i.e. the site-wide footprint to floor area ratio) is greater than the area weighted average of the two target ratios above (see Calculation Procedures)	1
For houses, where the net internal floor area: net internal ground floor area ratio is greater than or equal to 3:1 **OR** For blocks of flats, where the net internal floor area: net internal ground floor area ratio is greater than or equal to 4:1 **OR** For a combination of houses and flats, the ratio of total net internal floor area: total net internal ground floor area of all houses and flats (i.e. the site-wide footprint to floor area ratio) is greater than the area weighted average of the two target ratios above (see Calculation Procedures)	2
Default Cases None	

Information Required to Demonstrate Compliance

Schedule of Evidence Required	
Design Stage	Post Construction Stage
Calculation of the building footprint ratio, stating the Net Internal Floor Area (NIFA) and the Net Internal Ground Floor Area (NIGFA)	For post construction stage only assessments include the calculations of the building footprint ratio, stating NIFA and the NIGFA **OR** Written confirmation from the developer in the form of detailed documentary evidence confirming that the dwellings and buildings have been constructed in accordance with the design stage calculations **OR** Where different from design stage, revised calculations of the building footprint ratio, stating the NIFA and the NIGFA

Definitions

Habitable space

A space typically occupied for more than 30 minutes during the day with safe access by a permanent stairway or other means of entrance which complies with the requirements of relevant national Building Regulations and where the space is 'finished' with floor, walls, lighting and electric sockets.

Net internal floor area

The area of all *habitable spaces*, including the area taken up by halls, stairwells, cupboards, internal partitions, habitable loft spaces and basements. This also includes common areas of blocks of flats and apartment buildings, including stairwells, circulation spaces and entrance lobbies.

For semi-detached or terraced dwellings, this excludes the area of the party walls.

For flats, the floor area includes the party walls and separating walls to common areas.

Where residential accommodation is constructed above *other occupied space* such as shops or offices (garages or car parking would not be included), the floor area of these spaces can be included within the net internal floor area of the dwelling provided the areas are directly beneath the residential space.

Net internal ground floor area

Also referred to as the building footprint, this is the area of land that is taken up by the permanent foundations of the dwelling (including any other outbuildings with permanent foundations that are associated with the dwelling), within the external walls of the building.

For this issue, this is measured as the total net internal floor area of the ground floor, excluding the area taken up by the external walls.

In blocks of flats, this also includes the area taken up by party walls and separating walls to common areas, with the exception of party walls to adjoining buildings.

For *staggered dwellings*, the footprint area equals the total net internal floor area of the floor with the largest plate.

- Areas that normally count towards the footprint include conservatories, garages, permanent outhouses, fully enclosed permanent waste storage areas, communal garages or storage rooms and any other permanent buildings used by the occupants

- Areas that will NOT normally count towards the footprint include hard landscaping, semi-enclosed external spaces, pergolas and carports

- Garden sheds will not count unless they are built on a permanent solid foundation and are fitted out as habitable space with heating, lighting and power

- If a dwelling is raised above ground level on columns or other structures, the net internal ground floor area must be measured from the lowest floor of the dwelling

- Where other occupied spaces (e.g. non-domestic spaces such as retail and offices etc) form the ground floor or lower floors under a block of flats, the net internal ground floor area must be measured as the net internal floor area of the lowest floor of the block of flats.

Other occupied space

Other occupied spaces include retail and office spaces and other non-domestic spaces which are occupied for more than 30 minutes during the day. Garages or car parking would not be included in this definition.

Staggered dwellings

These are dwellings on several levels which are of unequal floor area. For example, a dwelling with a first floor area greater than the ground floor area which may overhang the ground floor.

Assessment Methodology

The assessment criteria should be read with the methodology and the definitions in this section. Credits are awarded where the performance requirements (set out in the assessment criteria table) have been met.

Design Stage

- Assess this issue on a site-wide basis using the ratio of combined net internal floor area to footprint area. This is measured as the total net internal ground floor area of all dwellings on site. Individual dwellings (i.e. detached, semi-detached and terraced, not individual flats) that are not subject to a Code assessment can be excluded from the assessment of this issue.

- Verify that the evidence demonstrates that all the assessment criteria have been met.

- Calculate the floor area: footprint ratio for each type of dwelling. Note that any outbuildings such as permanent garages and cycle stores must be taken into account in the footprint area.

Post Construction Stage

- Confirm which specifications and evidence provided at the design stage are still valid.

- Assess any new specifications and evidence provided at the post construction stage.

Calculation Procedures

1. Where there is a mixture of houses and flats, to calculate the area weighted target ratio for the site, use the following formula:

For one credit:

$$\text{Area Weighted Target Ratio} = \frac{(\text{Total NIFA Houses} \times 2.5) + (\text{Total NIFA Flats} \times 2.5)}{\text{Total NIFA of all Houses and Flats}}$$

For two credits:

$$\text{Area Weighted Target Ratio} = \frac{(\text{Total NIFA Houses} \times 3.2) + (\text{Total NIFA Flats} \times 4.0)}{\text{Total NIFA of all Houses and Flats}}$$

2. The site wide ratio should then be calculated using the following formula and assessed against the above target ratio. Credits can be awarded where the ratio calculated using the following formula is greater than the target area weighted ratio as described in point 1 above.

$$\text{Site Wide Footprint to Floor Area Ratio} = \left(\frac{\text{Total NIFA of all Dwellings}}{\text{Total NIGFA of all Dwellings}} \right)$$

Where:

NIFA = Net Internal Floor Area

NIGFA = Net Internal Ground Floor Area

Checklists and Tables

None.

Common Cases of Non-Compliance

Two-storey dwellings will not achieve the credit criteria unless a habitable loft space or basement is provided, depending on the provision of any other permanent structures such as garages or outhouses which may impact on the footprint area.

Special Cases

None.

Eco

Annex 1: Acronyms

ACoP	Approved Code of Practice
ACPO	Association of Chief Police Officers
AD L1A	Approved Document L1A
ADE	Approved Document E
ALO	Architectural Liaison Officer
ANC	Association of Noise Consultants
AWTC	Association of Wildlife Trust Consultancies
BRE	Building Research Establishment
BREEAM	Building Research Establishment Environmental Assessment Method
BS	British Standard
BSRIA	Building Services Research and Information Association
CABE	Commission for Architecture and the Built Environment
CCS	Considerate Constructors Scheme
CEH	Centre for Ecology and Hydrology
CFL	Compact fluorescent lamp
CH_4	Methane
CIBSE	Chartered Institution of Building Services Engineers
CIE	Commission Internationale de l'Eclairage (International Commission on Illumination)
CIRIA	Construction Industry Research and Information Association
CITES	Convention on International Trade in Endangered Species of Wild Fauna and Flora
CIWEM	Chartered Institution of Water and Environmental Management
CO_2	Carbon dioxide
CoC	Chain of custody
Code	Code for Sustainable Homes
CPDA	Crime Prevention Design Advisor
CPET	Central Point of Expertise on Timber
CSA	Canadian Standards Association
CSH	Code for Sustainable Homes

DECC	Department for Energy and Climate Change
DEFRA	Department for Environment, Food and Rural Affairs
DER	Dwelling Emission Rate
DF	Average daylight factor
DfT	Department for Transport
DIY	Do It Yourself
DS	Design stage
DTI	Department of Trade and Industry
Eco	Ecology
EMAS	Eco-Management and Audit Scheme
EMS	Environmental management system
EN	European Normalization
Ene	Energy and CO_2 Emissions
EPC	Energy Performance Certificate
EPDM	Ethylene propylene diene monomer
EPIs	Environmental performance indicators
ESCO	Energy services company
EST	Energy Saving Trust
EU	European Union
FEH	Flood Estimation Handbook
FRA	Flood risk assessment
FSC	Forest Stewardship Council
GLS	General Lighting Services
GRP	Glass reinforced plastic
GWP	Global Warming Potential
HCR Hea	Home Condition ReportHealth and Wellbeing
HFCs	Hydrofluorocarbons
HIP	Home Information Pack
HMSO	Her Majesty's Stationery Office
HSE	Health and Safety Executive
ICoP IDP	Interim Code of PracticeInclusive Design Principles

Annex

IEEM	Institute of Ecology and Environmental Management
IEMA	Institute of Environmental Management and Assessment
IPCC	Intergovernmental Panel on Climate Change
ISO	International Organization for Standardisation
KPI	Key performance indicators
LCA	Life cycle assessment
LED	Light emitting diode
LI	Landscape Institute
LZC	Low or zero carbon
Man	Management
Mat	Materials
MCS	Microgeneration Certification Scheme
MDF	Medium density fibreboard
MTCC	Malaysian Timber Certification Council
MVHR	Mechanical ventilation with heat recovery
NAEI	National Atmospheric Emissions Inventory
NaFRA	National Flood Risk Assessment
NIFA NIGFA	Net internal floor areaNet internal ground floor area
NOx	Nitrogen oxides
O_2	Oxygen
ODPM	Office of the Deputy Prime Minister
OSB	Oriented strand board
PCS	Post construction stage
PEFC	Programme of Endorsement of Forest Certification Schemes
PFCs	Perfluorocarbons
PIR	Passive infra red (movement detecting devices)
Pol	Pollution
PPG	Planning Policy Guidance
PPS	Planning Policy Statement
PU	Polyurethane
PVC	Polyvinyl chloride

Annex

QA	Quality assurance
RDL	Robust Details Limited
RIBA	Royal Institute of British Architects
SAP	Standard Assessment Procedure
SF_6	Sulphur hexafluoride
SFI	Sustainable Forestry Initiative
SGS	Société Générale de Surveillance
SMP	Shoreline management plan
SQE	Suitably qualified ecologist
SSSI	Site of Special Scientific Interest
SUDS	Sustainable drainage systems
Sur	Surface Water Run-off
SWMP	Site Waste Management Plan
TER	Target emission rate
TFT	The Forest Trust
TPO	Thermoplastic olefin
UK	United Kingdom
UKAS	United Kingdom Accreditation Service
UKPIA	United Kingdom Petroleum Industry Association
UNEP	United Nations Environment Programme
VOC	Volatile organic compound
Was	Waste
Wat	Water
WMO	World Meteorological Organization
WRAP	Waste and Resources Action Programme

Annex

Annex 2: References

BRE Global. *Code for Sustainable Homes – provision of scheme management services: Guidance notes for prospective service providers*. BRE Global, Garston, Watford, December 2007. Available from www.breeam.org/filelibrary/CSH_Guidance_Notes-_for_Prospective_Service_Providers.pdf

BRE. *The Government's Standard Assessment Procedure for energy rating of dwellings March 2010 Version (SAP 2009, version 9.90, March 2010, revision October 2010)*. Published on behalf of DECC by BRE, Garston, Watford, 2009. Available from http://www.bre.co.uk/filelibrary/SAP/2009/SAP-2009_9-90.pdf

Department for Communities and Local Government. *Approved Document* L1*A Conservation of fuel and power (New dwellings)*. CLG, London, 2010. Available from www.planningportal.gov.uk/approveddocuments

Department for Communities and Local Government. *Building Regulations Approved Document F – Ventilation* (2010) available from www.planningportal.gov.uk/approveddocuments

Communities and Local Government. *Code for Sustainable Homes: A step-change in sustainable home building practice*. Communities and Local Government, London, 2006. Available from www.communities.gov.uk

Convention on International Trade in Endangered Species of Wild Fauna and Flora (CITES). www.cites.org

ISO 17024 (General Requirements for Bodies Operating Certification of Persons)

Royal Institute of British Architects. *RIBA Outline Plan of Work*. RIBA Publications, London, 2008. Available from;
www.architecture.com/Files/RIBAProfessionalServices/Practice/OutlinePlanofWork(revised).pdf

UKAS Standard EN 45011 (General Requirements for Bodies Operating Product Certification Schemes)

Yates, A.; Brownhill, D.; Crowhurst D. *BRE's Environmental Assessment Methods for Buildings – BREEAM, including EcoHomes*. Prepared for the Sustainable Buildings Task Group, BRE, Garston, Watford, January 2004

Ene 1

BRE. *The Government's Standard Assessment Procedure for energy rating of dwellings March 2010 Version (SAP 2009, version 9.90, March 2010, revision October 2010). Published on behalf of DECC by BRE, Garston, Watford, 2009. Available from http://www.bre.co.uk/filelibrary/SAP/2009/SAP-2009_9-90.pdf*

Department for Communities and Local Government. *Approved Document* L1A *Conservation of fuel and power (New dwellings)*. CLG, London, 2010. Available from www.planningportal.gov.uk/approveddocuments

Ene 2

BRE. *The Government's Standard Assessment Procedure for energy rating of dwellings March 2010 Version (SAP 2009, version 9.90, March 2010, revision October 2010). Published on behalf of DECC by BRE, Garston, Watford, 2009. Available from http://www.bre.co.uk/filelibrary/SAP/2009/SAP-2009_9-90.pdf*

Department for Communities and Local Government. *Approved Document* L1A *Conservation of fuel and power (New dwellings))*. CLG, London, 2010. Available from www.planningportal.gov.uk/approveddocuments

Ene 3

Ene 4

Chartered Institution of Building Services Engineers (CIBSE): Low Carbon Consultants and Energy Assessors, CIBSE Certification Ltd www.cibse.org

Department for Communities and Local Government. *Approved Document* L1A *Conservation of fuel and power (New dwellings)*. CLG, London, 2010. Available from www.planningportal.gov.uk/approveddocuments

Department for Communities and Local Government. *Building Regulations Approved Document F – Ventilation* (2010) available from www.planningportal.gov.uk/approveddocuments

Ene 5

Energy Saving Trust (EST). Helps you find energy efficient products and provides information on the EU energy efficiency labelling scheme. www.energysavingtrust.org.uk/cym/Home-improvements-and-products/Home-appliances www.energysavingtrust.org.uk/cym/Home-improvements-and-products/About-Energy-Saving-Recommended-products/Other-energy-labels

Energy Saving Trust's Energy Saving Recommended scheme http://www.energysavingtrust.org.uk/business/Business/Energy-Saving-Trust-Recommended

Ene 6

British Standard BS 5266: *Emergency Lighting*. BSI, London, 2008.

Department for Communities and Local Government. *Approved Document* L1A *Conservation of fuel and power (New dwellings)*. CLG, London, 2010. Available from www.planningportal.gov.uk/approveddocuments

Department for Communities and Local Government. *Building Regulations Approved Document F – Ventilation* (2010) available from www.planningportal.gov.uk/approveddocuments

Chartered Institution of Building Services Engineers (CIBSE). *LG9, Lighting for Communal Residential Buildings.* CIBSE, London, 1997.

Ene 7

BRE. *The Government's Standard Assessment Procedure for energy rating of dwellings March 2010 Version (SAP 2009, version 9.90, March 2010, revision October 2010). Published on behalf of DECC by BRE, Garston, Watford, 2009. Available from http://www.bre.co.uk/filelibrary/SAP/2009/SAP-2009_9-90.pdf*

Department for Communities and Local Government. *Approved Document L1A Conservation of fuel and power (New dwellings).* CLG, London, 2010. Available from www.planningportal.gov.uk/approveddocuments

Department for Communities and Local Government. *Building Regulations Approved Document F – Ventilation* (2010) available from www.planningportal.gov.uk/approveddocuments

European Parliament. *Directive 2009/28/EC of the European Parliament and of the Council of 23 April 2009 on the promotion of the use of energy from renewable sources and amending and subsequently repealing Directives 2001/77/EC and 2003/30/EC.*

Available from http://eur-lex.europa.eu/LexUriServ/LexUriServ.do?uri=OJ:L:2009:140:0016:0062:EN:PDF

Microgeneration Certification Scheme (MCS) information available from; www.microgenerationcertification.org

Ene 8

Architectural Press. *New Metric Handbook – Planning and Design Data.* Architectural Press, Oxford, 2007.

British Standard BS 3621: *Thief-resistant lock assembly – Key egress.* BSI, London, 2007.

www.soldsecure.com

Wat 1

The Water Efficiency Calculator for New Dwellings, Communities and Local Government. September 2009. Available from http://www.communities.gov.uk/publications/planningandbuilding/watercalculator

British Standard EN 997: WC pans and WC suites with integral trap. BSI, London, 2003.

British Standard BS EN 12056-3: *Gravity drainage inside buildings – Roof drainage, layout and calculations.* BSI, London, 2000.

British Standard BS 8515: *Rainwater Harvesting Systems – Code of Practice.* BSI, London, 2009.

BSRIA Technical Note TN 7/2001. Available at
 https://infonet.bsria.co.uk/bookshop/books/rainwater-and-greywater-in-buildings-project-report-and-case-studies-tn-72001/?v=302&search=TN+7%2F2001

CIBSE TM13: *Minimising the risk of Legionnaire's disease.* 2002

CIRIA Publication C539: *Rainwater and Greywater Use in Buildings – Best Practice Guidance.* 2001

EN200: *Sanitary tapware. General technical specifications.* 2008

EN1112: *Sanitary tapware. General technical specifications.* 2008

HSE. *Approved Code of Practice and Guidance L8.* 1999

The Meteorological Office (incl. figures for UK rainfall) http://www.metoffice.gov.uk/

Water efficiency in new homes, an introductory guide for housebuilders. NHBC Foundation, 2009

Mat 1

The Green Guide to Specification. Available from www.thegreenguide.org.uk

The Green Guide Calculator http://www.bre.co.uk/greenguide/calculator/page.jsp?id=2071

Mat 2 and Mat 3

Arena Network & Groundwork Wales, 2006, *Green Dragon Environmental Standard*® *2006 Requirements.* Available from www.greendragonems.com

BES6001:2008 Issue 1 *Framework Standard for the Responsible Sourcing of Construction Products*, BRE Global, 2008.

British Standard BS 8555: *Environmental management systems – Guide to the phased implementation of an environmental management system including the use of environmental performance evaluation.* BSI, London, 2003

Briefing Sheets – The UK's Footprint: *The UK Timber Industry and its Impact on the World's Forest.* Friends of the Earth, 2000

Canadian Standards Association. www.csa.ca

Central Point of Expertise on Timber (CPET). www.proforest.net/cpet

Central Point of Expertise on Timber. *Evaluation of Category A Evidence – Review of forest certification schemes – Results.* December 2006

Certification of Forest Products. BRE, 1999

Convention on International Trade in Endangered Species of Wild Fauna and Flora (CITES). www.cites.org

Companies Act 1985

EU Eco-Management and Audit Scheme (EMAS). www.emas.org.uk/aboutemas/mainframe.htm

EU Forest Law Enforcement, Governance and Trade (FLEGT) Action Plan. http://europa.eu.int

FERN – European NGO campaigning for forests. www.fern.org

Forest Stewardship Council (FSC) www.fsc.org/en/

Forests Forever Campaign. www.forestsforever.org.uk

Green Book Live www.greenbooklive.com

Greenpeace Ancient Forest Campaign. www.greenpeace.org.uk

International Organization for Standardization (ISO), ISO 14001. Available at www.iso14000-iso14001-environmental-management.com

ProForest. www.ProForest.net

Programme for the Endorsement of Forest Certification Schemes (PEFC). www.pefc.org/

Scottish Procurement Policy Note (SPPN-09): *Procurement of Timber and Timber Products*. Scottish Procurement Directorate, 2005

Société Générale de Surveillance (SGS) timber tracking programme. www.sgs.com

Sustainable Forestry Initiative (SFI). www.sfiprogram.org

The Environment in Your Pocket. DEFRA, London, 2001

Malaysian Timber Certification Council (MTCC). www.mtcc.com.my

The Forest Trust (TFT). www.tropicalforesttrust.com

UK Government Timber Procurement Policy. *Definition of Legal and sustainable for timber procurement*. Second edition. CPET, 2006

UK Woodland Assurance Scheme. www.forestry.gov.uk/ukwas

Wood for Good. www.woodforgood.com

WRAP. Calculating and declaring recycled content in construction products: Rules of Thumb Guide. WRAP, February 2008

WWF. www.panda.org

Sur 1

BRE Digest 365 – Soakaway design 1991 (BRE)

BS EN 752:2008 – Drain and sewer systems outside buildings

Building Greener – Guidance on the use of green roofs, green walls and complementary features on buildings, C644, CIRIA (2007)

Centre for ecology and hydrology. *Flood estimation handbook*. 5 Volumes. National Environmental Research Council. ISBN 0 94854094X. 1999. Available from www.nwl. ac.uk

CIRIA SUDS information http://www.ciria.org/suds/

DEFRA / Environment Agency. *Preliminary rainfall runoff management for developments*. Flood and Coastal Defence R&D Programme. R&D Technical Report W5-074/A/TR/1. Contractor HR Wallingford. (2005).

Designing for exceedance in urban drainage – good practice, C635, CIRIA (2006)

Environment Agency Flood information http://www.environment-agency.gov.uk/ subjects/flood/

Environment Agency website www.environment-agency.gov.uk

Environment Agency website: Your environment > Environmental Facts and Figures > Climate > Flooding. See www.environment-agency.gov.uk

Foresight Future Flooding website: Previous Projects > Flood and Coastal Defence > Index. See www.foresight.gov.uk

Lancaster JW, Preene M, and Marshall. *Development and flood risk – guidance for the construction industry*. CIRIA Report C624. CIRIA, London. 2004. Available from www.ciriabooks.com

Marshall DCW and Bayliss AC. *Flood estimation for small catchments*. IOH Report No.124. Institute of hydrology, Wallingford (1994). Currently out of print. Available to download from http://www.ceh.ac.uk/products/publications/documents/ IH124FLOODESTIMATIONSMALLCATCHMENTS.PDF

Planning and Flood Risk, Planning Policy Statement 15 (PPS15), Department of the Environment Northern Ireland, Planning Service (2006)

PPS 25 (Planning Policy Statement 25), "Development and flood risk", ODPM (2006)

Preliminary rainfall runoff management for developments, EA/DEFRA, 2007

Technical Advice Note (TAN) 15: Development and Flood Risk, Welsh Assembly Government (2004)

The Met Office (incl. figures for UK rainfall) www.metoffice.gov.uk

The SUDS Manual – 2007 (CIRIA C697) This replaces C522 and includes revised and rationalised elements of C523 and C609

Town and Country Planning Act 1990

Water Industry Act 1991

Sur 2

See applicable references in Sur 1

BS EN 752:2008 – Drain and sewer systems outside buildings

Environment Agency Flood information http://www.environment-agency.gov.uk/subjects/flood/

Environment Agency website www.environment-agency.gov.uk/

PPS 25 (Planning Policy Statement 25), "Development and flood risk", ODPM (2006)

Technical Advice Note (TAN) 15: Development and Flood Risk, Welsh Assembly Government (2004)

Was 1

British Standard BS 8300: *Design of buildings and their approaches to meet the needs of disabled people – Code of practice.* BSI, London, 2009

British Standard BS 5906: *Code of Practice for Storage and On-Site Treatment of Solid Waste from Buildings.* BSI, London, 2005

British Standards Institution. *Design of accessible housing – Lifetime home – Code of practice.* Draft for Development DD 266. BSI, London, 2007

British Standard BS 5709: *Gaps, gates and stiles. Specification.* BSI, London, 2006

British Standard BS1703: *Refuse chutes and hoppers specification.* BSI, London, 2005

Building Regulations Part M and Approved Document M – *Access to and use of Buildings* (2004 Edition). Communities and Local Government, London, 2006. Available from http://www.planningportal.gov.uk/england/government/buildingregs/technicalguidance/bcapproveddocumentslist/

BRE Digest 505. *Access to Building.* BRE, 2008

Commission for Architecture and the Built Environment (CABE). *The principles of inclusive design. (They include you.)* CABE, 2006. Available from www.cabe.org.uk

Commission for Architecture and the Built Environment (CABE). *Homes for our old age. Independent living by design.* CABE, 2009. Available from www.cabe.org.uk

Commission for Architecture and the Built Environment (CABE). *Inclusion by design Equality, diversity and the built environment.* CABE, 2008. Available from www.cabe. org.uk

Building Regulations Approved Document H: *Drainage and Waste Disposal.* (2002 Edition), Communities and Local Government, London, 2006. Available from http:// www.planningportal.gov.uk/england/government/buildingregs/technicalguidance/ bcapproveddocumentslist/

Disability Discrimination Act, 1995

Disability Equality Duty, 2006

Environmental Protection Act, 1991

Household Waste Recycling Act, 2003

Waste Strategy for England (2007). Available from http://www.defra.gov.uk/ environment/waste/strategy/incentives/

Was 2

BRE: SMARTWaste Plan (Site waste management planning tool), *SMARTStart, waste benchmarks/EPIs and guidance: Reduction of Site Construction Waste, Recycling and Reuse of materials. A Site Guide and a Project Management Guide.* Available from www.smartwaste.co.uk

BREMAP - geographical information system of waste management facilities. www. bremap.co.uk

Constructing Excellence. Annual benchmarks for KPIs. www.constructingexcellence. org.uk

DEFRA (Department for Environment, Food and Rural Affairs). *Non Statutory Guidance for Site Waste Management Plans.* Available from www.defra.gov.uk/ constructionwaste

Environment Agency. Technical guidance available from www.environment-agency. gov.uk/subjects/waste

Envirowise GG493: *Saving money and raw materials by reducing waste in construction*: case studies. Available from www.envirowise.gov.uk

Envirowise GG642: *An Introduction to Site Waste Management Plans.* Available from www.envirowise.gov.uk

European Waste Catalogue. Available from http://www.environment-agency.gov.uk/ business/topics/waste/31873.aspx

Site Waste Management Plans, Guidance for Construction Contractors and Clients. Voluntary Code of Practice. DTI, 2004

DEFRA (Department for Environment, Food and Rural Affairs). *Waste Strategy for England 2007*. Available from http://www.defra.gov.uk/environment/waste/strategy/incentives/

Department for Communities and Local Government. *Approved Document* L1A *Conservation of fuel and power (New dwellings)*. CLG, London, 2010. Available from www.planningportal.gov.uk/approveddocuments

Department for Communities and Local Government. *Building Regulations Approved Document F – Ventilation* (2010) available from www.planningportal.gov.uk/approveddocuments

WRAP: SWMP templates for standard, good and best practice. Details and registration for download available from: www.wrap.org.uk/construction

WRAP: The requirements suite for setting SWMPs early within projects (client summary and waste minimisation and management guidance for delivering on the requirements). Available from www.wrap.org.uk/construction

Was 3

British Standard BS 8300: *Design of buildings and their approaches to meet the needs of disabled people – Code of practice*. BSI, London, 2001

British Standard BS 5709: *Gaps, gates and stiles. Specification*. BSI, London, 2006

British Standard BS 1703. *Refuse chutes and hoppers. Specification*. BSI, London, 2005

British Standard BS 5906. *Code of Practice for Storage and On-Site Treatment of Solid Waste from Buildings*. BSI, London, 2005

Building Regulations Part M and Approved Document M – *Access to and use of Buildings* (2004 Edition). Communities and Local Government, London, 2006. Available from http://www.planningportal.gov.uk/england/government/buildingregs/technicalguidance/bcapproveddocumentslist/

Disability Discrimination Act, 1995

The Animal By-Products Regulations 2005, Regulation (EC) No 1774/2002

DEFRA composting website. http://www.defra.gov.uk/environment/waste/topics/compost/index.htm

DEFRA. *Guidance on the treatment in approved composting or biogas plants of Animal by-Products and catering waste*. Version 8, September 2008. Available from http://www.defra.gov.uk/foodfarm/byproducts/documents/compost_guidance.pdf

Pol 2

British Standards EN 297:1994. A1:1995, A2:1996, A3:1996, A5:1998 and A6:2003 *Gas-fired central heating boilers*, page 42, table 14, section 3.6.2

Hea 1

Building Research Establishment. BRE IP 23/93: *Measuring daylight.* BRE, 1993

British Standard BS 8206-2. Lighting for buildings. Code of practice for daylighting. BSI, London, 2008

Chartered Institution of Building Services Engineers (CIBSE). *Lighting Guide 10: Daylighting and window design.* CIBSE, London, 1999

P.J. Littlefair, *Site layout planning for daylight and sunlight: a guide to good practice.* 1998

Building Research Establishment. BRE IP4/92: *Site layout for sunlight and solar gain.* BRE, 1992

Hea 2

Association of Noise Consultants (ANC). www.association-of-noise-consultants.co.uk

British Standard BS 8233: *Sound insulation and noise reduction for buildings – Code of practice.* BSI, London, 199Communities and Local Government. *Building Regulations Approved Document E – Resistance to the passage of sound.* (2003 edition incorporating 2004 amendments). Communities and Local Government, London, 2006. Available from http://www.planningportal.gov.uk/england/ government/buildingregs/technicalguidance/bcapproveddocumentslist/

Institute of Acoustics. www.ioa.org.uk

Robust Details Limited. www.robustdetails.com

United Kingdom Accreditation Service (UKAS). www.ukas.com

Hea 3

Architectural Press. *New Metric Handbook – Planning and Design Data*, Section 2.09. Oxford 2007.

British Standard BS 8300: *Design of buildings and their approaches to meet the needs of disabled people – Code of practice.* BSI, London, 2001

Commission for Architecture and the Built Environment (CABE). *The Value of Public Space.* 2004. Available at www.cabe.org.uk

Building Regulations Part M and Approved Document M – *Access to and use of Buildings* (2004 Edition). Communities and Local Government, London, 2006. Available from http://www.planningportal.gov.uk/england/government/buildingregs/ technicalguidance/bcapproveddocumentslist/

Hea 4

Habinteg Housing Association. www.habinteg.org.uk/

Joseph Rowntree Foundation. www.jrf.org.uk

Lifetime Homes. 2010. Available from http://www.lifetimehomes.org.uk/pages/revised-design-criteria.html

Lifetime Home Standards. www.lifetimehomes.org.uk/codeassessors

Meeting Part M and Designing Lifetime Homes Carroll, C.; Cowans, J.; Darton, D. (eds). Available from http://www.jrf.org.uk/publications/meeting-part-m-and-designing-lifetime-homes

Man 1

Department for Communities and Local Government. *Approved Document* L1*A Conservation of fuel and power (New dwellings)*. CLG, London, 2010. Available from www.planningportal.gov.uk/approveddocuments

Department for Communities and Local Government. *Building Regulations Approved Document F – Ventilation* (2010) available from www.planningportal.gov.uk/approveddocuments

Energy Performance Certificate (EPC). www.communities.gov.uk

Energy Saving Trust. www.energysavingtrust.org.uk

Info4local. One-stop information gateway for local public services. www.info4local.gov.uk

Sustrans. www.sustrans.org.uk

WRAP – The Waste and Resource Action Plan. www.wrap.org.uk

Man 2

Considerate Constructors *Scheme*. www.ccscheme.org.uk

Considerate Contractor Scheme. http://www.cityoflondon.gov.uk/Corporation/LGNL_Services/Business/Business_support_and_advice/considerate_contractor_scheme.htm#gold

Rethinking Construction. Available from www.constructingexcellence.org.uk/pdf/rethinking%20construction/rethinking_construction_report.pdf

Man 3

Construction Site Transport., April 2003. Measures for traffic movements and distances, BRE and DTI. www.bre.co.uk/pdf/constructiontraffic.pdf

Control of Dust from Construction and Demolition Activities. BRE, February 2003 Pollution Control Guide Parts 1–5, BRE, 2003

UK Construction Industry Key Performance Indicators. www.kpizone.com

Environment Agency. www.environment-agency.gov.uk

Guidelines for Company Reporting on Greenhouse Gas Emissions, Annex 6 Transport Conversion Tables. DEFRA, 2002, annexes updated July 2005.

NAEI (Netcen, 2005) based on data from DfT combined with factors from TRL as functions of average speed of vehicle derived from test data under real world testing cycles.

National Atmospheric Emissions Inventory for 2003. Developed by Netcen, 2005

Pollution Prevention Guideline PPG 1: *General guide to the prevention of pollution*. Environment Agency. Available from www.environment-agency.gov.uk

Pollution Prevention Guideline PPG 5: *Works and maintenance in or near water*. Environment Agency. Available from www.environment-agency.gov.uk

Pollution Prevention Guideline PPG 6: *Working at demolition and construction sites*. Environment Agency. Available from www.environment-agency.gov.uk/business/topics/pollution/39083.aspx

Sustainability Action Plan (or Achieving Sustainability in Construction Procurement); Government Construction Client's Panel (GCCP), Office of Government Commerce (OGC). Available from www.ogc.gov.uk/documents/AchievingSustainabilityConstructionProcurement.pdf

Man 4

BS 3621: 2004 Thief resistant lock assemblies - Key egress

BS 5588 Part 1:1990 Fire precautions in the design, construction and use of buildings. Code of practice for residential buildings

BS 7950:1997 Specification for enhanced security performance of windows for domestic applications

PAS 24:2007 Enhanced security performance requirements for door assemblies. Single and double leaf, hinged external door assemblies to dwellings

Safer Places – The Planning System & Crime Prevention. ODPM. Available from www.communities.gov.uk

Secured by Design – New Homes 2009 Available from www.securedbydesign.com/pdfs/newHomes2009.pdf

Secured by Design. www.securedbydesign.com

Eco 1

Association of Wildlife Trust Consultancies (AWTC) – Please contact the current chairman of the Association who will provide details of your local advisor. www.awtc.co.uk/contact.htm

Chartered Institution of Water and Environmental Management (CIWEM),15 John Street, London, WC1N 2EB. Tel: 020 78313110 Fax: 020 74054967 Email: admin@ ciwem.org www.ciwem.org

Institute of Environmental Management and Assessment (IEMA), St Nicholas House, 70 Newport, Lincoln, LN1 3DP. Tel 01522 540069. Fax 01522 540090
E-mail info@iema.net www.iema.net

The Institute of Ecology and Environmental Management (IEEM), 45 Southgate Street, Winchester, Hampshire SO23 9EH. www.ieem.co.uk

Landscape Institute (LI) – The Chartered Institute of the UK for Landscape Architects, 33 Great Portland Street, W1W 8QG http://www.landscapeinstitute.org/

Eco 3

Pollution Prevention Guideline PPG 5: *Works and maintenance in or near water.* Environment Agency. Available from www.environment-agency.gov.uk

Eco 4

Construction Industry Key Performance Indicators. www.kpizone.com

Department of the Environment, Transport and the Regions. *Digest of Environmental Statistics*, No 20. DEFRA, 1998

Annex 3: Sources of further information

Ene 4

Good Practice Guide 268: *Energy efficient ventilation of dwellings - a guide for specifiers*. 2006. Available from www.feta.co.uk/rva/downloads/GPG268%20-%20 Energy%20efficient%20ventilation%20in%20dwellings.pdf

Ene 5

Energy Saving Trust (EST). www.energysavingtrust.org.uk

Ene 6

Energy Efficiency Best Practice and Housing (EEBPH). www.est.org.uk/housingbuildings/professionals

Energy Saving Trust (EST). www.est.org.uk

Secured by Design – Guidance for New Homes 2009, Section 2 Available from www. securedbydesign.com/pdfs/newHomes2009.pdf

The Carbon Trust. www.thecarbontrust.co.uk/energy/pages/home.asp

Ene 7

Quality Assurance for Combined Heat and Power www.chpqa.com

Ene 8

Cycling England. National body charged with co-ordinating the development of cycling across England. Includes design guidance, examples, best practice etc. www.cyclingengland.co.uk

Cyclists Touring Club (CTC). The UK's national cyclist's organisation. www.ctc.org.uk

Communities and Local Government. *Better places to live by design: a companion guide to PPG3*. 2001

Planning guidance and advice. www.communities.gov.uk

London Cycling Campaign. www.lcc.org.uk

Sustrans, Cycle Parking Information Sheet FF37. www.sustrans.org.uk

Sustrans, National Cycle Routes. www.sustrans.org.uk

Annex

Ene 9

Communities and Local Government. *Better places to live by design: a companion guide to PPG3*. 2001

Department for Communities and Local Government. www.communities.gov.uk
Planning Policy Guidance Note 08: *Telecommunications*. 2001
Planning Policy Guidance Note 13: *Transport*. 2002

Wat 1

Building Research Establishment. BRE IP 1/04: *Drainage design for buildings with reduced water use.* BRE

Environment Agency National Water Demand Management Centre. *Conserving Water in Buildings.* 2007, available at http://publications.environment-agency.gov.uk/pdf/GEHO1107BNJR-E-E.pdf

Environment Agency. *Assessing The Cost Of Compliance With The Code For Sustainable Homes.* WRc Ref: UC7231

Statutory Instruments 1999 No. 1148, *Water Supply, (Water Fittings) Regulations*

Market Transformation Programme (MTP), BN DW BATHS: *Bath design and efficiency.* Briefing Note relating to Policy Scenario Objectives in Policy Brief

Market Transformation Programme (MTP), BNWAT02: *Domestic baths specification and stock model information*

Office of the Deputy Prime Minister (ODPM). Buildings Regulations Approved Document H: *Drainage and waste disposal*. 2002

Water Regulations Advisory Scheme. Information and Guidance Note 09-02-04: *Reclaimed Water Systems. Information about Installing, Modifying or Maintaining Reclaimed Water Systems*. 1999 Available at http://www.wras.co.uk/pdf_files/IGN%209-02-04%20Reclaimed.pdf

Wat 2

UK Rainwater Harvesting Association (UKRHA). www.ukrha.org

Water UK. www.water.org.uk

Mat 1

The Green Guide to Specification. www.thegreenguide.org.uk

Mat 2 and Mat 3

Arena Network & Groundwork Wales. *Green Dragon Environmental Standard® 2006 Requirements*. 2006. Available from www.greendragonems.com/

Annex

British Standard BS 8555: *Environmental management systems – Guide to the phased implementation of an environmental management system including the use of environmental performance evaluation*. BSI, London, 2003

Canadian Standards Association. www.csa.ca

Central Point of Expertise on Timber (CPET). http://www.cpet.org.uk/

Central Point of Expertise on Timber. *Evaluation of Category A Evidence – Review of forest certification schemes – Results*. December 2008

Convention on International Trade in Endangered Species of Wild Fauna and Flora (CITES). www.cites.org

EU Eco-Management and Audit Scheme (EMAS). (www.emas.org.uk/aboutemas/mainframe.htm)

EU Forest Law Enforcement, Governance and Trade (FLEGT) Action Plan. http://ec.europa.eu/environment/forests/flegt.htm

FERN – European NGO campaigning for forests. www.fern.org

Forest Stewardship Council (FSC). www.fsc.org/en

Greenpeace Ancient Forest Campaign. www.greenpeace.org.uk

International Organization for Standardization (ISO). ISO 14001. Available at www.iso14000-iso14001-environmental-management.com/

ProForest. www.ProForest.net

Programme of Endorsement of Forest Certification Schemes (PEFC). www.pefc.org/

Scottish Procurement Policy Note SPPN-09: *Procurement of Timber and Timber Products*. Scottish Procurement Directorate, 2005

Société Générale de Surveillance (SGS) timber tracking programme. www.sgs.com

Sustainable Forestry Initiative (SFI). www.sfiprogram.org

The Environment in Your Pocket, DEFRA, 2001

Malaysian Timber Certification Council (MTCC). www.mtcc.com.my

The Forest Trust (TFT) available at www.tropicalforesttrust.com/

UK Government Timber Procurement Policy. *Definition of Legal and Sustainable for Timber Procurement*. Second edition, CPET, 2006

UK Woodland Assurance Scheme. www.forestry.gov.uk/ukwas

Wood for Good. www.woodforgood.com

WRAP. *Calculating and declaring recycled content in construction products: Rules of Thumb Guide.* WRAP, February 2008

WWF. www.panda.org

Sur 1

BRE Digest 365 – Soakaway design 2007 (BRE)

BS EN 752:2008 – Drain and sewer systems outside buildings

The Met Office (incl. figures for UK rainfall) www.met-office.gov.uk

The SUDS Manual – 2007 (CIRIA C697) This replaces C522 and includes revised and rationalised elements of C523 and C609.

Sur 2

Approved Document H Drainage and waste Disposal ODPM (2002)

BRE – Repairing flooded buildings: an insurance industry guide to investigation and repair of flood damage to housing and small businesses

BRE Digest 365, *"Soakaway design"*, Building Research Establishment (2007).
BRE Good Repair Guide 11, "Repairing Flood Damage" Part 1–4, CRC Ltd, (1997)

BS EN 12056-3: 2000, "Gravity drainage inside buildings – Part 3: Roof drainage, layout and calculation", British Standard Institute (2000)

CIRIA – Flood repair standards for buildings, 2005

CIRIA – New development and flood risk, 2005

DEFRA / Environment Agency. *Preliminary rainfall runoff management for developments.* Flood and Coastal Defence R&D Programme. R&D Technical Report W5-074/A/TR/1. Contractor HR Wallingford. (2005).

Development and flood risk, guidance for the construction industry, Lancaster et. al, CIRIA (2004).

ODPM. PPS 25 (Planning Policy Statement 25), "Development and flood risk" A practice guide, (2006). Available from www.communities.gov.uk

CIRIA – Standards for the repair of buildings following floods - C632, 2005 (http://www.ciria.org/service/bookshop/core/orders/product.aspx?prodid=112)

CIRIA - Development and Flood Risk: Guidance for the Construction Industry - C624 (2004)

Was 1

Department for Environment, Food and Rural Affairs (DEFRA). www.defra.gov.uk/environment/waste

Commission for Architecture and the Built Environment (CABE). www.cabe.org.uk

Recycle Now. www.recyclenow.com

WRAP (Waste and Resources Action Programme). www.wrap.org.uk

Was 3

Community Composting. www.communitycompost.org

Community Recycling Network UK. www.crn.org.uk (further information to set up community composting).

Compost Information Sheet 2005: *Composting and disposing of garden and kitchen waste.* Available from www.wasteonline.org.uk

Composting troubleshooting. www.compostguide.com

Project: Growing with compost, which contains a technical guidance library on different subjects regarding community composting, at www.growingwithcompost.org

Recycle Now. www.recyclenow.com

Waste and Resources Action Programme (WRAP). www.wrap.org.uk

Pol 1

Guidance on EC Regulation No 2037/2000 on substances that deplete the ozone layer. October 2000, DTI. Available from http://webarchive.nationalarchives.gov.uk/+/ http://www.berr.gov.uk/sectors/sustainability/ods/page29091.html

National Atmospheric Emissions Inventory, *UK Emissions of Air Pollutants 1970–2006.* DEFRA, 2008

IPCC/TEAP Special Report: *Safeguarding the Ozone Layer and the Global Climate System.* 2005

Pol 2

Nitrogen Dioxide in the United Kingdom. DEFRA, (2004) Summary report also available http://www.defra.gov.uk/environment/quality/air/airquality/publications/ nitrogen-dioxide/nd-summary.pdf

Hea 1

BR 288. *Designing buildings for daylight.* James Bell and Bill Burt, 1995

Man 1

Coach Information/Enquiries. www.nationalexpress.co.uk

General Travel Information. www.traveline.org.uk

Rail Information/Enquiries. www.nationalrail.co.uk

Recycle Now. www.recyclenow.com

UK water companies. www.water.org.uk

WRAP Waste and Resources Action Programme www.wrap.org.uk

Man 2

Considerate Builders Scheme. www.westminster.gov.uk/Business/
businessandstreettradinglicences/highways/considerate_builders.cfm

Constructing Excellence. www.constructingexcellence.org.uk

Man 3

COPERT II: Computer programme to Calculate Emissions from Road Transport – Methodology and Emissions Factors. Technical Report No 6, 1999.

Good Practice Guide GPG 273: Computerised Routing and Scheduling for Efficient Logistics

NERA Report on lorry track and environmental costs –Available at http://webarchive.
nationalarchives.gov.uk/+/http://www.dft.gov.uk/pgr/roads/environment/nera/

The Carbon Trust. www.thecarbontrust.co.uk/energy

Man 4

British Standards Online. http://www.bsigroup.com/

British Standard BS 7950: *Specification for enhanced security performance of windows for domestic applications.* BSI, London, 1997

Guide to Security Standards for Doors and Windows (May 2002) prepared with the support of LPCB, Secured by Design and BSIA. Available from www.securedbydesign.com/pdfs/standards_doors_2002.pdf

PAS 24:2007 *Enhanced security performance requirements for door assemblies. Single and double leaf, hinged external door assemblies to dwellings.*

Eco 1

British Standard BS 5837:*Trees in relation to construction.* BSI, London, 2005. Available from http://www.bsigroup.com/

CIRIA C502: *Environmental Good Practice on Site.* Available from www.ciria.org.uk

CIRIA C567: *Working with Wildlife Site Guide.* Available from www.ciria.org.uk

Environment Agency. www.environment-agency.gov.uk

The Hedgerows Regulations. London: Office of Public Sector Information (formerly The Stationery Office). London, 1997

UK Biodiversity Action Plan. www.ukbap.org.uk

Eco 2

Biodiversity By Design. TCPA, 2004

British Standard BS5837: *Trees in relation to construction*. BSI, London, 2005. Available from www.bsigroup.com

CIRIA C502: *Environmental good practice on site*. Available from www.ciria.org.uk

CIRIA C567: *Working with wildlife site guide*. Available from ww.ciria.org.uk

Environment Agency. www.environment-agency.gov.uk

Grant G., *Green Roofs and Facades*. BRE, 2006

Eco 3

CIRIA C502: *Environmental good practice on site.* Available from www.ciria.org.uk

CIRIA C567: *Working with wildlife site guide*. CIRIA, 2005. Available from www.ciria.org.uk

Pollution Prevention Guideline PPG06: *Working at construction and demolition sites.* Environment Agency. Available from www.environment-agency.gov.uk

UK Biodiversity Action Plan. www.ukbap.org.uk

Eco 4

CIRIA C644: *Building greener – Guidance on the use of green roofs, green walls and complementary features on buildings*. CIRIA, 2007

Countryside Survey 2000. www.cs2000.org.uk

Environment Agency. www.environment-agency.gov.uk

Government Planning Department. www.communities.gov.uk

Eco 5

CIRIA. www.ciria.org.uk

Government Planning Department. www.communities.gov.uk